THE PENGUIN POETS
D101

THE PENGUIN BOOK OF
SATIRICAL VERSE

THE
PENGUIN BOOK OF
SATIRICAL VERSE

INTRODUCED AND EDITED BY
EDWARD LUCIE-SMITH

PENGUIN BOOKS

Penguin Books Ltd, Harmondsworth, Middlesex, England
Penguin Books Inc., 3300 Clipper Mill Road, Baltimore, Md 21211, U.S.A.
Penguin Books Australia Ltd, Ringwood, Victoria, Australia

—

First published 1967

—

Copyright © Edward Lucie-Smith, 1967

—

Made and printed in Great Britain
by Richard Clay (The Chaucer Press) Ltd,
Bungay, Suffolk
Set in Monotype Bembo

CONTENTS

7

CONTENTS

CONTENTS

CONTENTS

ACKNOWLEDGEMENTS

Many people were kind enough to offer me suggestions and ideas for this book. I owe particular gratitude to Martin Bell, Philip Hobsbaum, Yann Lovelock, Christopher Logue, George MacBeth, and Christopher Ricks.

For permission to reproduce copyright poems in this anthology, acknowledgement is made to the following:

For 'The Unknown Citizen' by W. H. Auden to Faber & Faber Ltd (publishers of *Collected Shorter Poems*) and to Random House, Inc; for 'Lord Lundy' by Hilaire Belloc to Gerald Duckworth & Co. Ltd (publishers of *Cautionary Tales* and to Alfred A. Knopf, Inc; for an extract from 'The Georgiad' by Roy Campbell to Curtis Brown Ltd; for 'The Evangelist' by Donald Davie to International Literary Management; for 'The Persian Version' by Robert Graves (published by Cassell & Co. Ltd in *Collected Poems*) to the author, to A. P. Watt & Son, and to Collins-Knowlton-Wing, Inc., Copyright © 1955 by Robert Graves; for 'I Shall Vote Labour' by Christopher Logue to the author; for 'Made in Heaven' by Peter Porter to Scorpion Press; for 'Mr Nixon' by Ezra Pound to Faber & Faber Ltd and to New Directions Publishing Corporation, New York (both publishers of *Personae*, copyright 1926, 1954 by Ezra Pound); for 'To the Wife of a Non-interventionist Statesman' by Edgell Rickword to the author; for 'Base Details and Memorial Tablet' by Siegfried Sassoon to the author; for 'If So the Man You Are' by P. Wyndham Lewis to Methuen and Co. Ltd (publishers of *One Way Song*).

INTRODUCTION

'THE END OF SATYR IS REFORMATION,' says Defoe, flatly, in the first sentence of his preface to *The True-Born Englishman*. And this indeed is what satire has always *pretended* to be about. The mask of the reformer is the one which the satirical poet most frequently assumes; it provides him with a justification for the release of his aggressive instincts, whatever topic he chooses to touch upon. The matter is not, however, to be so easily settled. The satiric impulse is complex rather than simple – good reason why satire so often seems self-conscious; why the chastisement of manners and morals is intermingled with a discussion of the genre itself. The satirist is afraid of his own instincts; he is afraid that matters will get out of control. The anonymous eighteenth-century author of a poem called *The Satirists* speaks for the whole tribe:

> How me mistake; th'abusive we think bold;
> But who calls names in Satire is a Scold:
> If such be Satire, and if such the use,
> Call it no longer Satire, but Abuse:
> Nor with such Ribaldry had I fill'd the Page,
> But to show Scandal's, not satirick rage.
> Scandal is what of all things I detest,
> And scarce endure an inoffensive Jest.
> Ingenious general Satire, I can love,
> While all that's personal I disapprove.

Here we find the 'official' programme of most satire. The satirist erects a pedestal, and leaps upon it himself. But can he maintain this position of aloof superiority? Very seldom, as the most amusing satires show us:

> Who'ere would *Comedy* or *Satire* write,
> Must never spare *Obscenity*, and *Spite*:
> A *Quantum sufficit* of Smut, will raise
> Crowds of Applauders to the dullest Plays;
> Whilst Scandal, Raillery, and pure ill Nature,
> Are found the best *Ingredients* for a Satire.
>   (*Harlequin Horace*, James Miller)

A satire, to succeed, very often has to invite a kind of complicity from the reader. The satirist buys attention with a flow of sly hints and titillating details, but the more personal he becomes, the more he tarnishes the image of moral purity which he is trying to create for himself. Unsophisticated satiric writers care very little about this – this is one reason why, in broadsides and 'popular' satires, we are often aware of jolting shifts of tone, sudden transitions between the high style and the low, for which the author has not prepared us. Political satires, in particular, tend to be morally naïve – the writers are too firmly committed to the cause they support to doubt its, or their own, righteousness. Authors who write a more general kind of satire are, by contrast, troubled by the ambiguity of their own position. But we cannot maintain a rigid distinction between one kind of satire and another, the noble and the ignoble. Satire, despite its mixed motives, always does have some general aim, a moral centre – otherwise it is not really satire at all. When satire concerns itself with individuals (as it so often does) these are being measured against an abstract thing, a standard of conduct. And it is this which gives force and resonance to the condemnations heaped upon the victims. Without some kind of moral code being implied by the poem, satire is helpless. It becomes merely abuse.

The whole question of satire – what it is and where it stands – can be examined in several different ways. The most obvious approach is through literature and literary history, which in this case provides a special kind of emphasis. Satire has two beginnings in English. One is lost in antiquity: men seem to have written lampoons and jingles ever since poetry began, and in England, as elsewhere, these gradually developed into something which is recognizably satiric. But, in another sense, English satire is the child of the Renaissance. When the Greek and Latin classics began to be studied with a new intensity, and became the basis of education, people naturally grew curious about the pagan satirists. Where poets were concerned, it was natural that they should begin to imitate the satiric poets, and we see the first attempts in the satires written by Wyatt and Surrey, which are quite different from those written by Skelton. These were followed by the fully-fledged Juvenalian satires of Hall and Marston. The earlier 'classical' satires are, in fact, less particular than the satiric verse written during the Middle Ages – there is a preference for satirizing types rather than personalities, and Skelton's political allusions are far more pointed than those of Marston. But the influence of the classics persisted, and by the end of the seventeenth century satire had become the dominant mode, and was to retain this pre-eminence for the first half of the eighteenth century as well. What impresses us, when we read satires written from the end of the sixteenth century to the beginning of our own, is the way in which the whole structure of classical allusion was put to work, to create a special kind of poetry for a special kind of public. This public had an absolutely homogeneous educational background. Its members were entirely familiar with Greek and Latin literature, and classical allusions had, for them, a special kind of resonance. We wonder at the extreme allusiveness of the Chinese scholar-poets, without perhaps realizing that the same phenomenon exists in our own literature.

The result was a kind of poetry which seemed to glory in its own derivativeness. The innumerable imitations of Horace's *Art of Poetry* written during the eighteenth century do indeed supply the modern reader with cause for wonder. Often the Latin text was printed in parallel with the English, or cited in footnotes, so that the reader could see at a glance how ingeniously the variations were being played on a familiar text. The comparison counted for far more than the integrity of the English poem. In certain poems – such as William King's *Art of Cookery* – Horace's terms and defini-tions were put to far-fetched uses. King ingeniously transfers the whole critical apparatus from literature to gastronomy.

Yet these classical satires are seldom as removed and rarefied as the literary background might lead us to think. The early Juvenalian satires are, in fact, splendidly earthy in language and image, often to the point of extreme coarseness. The reason is that these characteristics were to be found in Juvenal himself. The general tendency, during the seventeenth and eighteenth centuries, was for the language of poetry to move farther and farther away from the vernacular. Satire resisted the trend. Because it dealt with 'low' subjects, 'low' language could be used, and poets were not so much bound by the rules of decorum. In the work of some satirists, Rochester and Dryden for example, we find a marvellously subtle use of contrasts: the classical allusion, the Latin word or phrase,

are juxtaposed with language which is entirely and racily collo-
quial.

Nevertheless, the satiric genre did enter into a period of
prolonged crisis at the beginning of the nineteenth century. The
nineteenth-century satirists are not, as many critics have asserted,
entirely worthless. A great deal of satire was written during the
period, and it well deserves the attention of scholars, and even, for
that matter, of the general reader. What was missing, at least after
the death of Byron, was a presiding genius, a writer of sufficient
force and vitality to revivify the whole genre. Byron himself plays
a very curious role in the history of satire. *English Bards and Scots
Reviewers* is satire already tinged with a fatal nostalgia for true
rigour. *Don Juan*, a greater and more original poem, cannot be
classified as satire at all. When it comes to the point, Byron opts
for appetite for life rather than judgements upon it; and thus,
though the poem contains satirical elements, its prevailing tone is
not at all that of satire. Rather, it is something in a new mode –
romanticism tinged with self-irony.

But, just because there is no presiding genius to distract our
attention, nineteenth-century verse satire allows us to examine
other things which are of great interest. We are struck, for example, by the preservation of forms; and by the strength of these
forms even when in the hands of lesser men. Every great literary
success produces a crop of imitations. *Don Juan*, just because it was
left unfinished, spawned a number of continuations by other
hands. Sometimes the continuations were actual forgeries, which
the writer was trying to pass off as the work of Byron himself.
These continuations form a fascinating commentary on the public
reaction to Byron's genius, and every now and again we find them
being used for satiric purposes. Here, for example, is a verse by
Gerard Noel Byron, the poet's nephew:

> Yet England has some noble institutions,
>   Our prisons, hospitals, and volunteers,
> And several others kept by contributions,
>   To cure our sickness or to calm our fears;
> And various yearly pageants and delusions,
>   At which 'John Bull', *en masse*, in state appears.
> Then we have a noble peerage, *vide* 'Burke',
> And several millions starving – out of work.

But, interesting as it is to find Don Juan speaking in the accents of 1880, it is far more so, I think, to note the persistence of the *Dunciad* convention, and even of the Hudibrastic one. A poem called *The Modern Hudibras* was published in 1831, and one entitled *The New Inferno*, by an author calling himself 'Junius Hudibras', came out in the 1880s. Both poems are, as it happens, worthless. Much more merit is to be found in *The Obliviad*, published in 1879. This is a really astonishing revival of the manner and method of *The Dunciad*, and the author almost brings it off. Here he is, hectoring Dickens:

> First Dickens see, known by an ugly mark
> Of hack reporter with attorney's clerk;
> His early trades, which told, no need to ask
> Whence still that rancid savour of the cask;
> The vulgar irony, the tap-room jest,
> Fine spoken fellow when he did his best;
> Verbatim dialogue, Alsatian scene,
> The Cockney classic, and colloquial mean;
> The upstart shewn when scarce the speech began,
> With effort vain to ape the gentleman.

But this passage offers us a glimpse of one of the great weaknesses of the Victorian satirists – the fact that gentility had begun to drive out morality. The Victorians tended to denounce a breach of convention in the tones which eighteenth-century authors reserved for a moral lapse. The old concept of the *honnête homme*, which lies behind so much satire from the Restoration onwards, had been replaced by mere good manners, as the books of etiquette preached them to the new middle class. If we look at the best of the high Victorian satires – and here one must give due honour to that despised poet Alfred Austin – we see that they are all afflicted with shallowness. Austin's couplets have an agreeable sparkle, but it is the sparkle of paste rather than diamonds.

What I have so far left out is any consideration of radical satirists. This is a topic to which I must now turn in order to explain what has happened to verse satire in our own century. People commonly say that satire is best written from a conservative point of view; that the satirist needs firm ground to stand on. It is also said that there is now no place for satire in the twentieth century because education is no longer based on the classics, and that a good knowledge of these, on the part of the reader as well as the poet, is necessary to poetry of this kind. Both these assertions are nonsensical. In fact, the effort to write radical satire had been fitfully at work ever since the French Revolution – an example in this book is the strange poem by Blake 'Let the Brothels of Paris be Opened'. The hard times in England at the beginning of the nineteenth century, when people and government had never seemed further apart, were responsible for some notable poetry – the opening lines of Shelley's *Masque of Anarchy*, and the best things in Ebenezer Elliott's *Corn Law Rhymes*. But the radical tradition failed to establish itself fully, and the running down of the whole revolutionary impetus during the last part of the nineteenth century in England meant that the poets I've just mentioned had to wait a long time to find their true successors.

The fact is, however, that most of the good satiric verse written during the twentieth century has been the satire of the Left, and in this it resembles what was written during the Middle Ages. Satiric writing seems to be engaged in a return to the vernacular tradition. It takes a pride not in sophistication but in roughness. It is prepared – so it seems – to sacrifice literary quality for the sake of immediate effect. There is much talk about 'getting through to people'. One should, I believe, be wary of taking these explanations at their face value. There has, for example, been a good deal of influence from abroad – the 'radical' poets of the fifties and sixties show the influence of Brecht's satirical ballads. Some of them have conducted their own researches into the folk and broadside tradition, and have been able to see that all along there existed an alternative to the conventions imposed by the classical tradition. But it is already evident that the twentieth-century satire which survives will owe this survival to the fact that it is well written, and, furthermore (if this needs saying), that good writing actually increases the impact which the satirist has on his contemporaries. It is just that we must be careful to define what 'good writing' is, in the terms of today.

And this brings me to a most important question: the way in which society and literature are related to one another. Satiric poetry is poetry at grips with what society is doing. It deals with man's relationship to his fellow-men. For the most part, it avoids the transcendental. The advantage offered to the satirist by his profession is, in fact, what appears to be its principal disadvantage – the writer is placed at the mercy of events. A book of this kind, an anthology of satires and of extracts from satires, is, among other things, a social history of England in miniature. It charts the way that society has developed from the late Middle Ages till the present day. Satire is not always direct (satirists have a long tradition of self-protective obscurity) but good satire is, almost without exception, vivid, racy, and sensual. The satirist wants to project us into a situation that already exists, and, in order to do this, he must screw our senses up to a high pitch, must involve us with the milieu or the personality which he is describing. This is why satire often presents us with a series of lurid vignettes: history seen by flashes of lightning.

I don't mean by this that the best satire is simply a kind of newsreel – brilliantly edited perhaps, but essentially outside the sphere of art. There is, in some of the greatest satires in the language, a misanthropy which is its own sphere, something which passes far beyond the description of follies and foibles. One thinks of Rochester, of Swift, and perhaps even of Johnson. In these writers we find a total distrust of the world and its purposes. The 'Verses on the Death of Dr Swift', for example, is a poem which does not succeed in disguising, behind that light, easy tone which Swift possesses in greater measure than any other English poet, an implacable irony.

The satire of total rejection, the celebration of misanthropy, is not, however, the only kind of satire that exists. Satire of this kind plays only a small part in our literature. It is perhaps worth trying to decide what are the categories that satire most usually falls into. They turn out to be surprisingly few.

Political satire is something which I have already touched upon. The reasons why such satires are written seem to me to be self-evident. So, too, are the reasons why they are comparatively lightly represented here. The majority do not survive the immediate occasion. Those that live on do so, most often, because of the sheer force of the hatred which they enshrine; and an anthology of such hatreds would be a burden to any reader. A few, however, remain alive. The broadside satire, 'Tyburne Cheated', which I print here, perhaps for the first time since its original publication, does strike me as a work which is interesting from the literary point of view, as well as from the historical one. We see in it that mixture of triumph and bitterness which filled the minds of Royalists immediately after the Restoration. The dispossessed had returned once more to their orchards, and the fruit, though ripe, was bitter:

> Did we not doe a pretty thing,
> To *Murder* a Religious *King*:
> Oh! how we quafft his guiltless blood,
> He onely dy'd for being *good*;
> Whilst all the Punishment we had
> Was but to live, for being *bad*;
> If this be all we must incurr,
> Who would not be a *Murtherer*. . . .

The particular bitterness which we find here prepares us for the more comprehensive and general bitterness of the 'misanthropic' satires which I have just mentioned – 'Tyburne Cheated' is both the consequence of the Civil War, and the forerunner of Rochester's far greater poem, the 'Satyr' against reason and mankind, which was published as a broadside some fourteen or fifteen years later. Another obvious category is the literary satire. I have already spoken of the self-conscious character of the satiric impulse, and it is no surprise to discover how large a part of the satirist's criticisms are levelled against literature itself. In literary satire there is often a kind of wholeness because style, as well as content, can be used as an instrument of attack. A satire like Henry Carey's 'Namby Pamby' is doubly vituperative because of the element of parody:

> *Namby Pamby Pilli-pis*
> Rhimy pim'd on Missy-Miss;
> *Tartaretta Tartaree*
> From the Navel to the Knee;
> That her Father's Gracy-Grace
> Might give him a Placy-Place.

Unfortunately, good literary satires seem to me to be even rarer than durable political ones. There are two extremes. One is the parody, or burlesque. This too easily slips out of the satiric category altogether. The author signals a despairing admission that he is unable to capture the qualities of his original – the burlesque is a gesture of aggression directed at something admired; the writer takes what he cannot equal, and tries to bring it down to his own level of mediocrity. A great deal of Victorian parody fails for this reason: it is facetious, and has no edge, no genuine point of view. At the other extreme lies the serious literary satire, equipped with copious footnotes – I mean the literary satire as practised by such writers as Richard Owen Cambridge, author of *The Scribleriad*, and Thomas James Mathias, who wrote *The Pursuits of Literature*. The space which these two poems occupy in the textbooks is undeserved. A line of verse bobs, like a bit of flotsam, at the top of a page packed with notes in small type. The author is his own annotator, and pseudo-learning proves, in nearly every case, to be a dangerous weapon. It is hard to distinguish mock-pomposity from the real thing. Worse still, intensity drains out of the verse, because the author is having his fun elsewhere.

Between these contrasted kinds of failure – the Scylla and the Charybdis of literary satire – there are to be found the very numerous poems in the *Dunciad* convention. It is worth pointing out that Pope did not invent this particular form. *MacFlecknoe* is already a miniature *Dunciad*, and there are traces of the attitudes which Pope adopts even in Joseph Hall's *Virgidemiarum*. But the form persisted with astonishing vitality for more than two centuries, not only throughout the Victorian age, as I have already noted, but right up to the time of Roy Campbell's *Georgiad*, published as recently as 1931.

What gives *The Dunciad* its vitality is the fact that it is a mixture of things. We find in it an elaborate and dignified allegorical apparatus, the serious criticism of literature, and then a racy admixture of social and political satire. In fact, one is justified in saying that *The Dunciad* is really a social satire which has taken a special form to meet special circumstances.

If writers form a special class of victim, where English satire is concerned, so do women. Misogyny plays a far more prominent part in our satiric literature than total misanthropy. The reasons why writers should often dislike other writers are plain enough; but the reasons why satirists should persecute women perhaps need disentangling. It is not generally realized, even today, how large a part aggressive instincts, using this phrase in a Freudian sense, have to play in the creation of works of art. Since satire is itself an aggressive form of writing, the Freudian impulse appears more nakedly here than elsewhere. The symbolic rape is common in satire – we find it in the coarse poems against women written by Rochester and Swift. Misogynistic satire is often distinguished by a peculiarly nagging tone. Images recur in a way which suggests, not writers borrowing consciously from one another, but a common stock in the collective male subconscious. A writer like Robert Gould presents us with a picture of the fantasies which the male has about the female, and also the fears – of deception, castration, loss of identity. Sexual guilt leads him to paint women as repulsive physically; satire against women often seems to dwell with special emphasis on diseases, and on bodily functions and malfunctions.

It would be a mistake, nevertheless, to regard such sexually motivated satires in isolation. For the most part, because of the images and the trappings which the writer chooses, they range themselves among the social satires, just like literary satire of the *Dunciad* type.

Earlier, I talked of satire in verse being essentially a matter of poetry coming to grips with society, and with the idea of social organization. If morality lies at the very heart of satire (and this, I think, is axiomatic), then satire is ineffective unless that morality is active rather than passive. Moral codes are barren, if we regard them as things apart; they become fruitful only when we allow them to inform our every action. All the great religious teachers have been at pains to make this clear, and it is an idea still especially congenial to a puritan country, such as our own. What, then, are the typical *subjects* (not the objects) of social satire in English? Many people would think this a foolish question. 'Surely,' they would answer, 'the subject is English society itself.' And, in a way, they are right. But if we examine a mass of examples we find that the definition can be narrowed. The satirist speaks about power, and men of power. And it is at this point that political satire crosses an invisible frontier, and becomes something else. The depiction of types – the man of fashion, the rich mercantile vulgarian, the lawyer, and the priest – is, for the satirist, a means of self-definition, as well as being a complaint about the world and its ways. The writer tells us what he aspires to be, how he wants to live as well as what standards he adheres to. Often, the satire goes farther than this. It is characteristic of satire to be obsessed with court life and with the life of cities (these traits go back to Juvenal). One of the central subjects of English satire from the time of the Tudors till the end of the nineteenth century is specifically London, the 'great wen', the maw that devours a man body and soul. It is true that the satirist sometimes assumes a mask, and proceeds, with metropolitan suavity, to make fun of the country bumpkins. Soame Jenyns's amusing description of a country dinner, in 'A Letter from S. J. Esq. in the Country, to Lord Lovelace in Town', is an example of this:

> And having nine times view'd the garden,
> In which there's nothing worth a farthing,
> In comes my lady, and the pudden:
> You will excuse sir, – on a sudden –
> Then, that we may have four and four,
> The bacon, fowls, and collyflow'r
> Their ancient unity divide,
> The top one graces, one each side;
> And by and by, the second course
> Comes lagging like a distanc'd horse. . . .

But we are always aware, I think, that these satires of rusticity are affectionate, and quite without the bite of those which are directed against metropolitan corruption.

Yet let me make a point here – satire of the metropolis offered poets an opportunity to make use of material, and of a range of experience, which would otherwise have been useless to them. It has always struck me as a common misconception that poets are free to write about anything – anything which they experience, or look at, or read about. An examination of the evidence suggests that, in most epochs, the poets have only a comparatively limited range of subject matter open to them. The subject matter they could use, the experiences they could tap, were those which fitted the common stock of forms. These forms were to some extent determined by the condition of society itself, and even by the accepted moral framework – for example, by the idea that rustic things were 'good' and urban ones 'corrupt', which we find persisting right to our own day. We tend to forget what an immense and radical creative effort is required to invent a new form – by which I mean not merely a new metre or a new kind of stanza – but a whole new framework for the imagination. Literary history shows us few such efforts, and fewer still which have been made deliberately. One thinks of Malherbe, of Baudelaire, of Wordsworth, of Pound and Eliot. Some forms seem to have been created almost by accident; others still, as with the Elizabethan satirists such as Hall and Marston, by poets who proclaimed that they were returning to something earlier.

City life, innovatory, restless, 'unnatural', is something which poetry finds it hard to come to grips with. As I have already noted, our own (extremely urbanized) epoch is still marked by a certain hostility to material of this kind. Some of the most widely praised of contemporary poets – R. S. Thomas, for instance, and Ted Hughes – continue to make use of natural images, plants, and beasts, and the progress of the seasons. And this is something which seems to offer comfort to their readers. Satire, because it condemns, opens a door for the poet who wants to deal with city life and urban imagery. He may, in fact, have far greater experience of these than of the morally sound countryside. The satirical form enables him to describe, and even to relish, while apparently re-jecting. The images spring directly and freshly from the way of life which most concerns him. The brio of the descriptions of town life which we find in English verse-satires may perhaps help to convince us of the truth of this theory – that satire allows a release of creative literary energy into a channel which might otherwise be blocked.

What I mean is that satire sometimes offers a kind of outlet which the poet may not always understand, and this does not conflict in any way with my earlier remarks about the self-consciousness of satire. What we see in satirical poems is some-thing very interesting, and, occasionally, moving. The poet is at grips with the ordinary, rather than the exalted: with society, and with men in their everyday relationships to one another. These relationships may be far from ideal, but they go to make a kind of poetry which has its own, very genuine, fascinations. Satiric poetry requires special talents. Many of the poets represented here are quite unknown; a high proportion are not, so far as I am aware, represented in other anthologies. But they each have a fragment of truth to bring us. The general (though not total) neglect of satire by modern scholars has led, in turn, to the neglect of many poets worth re-reading. The making of this book has certainly provided me with a number of surprises, as well as a great deal of pleasure. I hope that this pleasure may be shared by those who read it. My aim has been primarily to show that the range of the English poets is perhaps even more extended than we think, and certainly all theories have been subordinated to that. To make new readers for an unjustly neglected writer seems to me one of the great services which an anthologist can perform.

EDWARD LUCIE-SMITH

NOTES ON THE SELECTION AND
THE TEXT

VERSE satire is a vast, ill-charted subject, as I know from my own experience in looking for material for this book. In order to preserve some kind of historical and social continuity I have kept to English satirists. Satires in dialect have been excluded, and translations (though not adaptations), and so has satire written by Americans, such as Lowell's *Fable for Critics*. I have, however, stretched this rule in order to include the work of W. H. Auden, and that of Ezra Pound (the poem I have chosen belongs to Pound's 'English' period).

In order not to cause undue difficulty to readers, poems printed before 1600 are presented in modernized versions, thus following the convention of my *Penguin Book of Elizabethan Verse*. After this date I have used either the first-edition text, or the generally accepted 'best' edition (as, for example, in the case of Cleveland, where the 1677 text edited by his friends and pupils is clearly preferable to earlier ones). Where there are good modern editions, these have been consulted. Punctuation, capitalization, italicization, and spelling have not been tampered with. Dates of publication (and of composition where these are significantly different) are given at the foot of each piece. I have provided such notes as I thought would be helpful, with special attention to the persons mentioned. Naturally there have been a few problems of annotation which I find myself unable to solve.

SATIRICAL
VERSE

WILLIAM LANGLAND

(*fl.* 1377)

It has been conjectured that the author of *Piers Plowman* was born
about 1332, and died around 1400. At one time, so he tells us in the
poem, he made a living by praying for those richer than himself.
He also tells us that he lived in London, in Cornhill, and that he had
a wife and a daughter. The poem exists in three distinct versions.

From *Piers Plowman*

AVARICE

THEN came Covetise · can I him not describe
So hungry-like and hollow · Sir Harvey[1] him looked.
He was beetlebrowed · and blabberlipped also,
With two bleared eyen[2] · as a blind hag;
And as a leathern purse · lolled his cheeks,
Well sydder[3] than his chin · they chiveled[4] for eld;
And as a bondman of his bacon · his beard was bedraveled.
With an hood on his head · a lousy hat above,
And in a tawny tabard[5] · of twelve winter age,
All to-torn and baudy · and full of lice creeping;
But if that a louse could · have lopen[6] the better,
She should not have walked on that welche[7] · so was it threadbare.
'I have been couvetous,' quod this caitiff. 'I beknow it here;
For some time I served · Sim at the Style,
And was his prentice y-plight · his profit to wait.
First I learned to lie · a leaf other twain,[8]
Wicked-like to weigh · was my first lesson.
To Wy[9] and Winchester · I went to the fair,
With many manner merchandise · as my master me hight;
Ne had the grace of guile · y-go among my ware,
It had be unsold this seven year · so God me help!
    Then drew I among drapers · my donet[10] for to learn,
To draw the lyser[11] along · the longer it seemed;
Among the rich rays[12] · I rendered a lesson,
To broach[13] them with a pack-needle · and plaited[14] them together,
And put them in a press · and pinned them therein,

Till ten yards or twelve · had tolled out thirteen.
  My wife was a webbe[1] · and woollen cloth made;
She spake to spinsters · to spinnen it out.
And the pound[2] that she payed by · poised a quartern more,
Than mine own auncel[3] · who-so weighed truth.
  I bought her barley-malt · she brew it to sell,
Penny-ale[4] and pudding-ale[5] · she poured together
For labourers and for low folk; · that lay by himself.[6]
  The best ale lay in my bower[7] · or in my bedchamber,
And who-so bummed[8] thereof · bought it thereafter,
A gallon for a groat · God wot, no less;
And yet it came in cupmel[9] · this craft my wife used.
Rose the regratour[10] · was her right name;
She hath holden hockery[11] · all her life-time.
  And I swear now, so the ik[12] · that sin I will let,
And never wicked-like way · ne wicked chaffer use,
But wenden to Walsingham[13] · and my wife also,
And bid the Rood of Bronholm[14] · bring me out of debt.'
  'Repentest thee ever,' quod Repentance · 'ne restitution[15]
    madest?'
  'Yes, once I was harboured,' quod he · 'with a heap of chapmen,
I rose when they were arest · and y-rifled[16] their males.'[17]

[B Text, Passus V, c. 1377, modernized text.]

A SONG AGAINST THE FRIARS:
ANONYMOUS

The Dominican order arrived in England in 1221, and the Franciscan in 1224. By the end of the fourteenth century, all the friars, but especially the Friars Minor, were under heavy fire. Wycliff, for example, wrote a number of pamphlets directed against the friars towards the end of his life. In one he asserts *'bonus enim fratrus rarus cum fenice'* – 'a good friar is as rare as the phoenix.' Chaucer and Langland also joined the attack. In general, the religious life of the period suffered because of the papal schism and other disorders of the time. The Friars Minor, who habitually mingled with the people, and who intruded upon the usual organization of diocese and parish, were open to many temptations, and were the target of much resentment. However, it is worth noticing that the commissioners of Henry VIII often remark that the Franciscan Friary was the poorest of the religious houses in a town.

From *A Song Against the Friars*

ALAS! that ever it should be so,
Such clerks as they about should go,
From town to town by two and two,
    To seek their sustenance.
By God that all this world won,
He that that order first begun,
Methink certes it was a man
    Of simple ordinance.
  For they have nought to live by,
    they wandren here and there,
And deal with divers mercery,
    right as they pedlars were.

They deal with purses, pins, and knives,
With girdles, gloves, for wenches and wives;
But ever backward the husband thrives
    There they are haunted till.
For when the good man is from home,

And the friar comes to our dame,
He spares neither for sin ne shame,
    That he ne does his will.
  If they no help of housewives had,
    when husbands are not in,
  The friars' welfare were full bad,
    for they should brew full thin.

Some friars bearen pelure[1] about,
For great ladies and wenches stout,
To reverse[2] with their clothes without;
    All after that they are.
For some vair,[3] and some gryse,[4]
For some bugee,[5] and for some byse,[6]
And also many a divers spice,
    In bags about they bear.
  All that for women is pleasand
    full ready certes have they;
  But little give they the husband,
    that for all shall pay.

Trantes[7] they ken, and many a jape;
For some shall with a pound of sape[8]
Get him a kirtle and a cape,
    And somewhat else thereto.
Whereto should I oathès swear?
There is no pedlar that pack can bear,
That half so dear can sell his gear,
    Than a friar can do.
  For if he give a wife a knife
    that cost but pennies two,
  Worth ten knives, so mot[9] I thryfe,
    he will have ere he go.

Each man that here shall lead his life,
That has a fair daughter or a wife,
Beware that no friar them shryfe,
    Neither loud ne still.

34

Though women seem of heart full stable,
With fair behest and with fable
They can make their hearts changeable,
 And their likings fulfil,
 Be ware aye with the limitour,[1]
  and with his fellow both,
 And they make mysteries in thy bower,
  it shall turn thee to scathe.

Were I a man that housè held,
If any woman with me dwelled,
There is no friar, but he were geld,
 Should come within my wones.
For may he till a woman win,
In privity, he will not blynne,[2]
Ere he a child put her within,
 And perchance two at once.
 Though he lour under his hood,
  with semblaunt[3] quaint and mild,
 If thou him trust, or does him good,
  by God, thou art beguiled.

[c. 1380, modernized text]

GEOFFREY CHAUCER

(*c.* 1340–1400)

The earliest record of Chaucer occurs in 1357, when he was a page in the household of the Countess of Ulster, later the Duchess of Clarence, the wife of the third son of Edward III. In 1359 Chaucer went abroad to soldier in France. He was captured by the enemy, and the king himself helped to ransom him. By 1367 he was in attendance on the king, and in that year he married. His wife was the sister of Catherine Swynford, the third wife of John of Gaunt. He was soon employed on various missions abroad – in 1372 he was sent to Genoa, and in 1378 to Milan. His official career prospered – in 1374 he became the Comptroller of customs and subsidies on wools, skins, and hides for the Port of London; in 1382 he was made the Comptroller of petty customs. In 1385 he became Justice of the Peace for Kent, and in 1386 Knight of the Shire. But 1386 also marked a setback in his fortunes. His constant patron John of Gaunt went to Spain, and Chaucer, deprived of this support, was also stripped of his offices. He was restored to favour in 1389, but the interval had allowed him to do most of the work on the *Canterbury Tales* – the culmination of a life's work as a writer.

From *The Prologue to The Canterbury Tales*

THE MONK

A Monk there was, a fair for the maistrie,[1]
An outrider,[2] that lovéd venery,[3]
A manly man, to been an abbot able.
Full many a dainty horse he had in stable,
And when he rode, men might his bridle hear
Jingling as in a whistling wind all clear
And eke as loud as doth the chapel bell.
There as[4] this lord was keeper of the cell,[5]
The rule of Saint Maure[6] or of Saint Beneit,[7]
By cause that it was old and somedel[8] strait
This ilké Monk let oldé thingés pace,[9]
And held after the new world the space.[10]
He yaf not of that text a pulléd hen,[11]
That saith that hunters be not holy men,

36

Ne that a monk, when he is recchelees,[1]
Is likned till a fish that is waterless, –
This is to seyn, a monk out of his cloister.
But thilkè text held he not worth an oyster;
And I said his opinion was good.
What should he study and make himselven wood,[2]
Upon a book in cloister alway to pore,
Or swynken[3] with his handès, and labour,
As Austin[4] bid? How shall the world be served?
Let Austin have his swynk to him reserved!
Therefore he was a prikasour[5] aright:
Greyhounds he had as swift as fowl in flight;
Of prikyng[6] and of hunting for the hare
Was all his lust, for no costs would he spare.
I seigh[7] his sleeves purfiléd at the hand[8]
With grys,[9] and that the finest of a land;
And, for to fasten his hood under his chin,
He had of gold y-wrought a full curious pin;
A love-knot in the greater end there was.
His head was bald, that shone as any glass,
And eke his face, as he had been enoynt,[10]
He was a lord full fat and in good point;
His eyen steep,[11] and rolling in his head,
That steamed as a furnace of a leed;[12]
His bootès supple, his horse in great estate.[13]
Now certainly he was a great prelate;
He was not pale as a forpynéd[14] ghost.
A fat swan loved he best of any roast.
His palfrey was as brown as is a berry.

[c. 1387, modernized text]

ON THE DEATH OF THE DUKE OF
SUFFOLK: ANONYMOUS

This poem is a parody of the Requiem Mass, and the fallen Suffolk's clients are represented as taking part in the service. The poem is in the form of a *sirventes*, a kind of political poem invented by the Provençal troubadours. William de la Pole, Duke of Suffolk, was born in 1396, and served in all the later French campaigns under Henry V. In the bad years after Henry's death, he was defeated and taken prisoner by Jeanne d'Arc at Jargeau, after the raising of the siege of Orleans (1429) but was soon ransomed. After the death of the Duke of Bedford, he attached himself to Cardinal Beaufort and the Beaufort party. He was largely responsible for the marriage between Henry VI and Margaret of Anjou. In 1447 both Cardinal Beaufort and Humphrey of Gloucester died, and Suffolk found himself the chief man in the state. His position was, however, far from secure, as he was held responsible for an unpopular peace. In 1449 there was a disastrous renewal of the war. Suffolk was impeached by the Commons, and eventually sentenced to banishment for five years. On 1 May 1450, he left England, but was intercepted and executed at sea.

On the Death of the Duke of Suffolk

In the month of May, when grass groweth green,
    Flagrant in her flourès, with sweet savour,
Jack Napes[1] would on the sea[2] a mariner to been,
    With his clog and his chain, to seek more treasure.
    Such a pain prickéd him, he asked a confessor.
Nicolas[3] said, 'I am ready thy confessor to be;'
    He was holden so that he ne passed that hour.
For Jack Napes' soul *Placebo* and *Dirige*.[4]

Who shall execute his exequies with a solemnity?
    Bishops and lordès, as great reason is;
Monks, canons, priests, and other clergy,
    Pray for this duke's soul that it might come to bliss;
    And let never such another come after this;

His interfectors[1] blessed might they be,
　　And grant them for their deed to reign with angelis;
And for Jack Napes' soul *Placebo* and *Dirige*.

'*Placebo*,' beginneth the bishop of Hertford.[2]
　　'*Dilexi*, for mine advancement,' saith the bishop of Chester.[3]
'*Heu mei*,' saith Salisbury,[4] 'this goeth to fair forth.'
　　'*Ad Dominum cum tribularer*,' saith the abbot of Gloucester.
　　'*Dominus custodit*,' saith the abbot of Rochester.
'*Levavi oculos*,' saith frere Stanbury, '*volavi*.'
　　'*Si iniquitates*,' saith the bishop of Worcester;[5]
'For Jack Napes' soul *de profundis clamavi*.'

'*Opera manuum tuarum*,' saith the cardinal[6] wisely,
　　That brought forth *confitebor*, for allè this Napes' reason.
'*Audivi vocem*,' sang Almighty God on high;
　　And therefore sing we '*Magnificat anima mea Dominum*.'
　　Unto this dirige most we gone and come
This paschal time, to say verily
　　Three psalms and lessons, that all is and some
For Jack Napes' soul *Placebo* and *Dirige*.

Executors of this office *Dirige* for to sing,
　　Shall begin the bishop of Saint Asse;[7]
'*Verba mea auribus*,' saith the abbot of Reading;
　　'All your joy and hope is come to alas.'
　　'*Committere, Domine*, yet grant us grace,'
Saith abbot of Saint Albans full sorrily.
　　The abbot of the Tower Hill, with his fat face,
Quaketh and tremuleth for '*Domine, ne in furore*.'

Master Walter Liard[8] shall sing '*Ne quando*.'
　　The abbot of Westminster, '*Domine Deus meus, in te speravi*;
Requiem aeternam grant them all to come to.'
　　Therto a pater-noster saith the bishop of Saint Davy[9]
　　For the soulès that wise were and mighty,
Suffolk, Moleyns,[10] and Roos,[11] these three;
　　And in especial for Jack Napes, that ever was wily,
For his soul *Placebo* and *Dirige*.

[Rise up, Say,[1] read *parce in Domine*,
  '*Nihil enim sunt dies mei*,' thou shalt sing;
The bishop of Carlyle sing '*Credo*' full sore.
  To such false traitors come foul ending!
  The baron of Dudley with great morning,
Readeth, '*Taedat animam meam vitae meae.*'
  Who but Daniel *qui Lasarum* shall sing?
For Jack Napes' soul *Placebo* and *Dirige*.

John Say readeth, '*Manus tuae fecerunt me.*'
  '*Libera me*,' singeth Trevilian, 'ware the rere,
That they do no more so, *requiescant in pace.*'
  Thus prays allè England far and near.
  Where is Somerset? why appears he not here,
To sing '*Dies irae et miseriae?*'
  God grant England allè in fear
For these traitors to sing *Placebo* and *Dirige*.

Many more there be behind, the sooth for to tell,
  That shall masses upon these do sing.
I pray some man do ring the bell,
  That these forsaiden may come to the sacring;
  And that in brief time, without more tarrying,
That this mass may be ended in such degree;
  And that all England joyful may sing
The commendation with *Placebo* and *Dirige*.

[1450, modernized text]

WOMEN, WOMEN . . .: ANONYMOUS

From an early sixteenth-century commonplace-book.

Women, Women, Love of Women,
Maketh Bare Purses with Some Men

SOME be merry, and some be sad,
And some be busy, and some be bad;
Some be wild, by Saint Chad,
   Yet all be not so;
     For some be lewd, and some be shrewd;
     Go, shrew, where-so-ever ye go.

Some be wise, and some be fond;
Some be tame, I understond;
Some will take bread at a mannès hond
   Yet all be not so;
     For some be lewd, and some be shrewd;
     Go, shrew, where-so-ever ye go.

Some be wroth, and cannot tell wherefore;
Some be scorning evermore;
And some be tuskéd like a boar;
   Yet all be not so;
     For some be lewd, and some be shrewd;
     Go, shrew, where-so-ever ye go.

Some will be drunken as a mouse;
Some be crooked, and will hurt a louse;
Some be fair, and good in a house;
   Yet all be not so;
     For some be lewd, and some be shrewd;
     Go, shrew, where-so-ever ye go.

Some be snouted like an ape;
Some can neither play ne jape;
Some of them be well shape;
   Yet all be not so;
     For some be lewd, and some be shrewd;
     Go, shrew, where-so-ever ye go.

Some can prate without hire;
Some make bate in every shire;
Some can play check-mate with our sire,
   Yet all they do not so:
     For some be lewd, and some be shrewd;
     Go, shrew, where-so-ever ye go.

[*c.* 1525, modernized text]

ALEXANDER BARCLAY

(1475?–1552)

Barclay seems to have been a Scotsman. In his will he describes himself as a Doctor of Divinity, but where he got his degree is unknown. As a young man, he apparently travelled in France and Italy. On his return, he was ordained priest, and became a member of the college of secular priests at Ottery St Mary, in Devonshire. Later he was a Benedictine monk at Ely, and it was here that the *Egloges* were written. At some later date, he assumed the habit of the more rigorous Franciscan order at Canterbury. He survived the dissolution of the monasteries, and in 1546 was presented to a vicarage in Essex and another in Somerset. He also survived the reign of Edward VI, and in 1552, just before his death, was presented to the rectory of All Hallows, Lombard Street. He was an enemy of Skelton's and attacks him at the end of *The Ship of Fools*, his most famous work.

From *The Egloges*

COURT MANNERS

CORIDON in court I tell thee by my soul
For most part thou must drink of a common bowl,
And where greasy lips and slimy beard
Hath late been dipped to make some mad afeard,
On that side must thou thy lips wash also,
Or else without drink from dinner thou must go.
In the mean season old wine and dearly bought,
Before thy presence shall to thy prince be brought,
Whose smell and odour so sweet and marvellous
With fragrant savour inbaumeth all the house,
As Muscadel, Caprike, Romney, and Malvesy,[1]
From Gene[2] brought, from Greece and Hungary.
Such shall he drink, such shall to him be brought,
Thou hast the savour thy part of it is nought,
Though thou shouldst perish for very ardent thirst
No drop thou gettest for to enslake thy lust,
And though good wines sometime to thee be brought
The taste of better shall cause it to be nought,

43

Oft wouldest thou drink yet darest thou not sup
Till time thy better have tasted of the cup.
No cup is filled till dinner be half done,
And some ministers it counteth then to sone,
But if thou begin for drink to call and crave
Thou for thy calling such good reward shall have,
That men shall call thee malapart or drunk,
Or an abbey lowne[1] or limner of a monk,
But with thy rebuke yet art thou never the near,
Whether thou demand wine, palled ale or beer,
Yet shalt thou not drink when thou hast need and thirst,
The cup must thou spare aye for the better lust.
Through many hands shall pass the piece or cup,
Before it come to thee is all drunk up,
And then if a drop or two therein remain
To lick the vessel sometime thou art full fain,
And then at the ground some filth if thou espy
To blame the butler thou gettest but envy.
And as men weekly new holy water pour,
And once in a year the vessel use to scour,
So cups and tankards in court as thou mayst think,
Wherein the commons are used for to drink,
Are once in the year empty and made clean,
And scantly that well as oftentime is seen.
For to ask water thy wines to allay
Thou shalt find no need if thou before assay,
With rinsing of cups it tempered is before
Because pure water perchance is not in store.

[1513/14, modernized text]

JOHN SKELTON
(c. 1460–1529)

Skelton is said to have been educated at Oxford. Afterwards he studied at Cambridge, and seems to have taken his M.A. degree in 1484. His first patron was the Countess of Richmond, Henry VII's mother. Later he was appointed tutor to Prince Henry, the future Henry VIII. In 1498 he was ordained priest and in 1504 retired from court to become rector of Diss in Norfolk, where he proved a troublesome and rather scandalous incumbent. He gained a reputation as a practical joker, and many legends began to gather about his character and conduct. Wolsey, who had been a patron of Skelton's, and the dedicatee of one of his works, became at a later period the object of Skelton's fiercest satire. The cardinal is said to have had him imprisoned several times. Eventually Skelton fled to sanctuary in Westminster Abbey. The abbot, John Islip, continued to protect him till his death.

From *Speak, Parrot*

My name is Parrot,[1] a bird of Paradise,
 By nature deviséd of a wondrous kind,
Daintily dieted with divers delicate spice
 Till Euphrates, that flood, driveth me into Ind;
 Where men of that countrý by fortune me find
And send me to greatè ladyès of estate:
Then Parrot must have an almond or a date.

A cage curiously carven, with a silver pin,
 Properly painted, to be my coverture;
A mirror of glassè, that I may toot therein:
 These, maidens full meekly with many a divers flower,
 Freshly they dress, and makè sweet my bower,
With 'Speak, Parrot, I pray you!' full curtesly they say,
'Parrot is a goodly bird, a pretty popinjay!'

With my bekè bent, my little wanton eye,
 My feathers fresh as is the emerald green,
About my neck a circulet like the rich rubý,

45

My little leggės, my feet both feat and clean,
    I am a minion to wait upon a queen.
'My proper Parrot, my little pretty fool!'
With ladies I learn, and go with them to school.

'Ha! Ha! Ha! Parrot, ye can laugh prettily!'
    Parrot hath not dinéd all this long day.
Like your puss-cat, Parrot can mew and cry
    In Latin, Hebrew, Araby and Chaldy;
    In Greekė tongue Parrot can both speak and say,
As Persius that poet, doth report of me,
    '*Quis expedivit psittaco suum chaire?*'[1]

Doucė French of Paris Parrot can learne,
    Pronouncing my purpose after my propertý,
With '*Parlez bien*, Parrot, *ou parlez rien!*'[2]
    With Dutch, with Spanish, my tongue can agree,
    In English to God Parrot can supply:
'Christ save King Henry the Eighth, our royal king,
The red rose in honour to flourish and spring!

With Katharine incomparable, our royal queen alsó,
    That peerless pomegranate, Christ save her noble grace!'
Parrot *sable hablar Castiliano*,[3]
    With *fidasso de cosso*[4] in Turkey and in Thrace;[5]
    Vis consilii expers, as teacheth me Horáce,
Mole ruit sua,[6] whose dictates are pregnánt,
Souventez foys, Parrot, *en souvenante*.[7]

My lady mistress, Dame Philology,
    Gave me a giftė, in my nest when I lay,
To learn all language, and it to speak apteIý.
    Now *pandez mory*, wax frantic, some men say,
    Phronesis for Phrenesis may not hold her way.
An almond now for Parrot, delicately drest:
In *Salve festa dies*, *toto* there doth best.[8]

Moderata juvant,[1] but *toto* doth exceed:
   Discretion is mother of noble virtues all.
Myden agan[2] in Greeke tongue we read.
   But reason and wit wanteth their provincial
   When wilfulness is vicar general.
Haec res acu tangitur,[3] Parrot, *par ma foy*:
Taisez-vous, Parrot, *tenez-vous coy*![4]

Busy, busy, busy, and business again!
   Que pensez-vous,[5] Parrot? what meaneth this business?
Vitulus[6] in Horeb troubléd Aaron's brain,
   Melchizadek[7] merciful made Moloch merciless:
   Too wise is no virtue, too meddling, too restléss.
In measure is treasure, *cum sensu maturato*,
Ne tropo sanno, ne tropo mato.[8]

Aran[9] was firéd with Chaldee's fire called Ur,
   Johab was brought up in the land of Hus,[10]
The lineage of Lot[11] took support of Assúr,
   Jereboseth[12] is Hebrew, who list the cause discuss –
   'Peace, Parrot, ye prate as ye wère *ebrius*:[13]
Hist thee, *lyver God van hemrik, ich seg*!'[14]
In Popering[15] grew pears when Parrot was an egg.

What is this to purpose? 'Over in a whinny Meg!'
   Hob Lobin of Lowdoon[16] would hae a bit a' bread;
The gibbet of Baldock was made for Jack Leg;[17]
   An arrow unfeatheréd and without an head,
   A bagpipe without blowing standeth in no stead:
Some run too far before, some run too far behind,
Some be too churlish, and some be too kind.

Ich dien[18] serveth for the ostrich feather,
   Ich dien is the language of the land of Beme;
In Afric tongue *byrsa*[19] is a thong of leather;
   In Palestina there is Jerusaleme.
   Colostrum[20] now for Parrot, white bread and sweet cream!
Our Thomasen she doth trip, our Jennet she doth shale:[21]
Parrot hath a blacké beard and a fair green tail.

'Morish mine own shelf!' the costermonger saith,
  'Fate, fate, fate!' ye Irish waterlag;
In flattering fables men find but little faith,
  But *moveatur terra*,[1] let the world wag;
  Let Sir Wrig-wrag wrestle with Sir Dalyrag;
Every man after his manner of ways,
Paub yn ei arver,[2] so the Welchman says.

Such shreddès of sentence, strewèd in the shop
  Of ancient Aristippus[3] and such other mo,
I gader together and close in my crop,
  Of my wanton conceit, *unde depromo*
  Dilemmata docta in paedagogio
Sacro vatem,[4] whereof to you I break.
I pray you, let Parrot have liberty to speak!

But 'Ware the cat, Parrot, ware the false cat!'
  With 'Who is there – a maid? Nay, nay, I trow!'
'Ware riot, Parrot! Ware riot, ware that!'
  'Meat, meat for Parrot, meat I say, ho!'
  Thus diverse of language by learning I grow,
With 'Buss me, sweet Parrot, buss me, sweet sweet!'
To dwell among ladyès Parrot is meet.

'Parrot, Parrot, Parrot, pretty popinjay!'
  With my beak I can pick my little pretty toe;
My delight is solace, pleasure, disport and play.
  Like a wanton, when I will, I reel to and fro.
  Parrot can say *Caesar, ave*![5] alsó.
But Parrot hath no favour to Esebon.[6]
Above all birdès, set Parrot alone.

Ulala,[7] Esebon, for Jeremy doth weep!
  Zion is in sadness, Rachel ruely doth look;
Madionita Jethro, our Moses keepeth his sheep;
  Gideon[8] is gone, that Zalmane undertook,
  Horeb *et* Zeb, of *Judicum* read the book
Now Gebal, Ammon, and Amaloch[9] – 'Hark, hark!'
Parrot pretendeth to be a Bible clerk!

O Esebon, Esebon! to thee is come again
  Sihon, the regent Amorraeorum,[1]
And Og, that fat hog of Bashan, doth retain
  The crafty *coistronus Cananaeorum*;[2]
    And *asylum*, whilom *refugium miserorum*,[3]
Non fanum, sed profanum,[4] standeth in little stead.
Ulala, Esebon, for Japhthah[5] is stark dead!

Esebon, Marylebone, Whetstone next Barnet;[6]
  A trim-tram[7] for an horse-mill it were a nice thing!
Dainties for damoiselles, chaffer far-fet:[8]
  Bo-ho[9] doth bark well, but Hough-ho[10] he ruleth the ring;
  From Scarpary[11] to Tartary renown therein doth spring,
With 'He said,' and 'We said,' ich wot now what ich wot –
Quod magnus est dominus Judas Iscariot.[12]

Ptolemy[13] and Haly[14] were cunning and wise
  In the volvel,[15] in the quadrant, and in the astroloby,
To prognosticate truly the chance of Fortune's dice;
  Some treat of their tirykis,[16] some of astrology,
  Some *pseudo-propheta*[17] with chiromancy.[18]
If Fortune be friendly, and grace be the guide,
Honour with renown will run on that side.

                    [1554, written *c.* 1521–3, modernized text]

From *Why Come Ye Not to Court?*

ON CARDINAL WOLSEY[19]

        ONCE *yet again*
        Of you I would frain,
        Why come ye not to court?
      To whichè court?
      To the kingès court,
      Or to Hampton Court?[20]
      Nay, to the kingès court.
      The kingès court
      Should have the excellence,

49

But Hampton Court
Hath the pre-eminence,
And Yorkės Place,[1]
With my lordės Grace!
To whose magnificence
Is all the confluence,
Suits and supplications,
Embassades of all nations.
Straw for Law Canon,
Or for the Law Common,
Or for Law Civil!
It shall be as he will.
Stop at Law Tancrete,[2]
An abstract or a concrete,
Be it sour, be it sweet,
His wisdom is so discreet
That, in a fume or an heat –
'Warden of the Fleet,
Set him fast by the feet!'
And of his royal power,
When him list to lower,
Then 'Have him to the Tower,
Sannz aulter remedy!
Have him forth, by and by,
To the Marshalsea,
Or to the Kingês Bench!'[3]
He diggeth so in the trench
Of the court royall
That he ruleth them all.
So he doth undermind,
And suchė sleights doth find,
That the kingês mind
By him is subverted,
And so straitly coarted
In credencing his talės
That all is but not-shellės
That any other saith –
He hath him in such faith.

Now, yet all this might be
Suffered and taken in gre
If that that he wrought
To any good end were brought.
But all he bringeth to nought,
By God, that me dear bought!
He beareth the king on hand
That he must pill his land
To make his coffers rich;
But he layeth all in the ditch,
And useth such abusíon
That in the conclusíon
All cometh to confusíon.

Perceive the cause why?
To tell the truth plainly,
He is so ambitíous,
So shameless, and so vicíous,
And so superstitíous,
And so much oblivíous
From whence that he came
That he falleth into a *caeciam,* –
Which, truly to express,
Is a forgetfulness,
Or wilful blindness,
Wherewith the Sodomites
Lost their inward sights,
The Gommorhians alsó
Were brought to deadly woe,
As Scripture recordès:
A caecitate cordis,
(In the Latin sing we)
Libera nos, Domine!

But this mad Amaleck,
Like to a Mamelek,
He regardeth lordès
No more than potsherdès!

He is in such elation
Of his exaltation,
And the supportation
Of our sovereign lordė,
That, God to recordė,
He ruleth all at will,
Without reason or skill.
Howbeit, the primordial
Of his wretched original,
And his base progeny,
And his greasy genealogy,
He came of the sang royall
That was cast out of a butcher's stall.

But however he was born,
Men would have the lessė scorn
If he couldė consider
His birth and roomė together,
And call to his mindė
How noble and how kindė
To him he hath found
Our sovereign lord, chief ground
Of all this prelacy,
That set him noblý
In great authority
Out from a low degree,
Which he cannot see.
For he was, pardee,
No doctor of divinity,
Nor doctor of the law,
Nor of none other saw;
But a poorė master of art,
God wot, had little part
Of the quatrivials,
Nor yet of trivials,
Nor of philosophy,
Nor of philology,
Nor of good policy,

Nor of astronomy,
Nor acquainted worth a fly
With honourable Halý,
Nor with royal Ptolemy,[1]
Nor with Albumazar,[2]
To treat of any star
Fixed or else mobile.
His Latin tongue doth hobble,
He doth but clout and cobble
In Tully's faculty
Calléd humanity.
Yet proudly he dare pretend
How no man can him amend.
But have yet not heard this, –
How a one-eyed man is
Well-sighted when
He is among blind men?

Then, our process for to stable,
This man was full unable
To reach to such degree
Had no our Princè be
Royal Henry the Eight,
Take him in such conceit
That he set him on height,
In exemplifying
Great Alexander the king,
In writing as we find
Which (of his royal mind,
And of his noble pleasure,
Transcending out of measure)
Thought to do a thing
That pertaineth to a king –
To make up one of nought,
And made him to be brought
A wretched poorè man
Which his living wan
With planting of leeks

By the days and by the weeks;
And of this poorè vassal
He made a king royall,
And gave him a realm to rule
That occupiéd a shule,[1]
A mattock, and a spade,
Before that he was made
A king, as I have told,
And ruléd as he wold.
Such is a kingès power, –
To make within an hour,
And work such a miracle
That shall be a spectacle
Of renown and worldly fame.
In likewise now the same
Cardinal is promoted,
Yet with lewd conditions coated,
As hereafter ben noted, –
Presumption and vainglory,
Envy, wrath, and lechery,[2]
Couvetise and gluttony,
Slothful to do good,
Now frantic, now starkè wood.[3]

[1545, modernized text]

FRIAR WILLIAM ROY AND FRIAR JEROME BARLOW

(fl. 1528)

Roy and Barlow were two exiled Franciscan friars. This satire, directed at Cardinal Wolsey, was printed before 8 May 1528. Wolsey ordered every copy bought up and destroyed.

From *Read Me and Be Not Wroth*

ON CARDINAL WOLSEY

Watkin:
Doth he use then on mules[1] to ride?

Jeffrey:
Yea! and that with so shameful pride,
  That to tell, it is not possible!
More like a God celestial,
Than any creature mortal!
  With worldly pomp incredible!
Before him rideth two priests strong,
And they bear two crosses right long,
  Gaping in every man's face.
After them follow two laymen secular;
And each of them holding a pillar
  In their hands, 'stead of a mace.
Then followeth my Lord, on his mule,
Trapped with gold under her cule,
  In every point most curiously.
On each side, a poleaxe is borne,
Which in none other use is worn;
  Pretending some hid mystery.
Then hath he servants five, or six, score;
Some behind, and some before,
  A marvellous great company!
Of which are lords and gentlemen,
With many grooms and yeomen,
  And also knaves among.

Thus daily he proceedeth forth;
And men must take it at worth,
   Whether he do right, or wrong!
A great carl he is, and a fat;
Wearing on his head a Red Hat,
   Procured with angels' subsidy:
And (as they say) in time of rain,
Four of his gentlemen are fain
   To hold over it a canopy.
Beside this, to tell thee more news,
He hath a pair of costly shoes;
   Which seldom touch any ground,
They are so goodly and curious!
All of gold and stones precious,
   Costing many a thousand pound.

Watkin:
And who did for these shoes pay?

Jeffrey:
Truly, many a rich Abbey,
   To be eased of his Visitation.

Watkin:
Doth he, in his own person, visit?

Jeffrey:
No! Another for him doth it,
   That can skill of the occupation.

                      [1528, modernized text]

SIR THOMAS WYATT

(1503?–42)

Wyatt's father was an opponent of Richard III and a favourite of Henry VII. Thomas Wyatt studied at St John's College, Cambridge, and spent much of his adult life on diplomatic missions for the English court, and, in particular, in the vain effort to conciliate Charles V. Wyatt married young (1520), but even before this had made the acquaintance of Anne Boleyn. Their relationship continued close even after his marriage, and she was widely regarded as his mistress. He apparently made a clean breast of the relationship to Henry VIII, before the king married her. In 1536, on Anne's fall, Wyatt was committed to the Tower. However, his role seems to have been that of a possible witness. He did not lose the king's favour, and was treated with marked confidence by Cromwell. He was again arrested on the fall of Cromwell, but was subsequently released and given marks of Henry's favour. He died possessed of large estates.

From *Satire I*

COUNTRY PURSUITS

THIS maketh me at home to hunt and to hawk
And in foul weather at my book to sit;

In frost and snow then with my bow to stalk.
No man doth mark whereso I ride and go.
In lusty leas at liberty I walk

(And of these news I feel nor weal nor woe,
Save that a clog doth hang yet at my heel –
No force for that, for it is ordered so)

That I may leap both hedge and dike full well.
I am not now in France to judge the wine,
With savoury sauce the delicates to feel;

Nor yet in Spain, where one must him incline
Rather than to be outwardly to seem –
I meddle not with wits that be so fine;

57

Nor Flanders cheer letteth not my sight to deem
Of black and white, nor taketh my wit away
With beastliness – they beasts do so esteem;

Nor am I not where Christ is given in prey
For money, poison and traison, at Rome –
A common practice uséd night and day:

But here I am in Kent and Christendom
Among the muses where I read and rhyme;
Where if thou list, my Poynz, for to come,
Thou shalt be judge how I do spend my time.

[c. 1536, modernized text]

HENRY HOWARD, EARL OF SURREY
(1517?–47)

Henry Howard was the eldest son of the 3rd Duke of Norfolk. Carefully educated, he seems to have written verse from an early age. In his teens he was selected to be the companion of Henry VIII's illegitimate son, the Duke of Richmond, and there was a project for marrying him to the Princess Mary. This, however, was soon abandoned. Surrey was an enemy of Cromwell's, one of whose agents described him as 'the most foolish proud boy that is in England'. His pride and hasty temper are attested by several incidents. The satire printed in part here refers to one of them, when in 1543 Surrey was charged before the Privy Council with having eaten flesh in Lent, and with having broken the windows of various citizens at night by shooting pebbles at them with a stone-bow. Surrey was the victim of the struggle for power between the Howards and the Seymours when Henry VIII was known to be dying. He was brought before the Privy Council on a charge of treason (given colour by his own rash conduct and ill-considered words), sent to the Tower, and beheaded on 21 January 1547 on Tower Hill.

From *A Satire on London*

> LONDON, hast thou accuséd me
> Of breach of laws, the root of strife?
> Within whose breast did boil to see,
> So fervent hot, this dissolute life,
> That even the hate of sins, that grow
> Within thy wicked walls so rife,
> For to break forth did convert so
> That terror could it not repress.
> The which, by words, since preachers know
> What hope is left for to redress,
> By unknown means, it likéd me
> My hidden burden to express,
> Whereby it might appear to thee
> That secret sin hath secret spite;
> From justice rod no fault is free;

But that all such as work unright
In most quiet, are next ill rest.
In secret silence of the night
This made me, with a reckless breast,
To wake thy sluggards with my bow;
A figure of the Lord's behest,
Whose scourge for sin the Scriptures show.

[Written 1543, modernized text]

ANDREW BOORDE

(1490?–1549)

Boorde was brought up at Oxford, and entered the Carthusian Order while still under age. About 1517 he was accused (apparently falsely) of being 'conversant with women'. In 1521 he was appointed suffragan bishop of Chichester, but seems not to have taken up the office. In 1528 he got a dispensation from his Carthusian vows, and went abroad to study medicine. By 1530 he was back in England, and again set off on his travels, returning in 1534. Cromwell now freed him from the London Charterhouse, and sent him on a third trip abroad, to report on the state of feeling in Europe about Henry VIII. This trip took him all over France and Spain, and even to Portugal. In 1536 Boorde was in Scotland, studying and practising physic at Glasgow University and heartily disliking the Scots. About 1537 he started on his last and longest tour which took him to the Low Countries, Germany, Venice, Rhodes, Joppa, and Jerusalem; and then, on the homeward trip, to Naples and Rome. Towards the end of his life, when he was living at Winchester, Boorde was proved before the justices to have kept three loose women 'in his chamber at Winchester'. The poem printed here is accompanied by a woodcut of a naked man, standing with a pair of shears in one hand, and a length of cloth in the other.

The Englishman Speaketh

I AM an Englishman; and naked I stand here,
Musing in my mind, What raiment I shall wear?
For now, I will wear this! and now, I will wear that!
Now, I will wear, I cannot tell what!
All new fashions be pleasant to me!
I will have them! whether I thrive, or thee.
　　Now, I am a frisker! All men doth on me look!
What should I do but set cock on the hoop!
What do I care, if all the world me fail?
I will get a garment shall reach to my tail!
　　Then, I am a minion! For I wear the new guise.
The year after this, I trust to be wise!
Not only in wearing my gorgeous array;

For I will go to Learning a whole summer's day!
I will learn Latin, Hebrew, Greek, and French;
And I will learn Douche, sitting on my bench!

    I do fear no man! All men feareth me!
I overcome my adversaries by land and by sea!
I had no peer, if to myself I were true!
Because I am not so, divers times I do rue!
Yet I lack nothing! I have all things at will,
If I were wise, and would hold myself still;
And meddle with no matters not to me pertaining:
But ever to be true to GOD and to my King!

    But I have such matters rolling in my pate,
That I *will* speak and do, I cannot tell what!
No man shall let me; but I will have my mind!
And to father, mother, and friend, I will be unkind!
I will follow mine own mind, and mine own trade!
Who shall let me? the Devil's nails unpared!

    Yet, above all things, new fashions I love well!
And to wear them, my thrift I will sell!

    In all this world, I shall have but a time;
Hold the cup, good fellow! Here is thine! and mine!

        [*The Fyrst Boke of the Introduction of Knowledge.*
        Written before 1542, published 1547 or later]

JOHN DONNE

(1572–1631)

Donne studied at both Oxford and Cambridge, and the *Satyres* are the very earliest of all his works, written just after he had been to university and during his period at Lincoln's Inn, which he entered in 1592. The *Satyres* are not usually considered to be among his most attractive or successful works. It is worth remembering, when reading the passage from *Satyre III* printed below, that Donne was brought up as a Catholic, and did not finally abandon Catholicism until around 1601.

From *Satyre III*

SEEKE true religion. O where? Mirreus
Thinking her unhous'd here, and fled from us,
Seekes her at Rome; there, because hee doth know
That shee was there a thousand yeares agoe,
He loves her ragges so, as wee here obey
The statecloth where the Prince sate yesterday,
Crantz to such brave Loves will not be inthrall'd,
But loves her onely, who at Geneva is call'd
Religion, plaine, simple, sullen, yong,
Contemptuous, yet unhansome; As among
Lecherous humors, there is one that judges
No wenches wholsome, but coarse country drudges.
Graius stayes still at home here, and because
Some Preachers, vile ambitious bauds, and lawes
Still new like fashions, bid him thinke that shee
Which dwels with us, is onely perfect, hee
Imbraceth her, whom his Godfathers will
Tender to him, being tender, as Wards still
Take such wives as their Guardians offer, or
Pay valewes. Carelesse Phrygius doth abhorre
All, because all cannot be good, as one
Knowing some women whores, dares marry none.
Graccus loves all as one, and thinkes that so
As women do in divers countries goe
In divers habits, yet are still one kinde,

So doth, so is Religion; and this blind-
nesse too much light breeds; but unmoved thou
Of force must one, and forc'd but one allow;
And the right; aske thy father which is shee,
Let him ask his; though truth and falshood bee
Neare twins, yet truth a little elder is;
Be busie to seeke her, beleeve mee this,
Hee's not of none, nor worst, that seekes the best.
To adore, or scorne an image, or protest,
May all be bad; doubt wisely; in strange way
To stand inquiring right, is not to stray;
To sleepe, or runne wrong, is. On a huge hill,
Cragged, and steep, Truth stands, and hee that will
Reach her, about must, and about must goe;
And what the hills suddennes resists, winne so;
Yet strive so, that before age, deaths twilight,
Thy Soule rest, for none can worke in that night.
To will, implyes delay, therefore now doe:
Hard deeds, the bodies paines; hard knowledge too
The minds indeavours reach, and mysteries
Are like the Sunne, dazling, yet plaine to all eyes.
Keep the truth which thou hast found; men do not stand
In so ill case here, that God hath with his hand
Sign'd Kings blanck-charters to kill whom they hate.
Nor are they Vicars, but hangmen to Fate.
Foole and wretch, will thou let thy Soule be tyed
To mans lawes, by which she shall not be tryed
At the last day? Oh, will it then boot thee
To say a Philip, or a Gregory,
A Harry, or a Martin taught thee this?
Is not this excuse for mere contraries
Equally strong? cannot both sides say so?
That thou mayest rightly obey power, her bounds know;
Those past, her nature, and name is chang'd; to be
Then humble to her is idolatrie.
As streames are, Power is; those blest flowers that dwell
At the rough streames calme head, thrive and do well,
But having left their roots, and themselves given

To the streames tyrannous rage, alas are driven
Through mills, and rockes, and woods, and at last, almost
Consum'd in going, in the sea are lost:
So perish Soules, which more chuse mens unjust
Power from God claym'd, than God himselfe to trust.

[*Poems*, 1633, written *c.* 1593]

JOSEPH HALL
(1574–1656)

Hall was Marston's chief opponent in the war of the satirists at the end of the sixteenth century. He was educated at Emmanuel College, Cambridge, took orders around 1600, and was successively Bishop of Exeter and Bishop of Norwich. He lived long enough to find himself expelled by the Commonwealth. Pope admired his satires. The present example gives a curious picture of Elizabethan manners.

Book II, Satire VI

A GENTLE squire would gladly entertain
Into his house some trencher-chaplain:
Some willing man that might instruct his sons,
And that would stand to good conditions.
First that he lie upon the truckle-bed,[1]
Whiles his young master lieth o'er his head.
Secondly, that he do, on no default,
Ever presume to sit above the salt.
Third, that he never change his trencher twice.
Fourth, that he use all comely courtesies:
Sit bare[2] at meals, and one half rise and wait.
Last, that he never his young master beat,
But he must ask his mother to define
How many jerks she would his breech should line.
All those observed, he would contented be
To give five marks, and winter livery.

[*Virgidemiarum*, Part I, 1597, modernized text]

JOHN MARSTON

(1575?–1634)

Apart from Donne, Marston is the leading writer of the brief satiric outburst at the end of Elizabeth's reign. He attended Brasenose College, Oxford, and wrote the satires at the beginning of his literary career. He turned from satire to the drama about 1600. In 1616 Marston (who took orders at some date unknown to us) was promoted to the living of Christchurch, Hampshire, and retired from the literary scene.

From *Certain Satires*, III

INAMORATO LUCIAN

BEDLAM, Frenzy, Madness, Lunacy,
I challenge all your moody empery[1]
Once to produce a more distracted man
Than is inamorato Lucian.
For when my ears received a fearful sound
That he was sick, I went, and there I found
Him laid of love, and newly brought to bed
Of monstrous folly, and a frantic head.
His chamber hanged about with elegies,
With sad complaints of his love's miseries;
His windows strowed with sonnets, and the glass
Drawn full of love-knots.[2] I approached the ass,
And straight he weeps, and sighs some sonnet out
To his fair love. And then he goes about
For to perfume her rare perfection
With some sweet-smelling pink[3] epitheton.
Then with a melting look he writhes his head,
And straight in passion riseth in his bed;
And having kissed her hand, stroke up his hair,
Made a French congé,[4] cries: 'Oh, cruel fair!'
To the antique bed-post. I laughed amain,
That down my cheeks the mirthful drops did rain.

[*The Metamorphosis of Pygmalion's Image*, 1598,
modernized text]

From *The Scourge of Villainy, V*

FAIR AGE!

WHEN 'tis a high and hard thing t'have repute
Of a complete villain, perfect, absolute,
And roguing virtue brings a man defame,
A packstaff epithet,[1] and scornéd name.
  Fie, how my wit flags! how heavily,
Methinks, I vent dull sprightless poesy!
What cold black frost congeals my numbéd brain?
What envious power stops a satire's vein?
Oh, now I know! The juggling God of sleights,
With caduceus nimble Hermes fights,
And mists my wits.[2] Offended that my rhymes
Display his odious world-abusing crimes.
  Oh be propitious, powerful God of Arts!
I sheathe my weapons and do break my darts;
Be then appeased, I'll offer to thy shrine
An hecatomb of many spotted kine.[3]
Myriads of beasts shall satisfy thy rage,
Which do profane thee[4] in this apish age.
  Infectious blood, ye gouty[5] humours quake,
  Whilst my sharp razor doth incision make.

[1598, modernized text]

From *The Scourge of Villainy, VIII*

  OH now, methinks, I hear swart Martius cry,
Souping[6] along in war's feigned maskery,
By Lais' starry front, he'll forthwith dye
In cluttered blood,[7] his mistress' livery.
Her fancy's colours[8] waves upon his head.
Oh, well-fenced Albion! mainly manly sped,
When those that are soldadoes in thy state,
Do bear the badge of base, effeminate,

Even on their plumy crests, brutes sensual,
Having no spark of intellectual.
Alack, what hope? when some rank nasty wench
Is subject of their vows and confidence?

[1598, modernized text]

From *The Scourge of Villainy*, XI

GALLANTS

METHINKS your souls[1] should grudge, and inly scorn
To be made slave to humours that are born
In slime of filthy sensuality.
That part not subject to mortality
(Boundless discursive apprehension
Giving it wings to act his function)
Methinks should murmur, when you stop his course,
And soil his beauties in some beastly source
Of brutish pleasures. But it is so poor,
So weak, so hunger-bitten, evermore
Kept from his food, meagre for want of meat,
Scorned and rejected, thrust out from his seat,
Upbrayed[2] by capon's grease, consuméd quite
By eating stews,[3] that waste the better spright.
Snib'd by his baser parts, that now-poor soul,
   (Thus peasanted to each lewd thought's control)
Hath lost all heart, bearing all injuries,
The utmost spite, and rank'st indignities,
With forcéd willingness. Taking great joy
If you will deign his faculties employ
But in the mean'st ingenious quality.
(How proud he'll be of any dignity!)
Put it to music, dancing, fencing school[4] –
Lord, how I laughed to hear the pretty fool,
How it will prate! his tongue shall never lie,
But still discourse of his spruce quality;
Egging his master to proceed from this
And get the substance of celestial bliss.

[1598, modernized text]

EDWARD GUILPIN

(*fl.* 1598)

Studied at Emmanuel College, Cambridge, and was later a member of
Gray's Inn. *Skialethia* shows him to have been interested in the
theatre. Guilpin was a friend of John Marston's, and is addressed by
him in the new satire (attacking Joseph Hall) which Marston added
to the second edition of *The Scourge of Villainy*. Guilpin and Marston
were both attacked in the anonymous *The Whipping of the Satyre* in
1601, and Guilpin replied in *The Whipping of the Satyre, His Penance*
(1601). He thus belongs firmly to the main group of late Elizabethan
satirists.

From *Satire I*

ALL things are different from their outward show:
The very poet, whose standish[1] doth flow
With nectar of Parnassus, and his brain
Melts to Castalian dew, and showers wit's rain,
Yet by his outward countenance doth appear
To have been born in wit's dearth's dearest year.
So that Zopirus,[2] judging by his face,
Will pronounce Socrates for dull and base.

This habit hath false larum'd-seeming won
In our affections, that whatsoe'er is done
Must be new coined with sly dissemblance stamp,
And give a sun-shine semblance to a lamp.

This makes the foisting traveller to swear,
And face out many a lie within the year.
And if he have been an hour or two aboard,
To spew a little gall: then, by the Lord,
He hath been in both the Indias, East and West,
Talks of Guiana, China, and the rest:
The straights of Gibraltar, and Aenian,
Are but hard by, no nor the Magellan,
Mandeville,[3] Candish,[4] sea-experienced Drake[5]
Came never near him, if he truly crake;
Nor ever durst come where he laid his head,

For out of doubt he hath discoveréd
Some half a dozen of th'infinity
Of Anaxarchus'[1] worlds. Like foppery
The Antiquary would persuade us to:
He shows a piece of black-jack for the shoe
Which old Aegeus[2] bequeathed his valiant son;
A piece of polished mother-of-pearl's the spoon
Cupid ate pap with; and he hath a dagger
Made of the sword wherewith great Charles did swagger.
Oh, that the whip of fools, great Aretine,[3]
Whose words were squibs and crackers, every line,
Lived in our days, to scourge these hypocrites,
Who taunts may be like goblins and sprites:
To haunt these wretches forth that little left them
Of airy wit (for all the rest's bereft them).
Oh, how the varges[4] from his black pen wrung,
Would sauce the idiom of the English tongue,
Give it a new touch, livelier dialect,
To hear this two-necked goose, this falsehood, checked.
    Methinks I see the pie-bald whoreson tremble
To hear of Aretine: he doth dissemble,
There is no trust to be had to his quaking.
To him once more, and rouse him from his shaking
Fever of feigned fear; hold whip and cord,
Muse, play the beadle, lash at every word!
No, no, let be: he's a true cozener still,
And like the cramp-fish darts, even through my quill,
His sly insinuating, poisonous juice,
And doth the same into my spirit infuse.
Methinks already I applaud myself,
For nettle-stinging thus this fairy elf;
And though my conscience says I merit not
Such dear reward, dissembling yet (God wot)
I hunt for praise, and do the same expect.
Hence, craft enchanter, welcome base neglect!
Scoffs make me know myself – I must not err.
Better a wretch than a dissembler.

[*Skialethia*, 1598, modernized text]

From *Satire IV*

A JEALOUS HUSBAND

HE hath as many hundred thousand eyes
As Argus had, like stars placed in the skies,
Though to no purpose, for blind love can see,
Having no eyes, farther than jealousy.
Gulf-breasted is he, silent, and profound,
Cat-footed for sly pace, and without sound,
Porpentine backéd, for he lies on thorns:
Is it not pity such a beast wants horns?
Is it not pity such a beast should so
Possess men's thoughts, and timpanize with woe
Their big swoll'n hearts? For let Severus hear
A cuckoo sing in June, he sweats for fear,
And coming home, he whurries through the house;
Each hole that makes an inmate of a mouse
Is ransacked by him for the cuckold-maker;
He beats his wife, and 'mongst his maids doth swagger
T'extort confession from th'one who hath been
Familiar with his wife, wreaking his teen
Upon her ruffs and jewels, burning, tearing,
Flinging and hurling, scolding, staring, swearing.
He's as discreet, civil a gentleman,
As Harry Peasecod, or a Bedlam man,
A drunken captain or a ramping whore,
Or swaggering blue-coat[1] at an ale-house door.
    What an infection's this, which thus doth fire
Men's most discreetest tempers, and doth tire
Their souls with fury? and doth make them thirst
To carouse bowls of poison till they burst?
Oh, this is to be too wise in sin,
Too well experienced and skilled therein!
'For false suspicion of another is
A sure condemning of our own amiss.'
Unless a man have into practise brought
The theoric art of love which Ovid wrote,

Unless his own lewd life have taught him more
Than Aretine's adventurous wandering whore,
Unless he have an ancient soldier been,
Brags of the marks, and shows the scars of sin,
How could he be so gored with loving hate,
As to think women so insatiate?
How could he know their stratagems and shifts,
Their politic delays and wily drifts?
No, no, 'tis true: he hath been naught himself,
And lewdness fathereth this wayward elf.
    Then take this for a maxim, general rule,
    No jealous man, but is or knave, or fool.

[*Skialethia*, 1598, modernized text]

RICHARD BRATHWAIT

(1588–1673)

Brathwait was born in Westmorland. He entered Oriel College, Oxford, in 1604, and later studied law at Cambridge and at the Inns of Court. On the death of his elder brother in 1618 he inherited his estates and became an important personage in his native Westmorland, being deputy-lieutenant of the county, and a justice of the peace. He was a prolific writer of verse, and his best-known work is the extraordinary burlesque poem, *Barnabee Itinerarium or Barnabee's Journal*, in English and Latin rhyme. This appeared anonymously in 1638.

An Epigramme Called the *Honest Lawyer*

SPRIGHTLY my muse, speake like the son of thunder
And with a full mouth, ring out *Albions* wonder:
No *Sussex Dragon*, no *Virginian*,
But of a Lawer that's an Honest man.
Whose definition if you wish to know,
Is a blacke Swan, faire Moore, or milke-white Crow.
He takes no fees, till he conceive the cause,
Nor with an Oyly bribe annoints his jawes.
He wants the use of feeling, feares Heavens curse,
Strings not his conscience with his Clients purse.
Hee'l not be tongue-tide, but for *Justice* sake,
He seeks to earne the mony he does take.
He hates aequivocation and delay,
Nor will he make his Threed-bare Client stay
For his dispatch: he will not have his fee,
Till he discusse the causes equity.
His Judgement will not vaile to wind nor wether,
Nor is his conscience made of retching lether.
His eye's on Justice, nor will ever he
Banke-rupt his soule, t'enrich posterity.
His tongue's no time-observer, made to please,
His fist is shut from taking double fees.
He will not forge a lye, nor wrest the fence,
Of law or right, for any faire pretence.

He will not backe his Clyent, or maintaine
An unjust suit, to reape a private gaine.
He speakes and stands too't, nor is sorry for't,
Though he by speaking truth, incense the Court.
He hates corruption, nor has ever sould,
His peace of Conscience, for a peece of gold,
He loves no perfumes, nor is one of those,
Whose peak't mouchatoes skirmish with their nose.
His beard's not starcht, he has no subtile sconce,
Nor *Janus*-like lookes he ten waies at once.
His Eare is never shut to poore mens mones,
His Coach-wheele is not made of Clients bones,
His Conscience nere did ought that needs relenting
Or ere made Clients pay for his wives painting.
His soule was never soild by corrupt dealing,
Nor stands he on a velvet gowne at sealing.
His face was nere at Braziers, nor his skin
Sy-sambris-like was hung up to be seene.
His tongue speakes truth, makes peace where ere he can.
This Lawer must be needs an honest man.
It's true, he must: but where now shall we finde
This man: I feare theres none left of his kind.
Yes one I know, and more there be no doubt
But that my dull pate cannot find them out,
Who's truely honest: Whom you may discerne,
You Clients you, that visit this throng Terme,
By no example in our *Albion* more,
Then by my Patron in my *Catch* before.
Aske you me why? Experience tells it me,
'None of's Profession honester then he.'

[*A Strappado for the Divell*, 1615]

ROBERT ANTON

(fl. 1616)

Anton is supposed to have been the son of a recorder of Lincoln, and
to have been educated at Magdalene College, Cambridge. *The
Philosophers Satyrs*, with seven pieces named each after one of the
planets, owe their plan to Ariosto. They are full of references to
Beaumont, Spenser, Jonson, Chapman, and Daniel. There is also an
allusion to Shakespeare's *Comedy of Errors*. These curious poems have
more merit than they are usually accorded, and are an interesting
example of 'general', rather than 'particular' satire.

A Dwarfish Satyre

A SATYRE sharpe and sweet, tastes like a Cherry,
It cheareth Wisedome, and doth make Wit merry,
It cooles hot Blouds, and (like a Phisicke potion)
Corects wilde humours in their gadding motion.
It tells the World her owne, that well it can
Discerne a Satyre from no honest man:
It may be sowre alone, and ill compos'd;
Then it offends both well and ill dispos'd.
Or, onely sweet and smouth; and then it is
Unlike a Satyre: so, as much amisse:
But (Cherry ripe, ripe, ripe) the Satyre should
Bee sweetely sharpe, and with it, sagely bold.
No Ballad-stile, no straine of vulgar stretch
Should come, but to be worryed in his reach.
Satyres doe use the Fang, and not the Whippe,
But Beggars-Beadles use to whippe and strippe.
A Satyrs Grinders scorne to scarre the skin:
But make small meale of greatest bones within:
And if he catch a Whipper in his way,
That stiles himself a Satyre, him hee'l flay
With his fore-tusses[1]; and, in sport, undoo
The Sotte, a Satyre, and a Whipper too.
Then, sottish Satyre, byte, and spare the Whippe,
Els, like a scourge, my Fang shall make thee skippe.

[*The Philosophers Satyres*, 1615/16]

ROBERT ANTON

From *Of Mars*

THE dull *Athenians* offered *sacrifice*
To *Mars*, when warres began to tyranize:
But when the *furie* of stearne *warre* did cease,
His hallowed *Altars* lay untoucht with *peace*.
Souldiers are *Saints* in *steele*, *Gods* in their *beavers*,
Ador'd like *Esculapius* in hot *Feavers*
Of *blood* and *warre*: but when their *steele-coates* rust,
And their bright *armes* ore-cast with *peacefull dust*.
Behould you *sonnes* of *thunder*, th'end of all
Are *Usurers almes*, and a poore *Hospitall*.

[*The Philosophers Satyres*, 1615/16]

From *Of the Moone*

BUT I enough have dwelt upon your *starre*,
Let it suffise, the *world* knowes what you are,
A *Bit-borne curse*, an *Eele*, a *Bee* to sting:
A *Cockatrice* to kill, *Syren* to sting.
But leaving you for *mans* eternal *bane*:
Bright *Cynthia*, let me sing th' *inconstant vaine*
Of these uncertaine *times*, and truly show
How all things change, and with thy *beames* do flow:
Nor *woman*, nor the *change* of *elements*,
Nor the *Moones changes* do more *change* present;
Then the inconstant monstrous *multitude*:
Whose giddy *Hydra-heads* all *formes* include,
Marke how the *winds* breaking their *brazen-guard*,
Changes each *point of compasse*, or of *card*:
Sometimes full *East*, sometimes againe full *west*.
So *change* the *furies* of the *poopels brest*:
A *great-mans fortune*, that like *full-Moones* rise
Like *Dolphins*, these adore; but when it dies,
And wants from fuller influence of *Respect*.
When his ambitious *beames* no more reflect,
Upon the baser *bodies*; then their *tide*

77

In shallow *ebbes*, and falling *currents* aside:
As *great mens* miserie, that like the *Sun*
Attended with *twelve-signes* their progresse run,
When their *bright honors* do ascend the *skie*
Like *Aries*[1] then they beare him companie,
In comfort of his *spring-tide* and *high state*.
Adore the high *Solstitiall* of his fate:
But when his *rising honors* do decline,
Then with his fall fals the *dissembling signe*
Into *Aquarius*,[2] and from their *eyes*
Drop onely *teares* to shroud him, when he dies.
The *Peacooketraine* of heavens all-colourd *bow*,
Paints not more *colours* then these *Jayes* do show
That have the *falling-sicknesse*: when such fall,
Moores at their *East*, *Dogs* at their *funerall*.
Oh *Popularitie* that cost more *heads*
Then there are *worms* within their *shamed beds*,
To eate their *treasons* with their honord *bones*
To their first *elements*, or weeping *stones*,
To wash their *shame* in *teares*: how have your *charms*
Betrayed the nobler parts of *Arts* and *Armes*
To an untimely grave, which *time* shall write
In bleeding *characters* to after-sight.

[*The Philosophers Satyres*, 1615/16

RICHARD CORBET

(1582–1635)

Corbet was educated at Westminster and Broadgate Hall (later Pembroke College), Oxford. In 1598 he was elected a student of Christ Church. Wood says that in his young days he was estimated 'one of the most celebrated wits in the university'. Aubrey described him as 'a very handsome man, but something apt to abuse, and a coward'. Corbet took holy orders, and James I made him one of the royal chaplains in consideration of his 'fine fancy and preaching'. In 1620 he became Dean of Christ Church at the early age of thirty-seven, and was at this time very friendly with the Duke of Buckingham. In 1628 he was elected Bishop of Oxford, and in 1632 was translated to the see of Norwich. Corbet strongly opposed the puritans, and frequently admonished his clergy for puritan practices. Throughout his life he was famous for his conviviality.

The Distracted Puritane

Am I madd, o noble Festus,[1]
When zeale and godly knowledge
Have put mee in hope
To deale with the Pope,
As well as the best in the Colledge?
   Boldly I preach, hate a Crosse, hate a Surplice,
     Miters, Copes, and Rotchets:
   Come heare mee pray nine times a day,
     And fill your heads with Crotchets.

In the howse of pure Emanuel[2]
I had my Education;
Where my friends surmise
I dazeld mine Eyes,
With the Light of Revelation.
   Boldly I preach, &c.

They bound mee like a Bedlam,
They lash't my foure poore quarters:
Whilst this I endure
Faith makes mee sure
To be One of Foxes Martyrs.
   Boldly I preach, &c.

These injuryes I suffer
Through Anti-Christs perswasions,
Take of this Chaine,
Neither Rome nor Spaine
Can resist my strong invasions.
   Boldly I preach, &c.

Of the Beasts ten hornes (God blesse us)
I have knock't of three allready:
If they let mee alone,
I'le leave him none;
But they say I am too heady.
   Boldly I preach, &c.

When I sack'd the Seaven-hilld Citty
I mett the great redd Dragon:
I kept him alloofe
With the armour of proofe,
Though here I have never a rag on.
   Boldly I preach, &c.

With a fiery Sword and Targete
There fought I with this monster:
But the sonnes of pride
My zeale deride,
And all my deedes misconster.
   Boldly I preach, &c.

I unhorst the whore of Babel
With a Launce of Inspirations:

I make her stinke,
And spill her drinck
In the Cupp of Abominations.
   Boldly I preach, &c.

I have seene two in a Vision,
With a Flying Booke betweene them;
I have bin in dispaire
Five times a yeare,
And cur'd by reading Greenham.[1]
   Boldly I preach, &c.

I observ'd in Perkins[2] Tables
The black Lines of Damnation:
Those crooked veines
Soe struck in my braines,
That I fear'd my Reprobation.
   Boldly I preach, &c.

In the holy tongue of Chanaan[3]
I plac'd my chiefest pleasure:
Till I prickt my foote
With an Hebrew roote,
That I bledd beyond all measure.
   Boldly I preach, &c.

I appear'd before the Arch-Bishopp,
And all the high Commission:
I gave him noe Grace,
But told him to his face
That he favour'd Superstition.
   Boldly I preach, hate a Crosse, hate a Surplice,
      Miters, Copes, and Rotchets:
   Come heare mee pray nine times a day,
      And fill your heads with Crotchets.

[First published 1647. This text from *Poetica Stromata*, 1648]

ABRAHAM COWLEY

(1618-67)

Cowley was the seventh and posthumous child of a stationer. He was a king's scholar at Westminster, and began to write verse very young. His first collection of poems was published in 1633 – one poem, according to the poet, was written at the age of ten. In 1637 Cowley was admitted to Trinity College, Cambridge. In 1643-4 he was ejected from Cambridge and retired to Oxford, where he attached himself to Henry Jermyn, afterwards Earl of St Albans, the favourite of Henrietta Maria. In 1646 he followed the queen to France and was employed on various diplomatic missions for the exiled court and in conducting a correspondence in cipher between the king and his wife. In 1656 he returned to England, and was arrested in mistake for another man. He remained under bail till the Restoration. He now took to medicine, and was created M.D. at Oxford in 1657, by an order of the government which caused some offence to his royalist friends. Later, he again retired to France. After the Restoration, he was one of the founder members of the Royal Society. His reputation was at its highest in his own lifetime, when he was regarded as the model of cultivated poetry, and when he died he was buried with great pomp in Westminster Abbey. By 1700 Dryden was remarking on the decline in his reputation. In 1737, Pope wrote:

> Who now reads Cowley? If he pleases yet,
> His moral pleases, not his pointed wit.

From *The Puritan and the Papist*

ADDRESS TO THE PURITAN PARTY

YE boundlesse *Tyrants*, how doe you outvy
Th' *Athenian Thirty*, *Romes Decemviri*?
In Rage, Injustice, Cruelty as farre
Above those men, as you in *number* are.
What *Mysteries* of *Iniquity* doe we see?
New *Prisons* made to defend *Libertie*;
Where without cause, some are undone, some dy.
Like men *bewitcht*, they know not *how*, nor *why*.
Our *Goods* forc'd from us for *Propriety's* sake;

And all the *Reall Non-sence* which ye make.
Ship-money[1] was unjustly ta'ne, ye say;
Unjustlier farre you take the *Ships* away.
The *High-Commission*[2] you calld Tyrannie,
Ye did; Good God! what is the *High-Committee*?[3]
Ye said that *gifts* and *bribes Preferments* bought,
By *Money* and *Bloud* too, they now are fought.
To the *Kings will* the *Lawes* men strove to draw;
The *Subjects will* is now become the *Law*.
'Twas fear'd a *New Religion* would begin;
All new Religions now are entred in.
The King *Delinquents* to protect did strive;
What Clubs, Pikes, Halberts, Lighters, sav'd the Five?[4]
You thinke the *Parliament*, like *your State of Grace*,
What ever sinnes men doe, they keepe their place.
Invasions then were fear'd against the *State*,
 And *Strode* swore that last year would be *'Eighty-Eight*.[5]
You bring in Forraine aid to your designes;
First those great *Forraine Forces of Divines*,
With which Ships from *America* were fraught;
Rather may *stinking Tobacco* still be brought
From thence, I say; next ye the *Scots* invite,
Which ye terme *Brotherly Assistants* right;
For with them you intend *England* to share:
They, who, alas, but *younger Brothers* are,
Must have the *Monies* for their *Portion*;
The *Houses* and the *Lands* will be your *owne*.
We thanke ye for the *wounds* which we endure,
Whil'st *scratches* and slight pricks ye seeke to *cure*.
We thanke ye for *true reall feares* at last,
Which free us from so many *false ones* past.
We thanke ye for the *Bloud* which *fats* our *Coast*,
(That fatall debt paid to great *Straffords* Ghost.)[6]
We thanke ye for the ills receiv'd, and all
Which by your *diligence* in good time we shall.
We thanke ye, and our *gratitude's* as great
As *yours*, when you thank'd *God* for being *beat*.

[1643]

JOHN CLEVELAND

(1613-58)

Cleveland's father was a schoolmaster. In his fifteenth year Cleveland
went to Cambridge, and was admitted as a student of Christ's
College. He became a fellow of St John's in 1634, and for nine years
was 'the delight and ornament' of the college. Cleveland was an
ardent royalist, and when Cromwell stood as candidate for Cambridge at the election for the Long Parliament, Cleveland opposed
him bitterly. When the Civil War came, Cleveland was ejected from
his fellowship, together with the Master of St John's and several
other fellows of the college. He went to the royalist army in Oxford,
and was later a judge-advocate. He was with the garrison of Newark
when this surrendered to the parliamentarians. After the surrender,
he was left at liberty, but had a hard job of it to make a living. In
1655 he was arrested at Norwich and imprisoned for three months,
but was released on Cromwell's orders. After this he continued to
live entirely retired from the world until his death. He was a friend
of Samuel Butler's, and Aubrey notes the influence of Cleveland's
satires on Butler. *The Rebel Scot* is his best-known poem, and ex-
presses his disgust with the conduct of the Scots towards Charles I.

The Rebel Scot

HOW! Providence! and yet a Scottish Crew!
Then Madam Nature wears black Patches too,
What shall our Nation be in bondage thus
Unto a Land that truckles under us?
Ring the Bells backward; I am all on fire,
Not all the Buckets in a Country-Quire
Shall quench my rage. A Poet should be fear'd
When angry, like a Comet's flaming Beard.
And where's the Stoick can his wrath appease
To see his Country sick of *Pym*'s disease;[1]
By Scotch Invasion to be made a prey
To such Pig-Widgin Myrmidons as they?
But that there's Charm in Verse, I would not quote
The Name of *Scot* without an Antidote;
Unless my head were red, that I might brew

Invention there that might be poyson too.
Were I a drowzy Judge, whose dismal Note
Disgorgeth Halters, as a Jugler's throat
Doth Ribbands? Could I in Sir Empericks tone
Speak Pills in phrase and quack destruction,
Or roar like *Marshal*[1] that *Geneva* Bull,
Hell and Damnation a Pulpit full.
Yet to express a *Scot*, to play that prize,
Not all those Mouth-Granados can suffice.
Before a *Scot* can properly be curst,
I must like *Hocus*,[2] swallow Daggers first.
Come keen Iambicks with your Badgers feet,
And Badger-like bite till your Teeth do meet:
Help ye tart Satyrists to imp my rage
With all the Scorpions that should whip this Age.
Scots are like Witches; do but whet your Pen,
Scratch till the blood come, they'l not hurt you then.
Now as the Martyrs were enforc'd to take
The shapes of Beasts, like Hypocrites at stake
I'll bait my *Scot* so, yet not cheat your eyes;
A *Scot*, within a Beast, is no Disguise.

No more let *Ireland* brag, her harmless Nation
Fosters no Venom since that *Scot*'s Plantation:
Nor can our feign'd Antiquity obtain;
Since they came in, *England* hath Wolves again.
The *Scot* that kept the Tower might have shown
Within the Grate of his own Breast alone,
The Leopard and the Panther, and ingross'd
What all those wild Collegiars had cost.
The honest high-shoes in their termly Fees,
First to the Salvage Lawyer, next to these.
Nature her self doth Scotchmen Beasts confess,
Making their Country such a Wilderness;
A Land that brings in question and suspence
God's Omnipresence, but that *Charles* came thence;
But that *Montross* and *Crawford*'s[3] Loyal Band
Atton'd their Sin, and Christned half their Land.
Nor is it all the Nation hath these Spots,

There is a Church as well as Kirk of *Scots*.
As in a Picture where the squinting paint
Shews Fiend on this side, and on that side Saint.
He that saw Hell in's melancholy Dream,
And in the Twy-light of his Phancie's Theme
Scar'd from his Sins, repented in a fright,
Had he view'd *Scotland* had turn'd Proselite.
A Land where one may pray with curst intent,
O may they never suffer Banishment!
Had *Cain* been *Scot*, God would have chang'd his Doom,
Not forc'd him wander but confin'd him home;
Like *Jews* they spread, and as Infection fly,
As if the Devil had Ubiquity.
Hence 'tis they live as Rovers and defie
This, or that place, Rags of Geography.
They'r Citizens oth' World, they'r all in all,
Scotland's a Nation Epidemical;
And yet they ramble not to learn the Mode,
How to be drest, or how to lisp abroad;
To return knowing in the Spanish Shrug,
Or which of the *Dutch* States a double Jug
Resembles most in belly, or in beard,
(The Card by which the Mariners are steer'd)
No, the *Scots* Errant fight, and fight to eat,
Their Ostrich Stomach make their Swords their Meat.
Nature with *Scots* as Tooth-drawers hath dealt,
Who use to string their Teeth upon their Belt.
　　Yet wonder not at this their happy choice,
The Serpent's fatal still to Paradise.
Sure *England* hath the Hemorrhoids, and these
On the North-postern of the Patient seize,
Like Leeches; thus they Physically thirst
After our blood, but in the Cure shall burst.

　　Let them not think to make us run oth' score
To purchase Villenage, as once before
When an Act past to stroak them on the Head;
Call them good Subjects, buy them Ginger-bread.

Not Gold, nor Acts of Grace, 'tis Steel must tame
The stubborn *Scot*, a Prince that would reclaim
Rebels by yielding, doth like him, or worse,
Who sadled his own back to shame his Horse.

Was it for this you left your leaner Soil,
Thus to lard *Israel* with *Egypt's* Spoyl.
They are the Gospel's Life-guard, but for them
(The Garrison of New *Jerusalem*)
What would the Brethren do? The Cause! The Cause!
Sack-Possets, and the Fundamental Laws?

Lord! what a godly thing is want of Shirts!
How a Scotch Stomach and no Meat converts!
They wanted Food and Rayment; so they took
Religion for their Seamstress, and their Cook.
Unmask them well, their Honours and Estate,
As well as Conscience, are sophisticate.
Shrive but their Title and their Moneys poize,
A Laird and twenty pence pronounc'd with noise,
When constru'd but for a plain Yeoman go,
And a good sober two pence, and well so.
Hence then you proud Impostors, get you gone,
You *Picts* in Gentry and Devotion.
You Scandal to the Stock of Verse, a Race
Able to bring the Gibbet in disgrace.
Hyperbolus[1] by suffering did traduce
The Ostracism, and sham'd it out of use.
The *Indian* that Heaven did forswear,
Because he heard some *Spaniards* were there;
Had he but known what *Scots* in Hell had been,
He would *Erasmus*-like[2] have hung between.
My Muse hath done. A Voyder for the nonce,
I wrong the Devil should I pick their Bones;
That Dish is his; for when the *Scots* decease,
Hell like their Nation, feeds on Barnacles.
A *Scot* when from the Gallow-tree got loose
Drops into *Styx*, and turns a *Soland* Goose.[3]

[1648. Text from the edition of 1677]

JOHN HALL

(1627–56)

Hall impressed his contemporaries by his precociousness. Educated at Durham School, and St John's College, Cambridge, he had a volume of essays published when he was only nineteen, and these are said to have 'amazed not only the university, but the more serious part of three nations'. Hall did not manage to live up to the expectations thus aroused. A contemporary remarks that 'had not his debauchery and intemperance diverted him from the more serious studies, he had made an extraordinary person, for no man had ever done so great things at his age'. Nevertheless, Hobbes is said to have had a high opinion of his abilities. He was on the parliamentary side in the Civil War, and supported Cromwell as a pamphleteer.

From *A Satire*

COUNTRY SCHOOLMASTERS

STRANGE hedly medly! who would make his swine
Turn greyhounds, or hunt foxes with his kine?
Who would employ his saddle nag to come,
And hold a trencher in the dining room?
Who would engage Sir James, that knows not what
His cassock's made of, in affairs of state?
Or pluck a Richelieu from the helm to try
Conclusions to still children when they cry?
Who would employ a country schoolmaster
To construe to his boys some new found star?
Poor leaden creatures! yet shap'd up to rule
Perpetual dictators in a school;
Nor do you want your rods, though only fed
With scraps of Tully and coarse barley bread;
Great threadbare princes, which like chess-kings, brave,
No longer than your masters give you leave,
Whose large dominions in some brew-house lies.
Asses commands o'er you, you over boys;
Who still possess the lodgings next the leads,
And cheat your ladies of their waiting maids;

JOHN HALL

Who, if some lowly carriage do befriend,
May grace the table at the lower end,
Upon condition that ye fairly rise
At the first entrance of th' potatoe pies,
And while his lordship for discourse doth call
You do not let one dram of Latin fall;
But tell how bravely your young master swears,
Which dogs best like his fancy, and what ears;
How much he undervalues learning, and
Takes pleasure in a sparrow-hawk well mann'd;
How oft he beats his foot-boy, and will dare
To gallop when no serving man is near;
How he blackberries from the bushes caught,
When antidoted with a morning's draught;
How rather than he'll construe Greek, he'll choose
To English Ovid's Art into prose:
Such talk is for his lordship's palate, he
Takes much delight in such like trumpery;
But still remember, ye forbear to press
Unseasonably some moral sentences;
Take heed, by all means, how rough Seneca
Sally into your talk; that man, they say,
Rails against drinking healths, and merits hate,
As sure as Ornis mocked a graduate.
What a grand ornament our gentry would
Soon lose, if every rug-gown might be bold
To rail at such heroic feats? pray who
Could honour's Mistress health, if this did grow
Once out of fashion? 'las, fine idols! they,
E'er since poor Cheapside cross in rubbage lay,
E'er since the play-houses did want their prease,
And players lay asleep like dormouses,
Have suffered, too, too much: be not so sour
With tender beauties, they had once some power;
Take that away, what do you leave them? what?
To marshal fancies in a youngster's hat.

[Poems, 1646]

89

ROBERT HEATH

(*fl.* 1650)

Not much is known of Robert Heath, except that he probably entered Corpus Christi College, Cambridge, in 1634. From the printer's address to the reader, his book of verse *Clarastella* seems to have been printed without the author's knowledge. It contains elegies to Sir Bevil Grenvil, to William Lawes, the musician, and to other friends who had fallen in the Civil Wars, but the bulk of it is love lyrics.

From *Satyr I*

THE PEDANTS

A FEW good books disgested wel do feed
The mind, much cloys or doth ill humours breed.
Seempot sets down in his *Ephemeris*
The trifles of each how'rs vain exercise,
Toys that should be *Ephemera* indeed
Dying the same day they were born and bred.
Things of so smal concern or moment, who
Would stuffe his Diarie with, or care to know?
As what he wore, thought, laugh't at, where he walkt,
When farted, where he pist, with whom he talkt.
Memento's more ridiculous than those
The City Chronicler made at Lord Mayors shows;
As who his Hinchboys were, who wav'd the sword,
Who brought the Custard to his *Honours* boord,
What year a Lyon whelpt i'th' Tower dy'd,
Pepper or corn was dear, whose child bestride
Each gilt Colossus Pageant in Cheapside,
Or in what year *Bartholomie* Fair forbid.
(Whereas Historians only things of weight,
Results of Persons or affairs of State,
Briefely with truth, and cleerness should relate)
Laconick shortness memorie feeds. I hate
A long spun story of one drawn to th' stake
Would reach from *Newgate* to *Smithfield*, and make

90

The martyr'd reader sweat as much or more
Than *Latimer*[1] i'th' flames, with a bald score
Of phars'd (*Quoth he's*) in every page at least,
As without them 'twere not to be exprest.
But *Dulman* barren of invention, wears
His time and books in reading only. Here's
Squire *Topas* spends his daies in killing flies,
And like *Domitian*[2] such a drone he dies.

[*Clarastella*, 1650]

ANDREW MARVELL
(1621–78)

Marvell was educated at Hull Grammar School and Trinity College, Cambridge. In 1650 he became tutor to Lord Fairfax's daughter Mary, who afterwards married George Villiers, 2nd Duke of Buckingham. It was at this period that the earlier, lyrical poems were written. In 1657 Marvell became assistant to Milton in the foreign secretaryship, and held this post till the Restoration – it was apparently due to him that Milton remained unmolested. In 1659 he was elected M.P. for Hull, and he continued to represent the town till his death, and was mostly in close attendance upon Parliament, though in 1663–5 he acted as secretary to the Earl of Carlisle, on the latter's diplomatic mission to Muscovy, Sweden and Denmark. Marvell was a puritan, but not a partisan. However, he soon became disillusioned with the King, and with the moral climate of the Restoration. He began by attacking Clarendon, but ended by attacking his master. Swift greatly admired Marvell's powers of irony.

From *The Character of Holland*

HOLLAND, that scarce deserves the name of *Land*,
As but th'Off-scouring of the *British Sand*;
And so much Earth as was contributed
By *English Pilots* when they heav'd the Lead;
Or what by th' Oceans slow alluvion[1] fell,
Of shipwrackt Cockle and the Muscle-shell;
This indigested vomit of the Sea
Fell to the *Dutch* by just Propriety.

Glad then, as Miners that have found the Oar,
They with mad labour fish'd the *Land* to *Shoar*;
And div'd as desperately for each piece
Of Earth, as if't had been of *Ambergreece*;
Collecting anxiously small Loads of Clay,
Less then what building Swallows bear away;
Or then those Pills which sordid Beetles roul,
Transfusing into them their Dunghil Soul.

How did they rivet, with Gigantick Piles,
Thorough the Center their new-catched Miles;

And to the stake a strugling Country bound,
Where barking Waves still bait the forced Ground;
Building their *watry Babel* far more high
To reach the *Sea*, then those to scale the *Sky*.
   Yet still his claim the Injur'd Ocean laid,
And oft at Leap-frog ore their Steeples plaid:
As if on purpose it on Land had come
To shew them what's their *Mare Liberum*.[1]
A daily deluge over them does boyl;
The Earth and Water play at *Level-coyl*;[2]
The fish oft-times the Burger dispossest,
And sat not as a Meat but as a Guest;
And oft the *Tritons* and the *Sea-Nymphs* saw
Whole sholes of *Dutch* serv'd up for *Cabillau*;[3]
Or as they over the new Level rang'd
For pickled *Herring*, pickled *Heeren* chang'd.
Nature, it seem'd, asham'd of her mistake,
Would throw their land away at *Duck* and *Drake*.

                   [*Miscellaneous Poems*, 1681, written *c.* 1653]

From *The Last Instructions to a Painter*

CASTLEMAINE[4] AND THE FOOTMAN

PAINT *Castlemaine* in Colours that will hold,
Her, not her Picture, for she now grows old.
She through her Lacquies Drawers as he ran,
Discern'd Love's Cause, and a new Flame began.
Her wonted joys thenceforth and *Court* she shuns,
And still within her mind the Footman runs:
His brazen Calves, his brawny Thighs (the Face
She slights) his Feet shapt for a smoother race.
Poring within her Glass she re-adjusts
Her looks, and oft-try'd Beauty now distrusts:
Fears lest he scorn a Woman once assay'd,
And now first, wisht she e're had been a Maid.
Great Love, how dost thou triumph, and how reign,
That to a Groom couldst humble her disdain!

Stript to her Skin, see how she stooping stands,
Nor scorns to rub him down with those fair Hands;
And washing (lest the scent her Crime disclose)
His sweaty Hooves, tickles him 'twixt the Toes.
But envious Fame, too soon, begun to note
More gold in's Fob, more Lace upon his Coat
And he, unwary, and of Tongue too fleet,
No longer could conceal his Fortune sweet.
Justly the Rogue was whipt in Porter's Den:[1]
And *Jermyn*[2] straight has leave to come agen.
Ah *Painter*, now could *Alexander*[3] live,
And this *Campaspe* thee *Apelles* give!

DE RUYTER[4] SAILS UP THE THAMES

R U Y T E R the while, that had our Ocean curb'd,
Sail'd now among our Rivers undisturb'd:
Surveyed their Crystal Streams, and Banks so green,
And Beauties e're this never naked seen.
Through the vain sedge the bashful *Nymphs* he ey'd;
Bosomes, and all which from themselves they hide.
The Sun much brighter, and the Skies more clear,
He finds the Air, and all things, sweeter here.
The sudden change, and such a tempting sight,
Swells his old[5] Veins with fresh Blood, fresh Delight.
Like am'rous Victors he begins to shave,
And his new Face looks in the *English* Wave.
His sporting Navy all about him swim,
And witness their complaisence in their trim.
Their streaming Silks play through the weather fair,
And with inveigling Colours Court the Air.
While the red Flags breath on their Top-masts high
Terrour and War, but want an Enemy.
Among the Shrowds the Seamen sit and sing,
And wanton Boys on every Rope do cling.
Old *Neptune* springs the Tydes, and Water lent:
(The Gods themselves do help the provident.)
And, where the deep Keel on the shallow cleaves,

With *Trident's* Leaver, and great Shoulder heaves.
Aeolus their Sails inspires with *Eastern* Wind,
Puffs them along, and breathes upon them kind.
With Pearly Shell the *Tritons* all the while
Sound the Sea-march, and guide to *Sheppy Isle*.¹

   So have I seen in *April*'s bud, arise
A Fleet of Clouds, sailing along the Skies:
The liquid Region with their Squadrons fill'd,
The airy Sterns the Sun behind does guild;
And gentle Gales them steer, and Heaven drives,
When, all on sudden, their calm bosome rives
With Thunder and Lightning from each armed Cloud;
Shepherds themselves in vain in bushes shrowd.
Such up the stream the *Belgick* Navy glides,
And at *Sheerness* unloads its stormy sides.

APPORTIONING THE BLAME

   AFTER this loss, to rellish discontent,
Some one must be accus'd by Punishment.
All our miscarriages on *Pett*² must fall:
His Name alone seems fit to answer all.
Whose Counsel first did this mad War beget?
Who all Commands sold thro' the Navy? *Pett*.
Who would not follow³ when the *Dutch* were bet?
Who treated out the time at *Bergen*?⁴ *Pett*.
Who the *Dutch* Fleet with Storms disabled met,
And rifling Prizes, them neglected? *Pett*.
Who with false news prevented⁵ the *Gazette*?
The Fleet divided?⁶ Writ for *Rupert*? *Pett*.
Who all our Seamen cheated of their Debt?
And all our Prizes who did swallow? *Pett*.
Who did advise no Navy out to set?
And who the Forts left unrepair'd? *Pett*.
Who to supply with Powder, didst forget
Languard,⁷ *Sheerness*, *Gravesend*, and *Upnor*? *Pett*.
Who all our Ships expos'd⁸ in *Chathams* Net?
Who should it be but the *Phanatick*⁹ *Pett*.

Pett, the Sea Architect,[1] in making Ships,
Was the first cause of all these Naval slips:[2]
Had he not built, none of these faults had bin;
If no Creation,[3] there had been no Sin.

[*Poems on Affairs of State*, 1689,
probably written in 1667]

SAMUEL BUTLER

(1612–80)

Butler was the son of a small farmer. He was educated at King's
School, Worcester. Later, he was a justice's clerk. He is supposed to
have modelled Hudibras on an acquaintance – Sir Samuel Luke, a
noted puritan and a colonel in the parliamentary army. On the
Restoration, Butler became secretary to the Earl of Carbery, Lord
President of the Principality of Wales, who made him steward of
Ludlow Castle. Early in 1663 the first genuine edition of *Hudibras*
appeared – it had been preceded in 1662 by an unauthorized one.
The poem summed up people's feelings about the long rule of the
puritans, and immediately achieved an extraordinary success, as
Pepys testifies. Butler received a gift of three hundred pounds from
Charles II. A second and third part of the poem followed, and two
years after the publication of the third part Butler died in poverty.
Aubrey describes him as being 'of a leonine-coloured hair, sanguine,
choleric, middle-sized, strong . . .' *Hudibras* is a poem which shows
the strong influence of *Don Quixote*, but Butler's supreme gift as a
satirist is not so much his humour or his ridicule in their own right,
as the irony with which he makes his characters condemn themselves
out of their own mouths.

From *Hudibras*, Part 1, Canto III

HUDIBRAS ON VALOUR

But *Hudibras*, who scorn'd to stoop
To Fortune, or be said to droop,
Chear'd up himself with ends of Verse,
And sayings of Philosophers
Quoth he, Th'one half of Man, his Mind
Is *Sui juris* unconfin'd,
And cannot be laid by the heels,
What e'er the other moiety feels.
'Tis not Restraint or Liberty
That makes Men prisoners or free;
But perturbations that possess
The Mind or Aequanimities.
The whole world was not half so wide

To *Alexander* when he cry'd,
Because h' had but one to subdue,
As was a paltry narrow tub to
Diogenes, who is not said
(For ought that ever I could read)
To whine, put finger i' th' eye, and sob
Because h' had ne'er another *Tub*.
The ancients make two several kinds
Of Prowess in heroick minds,
The *Active* and the *Passive* valiant;
Both which are *pari libra* gallant:
For both to give blows and to carry,
In fights are equenecessary;
But in defeats, the *Passive* stout
Are always found to stand it out
Most desp'rately, and to out-doe
The Active, 'gainst a conquering foe.
Though we with blacks and blews are suggil'd,
Or, as the vulgar say are *cudgel'd*:
He that is valiant, and dares fight,
Though drubb'd, can lose no honor by't.
Honor's *a lease for lives to come*,
And cannot be *extended* from
The legal Tenant: 'tis a Chattel,
Not to be forfeited in Battel.
If he that in the field is slain,
Be in the *Bed of Honor* lain:
He that is beaten may be sed
To lie in Honor's *Truckle-bed*.[1]
For as we see th' eclipsed Sun
By mortals is more gaz'd upon,
Than when adorn'd with all his light
He shines in Serene Sky most bright:
So Valor in a low estate
Is most admir'd and wondered at.

[1663]

From *Hudibras*, Part 2, Canto III

ON ASTROLOGERS

SOME *Towns* and *Cities*, some, for brevity,
Have cast the Versal World's *Nativity*;
And made the Infant-Stars confess,
Like Fools or Children, what they please:
Some calculate the hidden fates
Of *Monkeys*, *Puppy-Dogs*, and *Cats*,
Some *Running-Nags*, and *Fighting-Cocks*;
Some *Love*, *Trade*, *Law-Suits*, and the *Pox*;
Some take a measure of the lives
Of Fathers, Mothers, Husbands, Wives,
Make *Opposition*, *Trine*, and *Quartile*;[1]
Tell who is barren, and who fertile,
As if the *Planet's* first aspect
The tender Infant did infect
In *Soul* and *Body*, and instill
All future good, and future ill:
Which, in their dark fatalities lurking,
At destin'd Periods fall a working;
And break out like the hidden seeds
Of long diseases into deeds,
In Friendships, Enmities, and strife,
And all th' emergencies of Life:
No sooner does he peep into,
The *World*, but he has done his do,
Catch'd all Diseases, took all *Physick*,
That cures, or kills a man that is sick;
Marry'd his punctual dose of Wives,
Is Cuckolded, and Breaks, or Thrives.
There's but the twinkling of a *Star*
Between a Man of *Peace* and *War*,
A *Thief* and *Justice*, *Fool* and *Knave*,
A huffing *Officer*, and a *Slave*,
A crafty *Lawyer* and *Pick-pocket*,
A great *Philosopher* and a *Blockhead*,

A formal *Preacher* and a *Player*,
A learn'd *Physitian* and *Man-slayer*.
As if Men from the Stars did suck
Old-age, Diseases, and *ill-luck,*
Wit, Folly, Honor, Virtue, Vice,
Trade, Travel, Women, Claps, and *Dice;*
And draw with the first Air they breath,
Battel, and *Murther, sudden Death.*
Are not these fine Commodities,
To be imported from the Skies?
And vended here among the Rable,
For staple Goods, and warrantable?
Like Mony by the *Druids* borrow'd
I' th' other *World* to be restor'd.

[1664]

From *Hudibras*, Part 3, Canto I

A DEVIL'S CATECHISM

WHAT makes a Knave a Child of God,
And one of us? – A Livelihood.
What renders Beating out of Brains
And Murther Godliness? – Great Gains.
What's tender Conscience? – 'Tis a Botch
That will not bear the gentlest touch,
But breaking out, dispatches more
Then th'Epidemical'st Plague-sore.
What makes y'encroach upon our Trade,
And damn all others? – To be paid.
What's Orthodox and true Believing
Against a Conscience? – A good Living.
What makes Rebelling against Kings
A Good Old Cause? Administrings.
What makes all Doctrines plain and clear?
About Two hundred pounds a year.
And that which was prov'd true before,
Prove false again? Two hundred more.

What makes the Breaking of all Oaths
A holy Duty? Food and Cloaths.
What Laws and Freedom, Persecution?
B'ing out of Pow'r, and Contribution.
What makes a Church a Den of Thieves?
A Dean and Chapter, and White Sleeves.
And what would serve, if those were gone,
To make it Orthodox? Our own.
What makes Morality a Crime,
The most notorious of the Time?
Morality, which both the Saints
And Wicked too cry out against?
'Cause Grace and Vertue are within
Prohibited Degrees of Kin:
And therefore no true Saint allows
They should be suffer'd to espouse.
For Saints can need no Conscience
That with Morality dispense;
As Vertue's impious, when 'tis rooted
In Nature onel', and not imputed.
But why the Wicked should doe so,
We neither know, nor care to do.
What's Liberty of Conscience,
I' th' Natural and Genuine Sense?
'Tis to restore with more security
Rebellion to its ancient Purity;
And Christian Liberty reduce
To th' elder Practice of the *Jews*.
For a Large Conscience is all one,
And signifies the same with None.

[1678]

HENRY BOLD

(1627–83)

Bold was educated at Winchester, and went on to Oxford. In 1645 he was elected a probationer fellow of New College, but was dislodged in 1648 by the Parliamentary visitors. Later he settled in London and is described as 'of the Examiner's Office in Chancery' on the title-page of a posthumous volume of verse published in 1685. The point of the satire printed here is that the coinage, which had been debased, was restored to its old standard with the Restoration.

Satyr on the Adulterate Coyn
Inscribed the Common-wealth

THAT *Common-wealth* which was our *Common-woe*,
Did *Stamp* for *Currant*, *That*, which must not *Goe*:
Yet it was well to *Passe*, till *Heaven* thought meet
To shew both *This*, and *That* were *Counterfeit*.
Our *Crosses* were their *Coyn*! Their *God* our *Hell*!
Till *Saviour Charles* became *Emanuel*.
But now – The *Devill* take their *God*! Avaunt
Thou molten *Image* of the *Covenant*!
Thou lewd *Impostor*! *State's*, and *Traffique's* Sin!
A *Brazen Bulk*, fac'd with a *Silver Skin*!
Badge of Their *Saints-Pretences*, without doubt!
A *Wolfe within*, and *Innocence without*!
Like to Their *Masqu'd Designs*! *Rebellion*
Film'd with the Tinsell of Religion!
Metall on *Metall*, here, we may disclose;
Like *Sear-cloth* stript from *Cromwell's Copper Nose*.

Thou *Bastard Relique* of the *Trayterous Crew*!
A mere *Invent*, to Give the *Devill's Due*!
Or (as a Learned Modern *Author* sayth)
In their *Own Coyn*, to *Pay* the *Publique Faith*!
Heavens! I thank you! that, in mine Extreme,
I never lov'd Their *Money More* than *Them*!

Curs'd be those *Wights*! whose *Godliness* was *Gain*,
Spoyling *Gods Image* in Their *Soveraign*!
They made *Our Angell's Evill*! and 'tis known,
Their *Crosse* and *Harp* were *Scandall* to the *CROWN*.
Had, 'mongst the *Jewes*, Their *Thirty Pence* been us'd
When *Judas* truckt for's *Lord*, 't had bin refus'd.
Worse than that *Coyn* which our *Boyes*, *Fibbs* do call!
A *Scottish Twenty-Pence* is *Worth* them *All*!

To their eternal *Shame*, be't brought to th'*Mint*!
Cast into *Medalls*; and Their *Names Stampt* in't!
That *Charon* (when they come for *Wastage* ore)
May dout *his Fare*, and make them wait on shore:
For, if *Repentance ransome* any thence,
Know! – *Charles* his *Coyn* must pay their *Peter-Pence*.

[1661]

TYBURNE CHEATED: ANONYMOUS

This anonymous broadside poem represents the state of royalis feeling immediately after the Restoration. The three protagonists were lesser regicides, who had sat among the king's judges, but who had not signed the warrant for his execution. They were condemned to perpetual imprisonment, and to be dragged upon hurdles to Tyburn every year, on the anniversary of the king's death. William Monson or Munson (*c.* 1598–1673) was one of the lesser favourites of James I. In 1618 we are told that there were some who 'took great pains in prinking and pranking him up, besides washing his face every day with posset-curd'. The triumphant Buckingham got the king to knight him and send him abroad. In 1628 he was made an Irish viscount. He changed sides very late in the Civil War, not till 1646, and sat as M.P. for Reigate from 1646 to 1653. He died, still in prison, before 11 April 1673. Sir Henry Mildmay was an equally dubious character. He was the Master of the King's Jewel House, and a notorious peculator. Clarendon describes him as 'a great flatterer of all persons of authority, and a spy in all places for them'. He voted against the attainder of Strafford in 1641, but deserted the king shortly thereafter. In 1664 his sentence of life-imprisonment was changed to one of transportation to Tangier, but he died at Antwerp shortly after setting out. Robert Wallop (1601–67) was member for Andover in the Long Parliament, and sat only three times as one of Charles's judges. He remained in the Tower till his death in 1667.

Qui Chetat Chetabitur

OR

TYRURNE Cheated

BEING

A POEME

UPON

The three Regicides *Munson*, *Mildmay* and *Wallopp*, who
were Drawn upon Hurdles to *Tyburne* on the
27th of January, 1661

GREAT, and grave *Tyburne*, Wee are sent
To court thee in a *Complement*;
Wee come, oh strange! to make no stay,
Only greet, and so away,

Take notice how we doe adore thee,
And in worship fall before thee;
Thus we fall before thy *Trine*,
And vow our selves for ever thine:
'Twas for thy sake we stirr'd up strife,
And now we love thee to the life;
Our humble hearts doe make request,
Not to be mounted, like the rest;
We are content all strife should cease,
And love, what once we hated, *Peace*.
Did we not doe a pretty thing,
To *Murder* a Religious *King*:
Oh! how we quafft his guiltless blood,
He onely dy'd for being *good*;
Whilst all the Punishment we had
Was but to live, for being *bad*;
If this be all we must incurr,
Who would not be a *Murtherer*:
We care not now we know our hope
Must be intayl'd upon a *Rope*.
Pray tell us Lawyers, can there be
A Fine, without Recoverie?
We'l satisfie our selves a None,
We now are reading *Little–ton*;
If *Cooke*[1] were living, he'd advise us
In our distress, though you dispise us;
But he (poore Wretch) was cast aside,
His Law was DUN before he dy'd:
Some of his Brethren smil'd to see,
Whilst others cry'd, And why not we?
Their Judgments did the thing enlarge,
Though he were Drawn that drew the *Charge*;
We see a boundance of our Gange,
(I hope they practice how to Hang)
That knew full well, the time was, when
Money made Knaves, now honest men:
Nor had we bin thus made a *Theame*,
Had we bin rul'd by QUARLES his *Dreame*;[2]

He call'd us *Rebells* in our prime,
And told us of this very time:
But he n'ere dream'd, as some recited,
That for his *Worke* he should be slighted:
Such *Caveleirs* we daily see
Are constant to their *Povertie*;
Their's was the danger, their's the paine,
But we can tell who reapes the gaine;
Now they may begg through Iron-grates,
That lost (by which we got) Estates.
Whilst once a yeare we pay our *Vows*,
To this our monstruous three legg'd *Spous*,
Who showes her love, in this our woe,
Poore Wretch she's loath to let us goe;
Oh! how she labours, and inclines
To make us understand her *Lines*;
How she seems to swell with pride,
With her *Champion* by her side,
Who invites us to our woes,
That the Knave might have our *cloathes*;
He tells us that we need not feare,
For old *Noll*, and *Bradshaw*'s there;
We know, and all the world may see't,
That 'tis not merry when Knaves meet;
But this old saying now proves true,
The *Gallows* always claimes her due;
Wer't not for fear, we would proceed,
And out of love, be hang'd indeed;
For unto us it does appeare
Sad to be hanged once a yeare,
For like old *Noll*, though breath be fled,
We may be hang'd when we be dead:
But one thing joyes us to the heart,
The *Caveleirs* can bare no part,
For if we see them but begin
To laugh we'le bid them laugh that win;
And if they chance to make their braggs,
We'le bid them looke upon their Raggs;

Alas poore *Creatures*, they can hope
Only in *Raggs*, and we in *Rope*.
But now, Grave *Tyburne* we must leave thee,
'Tis no wonder we deceive thee;
Pray doe not weep, for 'tis in vaine
Next yeare, we'le see the here againe;
Till then, with a submissive bow
We make to thee, each *Man* his *vow*:
And first we doe resolve to bee
Obedient unto none but thee;
Next, during life, we vow t'appeare
And doe thee *homage* once a *yeare*;
These *promises* thou well mayst trust,
Necessety will make us just.
Thus we *thy Servants*, every one,
Wallopp, *Mildmay*, and *Munson*,
With all our might and power, will
Be allwayes carefull to fullfill
Thy sweet commands, nor *time*, nor *season*
Shall hinder us, from thinking *Treason*;
What though we never lov'd our *King*?
Thou lov'st *us* for that very thing;
In all things thou shalt be our *Cheife*,
Thou lov'st a *Traitor*, and a *Theife*,
Therefore thou need'st take no care
For we can fitt thee to a haire;
For our *Deeds* are so much fam'd
That *Hell* will blush to hear *us* nam'd,
And thus for our Rebellious Pride,
Wee'l once a *yeare* on Hurdles ride,
And if Squire *Dun* will not oppose,
Wee'l every *Winter* finde him cloaths.
And now, *great Charles*, to thee we bow,
And *Satan-like*, we all alow
And owne thee for a gratious King,
Though unto us th'art no such thing;
We tooke away thy *Fathers life*,
His *Blood* still reekes upon our *knife*;

Then how can *we* expect thy *Grace*,
When *Justice* takes up *Mercies* place.
Therefore, if extracted be
The *Quintescence* of Tyrannie,
'Tis Love, compared to our *Deeds*,
Till *we* are dead, thy Father bleeds;
But if thy *Mercy* should out shine
Thy *Justice*, Thou would'st prove Devine;
Add Plagues, to Plagues, and even then
Thou art the mildest of all *Men*.
Thus we conclude, and from this houre
We will acknowledge *Thee* in *Power*.

[1661]

THE GENEVA BALLAD: ANONYMOUS

One of the most popular of all political broadside ballads, many times reprinted.

The Geneva Ballad
To the Tune of 48[1]

O FALL the *Factions* in the Town,
Mov'd by *French Springs* or *Flemish Wheels*,
    None treads *Religion* upside down,
Or tears *Pretences* out at heels,
        Like *Splay-mouth* with his brace of Caps,
        Whole Conscience might be scan'd perhaps
        By the Dimensions of his Chaps.

He whom the Sisters so adore,
Counting his Actions all Divine,
    Who when the Spirit hints, can roar,
And if occasion serves can whine;
        Nay he can bellow, bray or bark;
        Was ever *sike a Beuk-larn'd Clerk*,
        That speaks all *Lingua's* of the Ark.

To draw in Proselytes like Bees,
With *pleasing Twang* he tones his Prose,
    He gives his Hand-kerchief a squeez,
And draws *John Calvin* through his Nose.
        Motive on Motive he obtrudes,
        With *Slip-stocking Similitudes*,
        Eight Uses more, and so concludes.

When *Monarchy* began to bleed,
And *Treason* had a fine new name,
    When *Thames* was *balderdash'd* with *Tweed*,
And Pulpits did like Beacons flame;
        When *Jeroboam's* Calves were rear'd,
        And *Laud*[2] was neither lov'd nor fear'd,
        This *Gospel-Comet* first appear'd.

Soon his unhallowed Fingers strip'd
His Sov'reign Liege of Power and Land,
   And having smote his Master slip'd
His Sword into his Fellows hand.
     But he that wears his Eyes may note,
     Ofttimes the Butcher binds a Goat,
     And leaves his Boy to cut her Throat.

Poor *England* felt his Fury then
Out-weigh'd Queen *Mary's* many grains;
   His very Preaching slew more men,
Than *Bonner's*[1] Faggots, Stakes and Chains.
     With *Dog-star Zeal* and Lungs like *Boreas*,
     He fought and taught; and what's notorious,
     Destroyed his Lord to make him *Glorious*.

Yet drew for King and *Parliament*
As if the Wind could stand *North South*;
   Broke *Moses's* Law with blest intent,
Murther'd and then he wip'd his mouth.
     Oblivion alters not his case,
     Nor Clemency nor acts of Grace
     Can blanch an *Æthiopian's* Face.

Ripe for Rebellion he begins
To rally up the Saints in swarms.
   He bauls aloud, *Sirs, leave your Sins*,
But whispers, *Boys, stand to your Arms*,
     Thus he's grown insolently rude,
     Thinking his Gods can't be subdu'd,
     Money, I mean, and *Multitude*.

Magistrates he regards no more
Than St *George* or the Kings of *Colen*;[2]
   Vowing he'l not conform before
The Old-wives winde their Dead in woollen.
     He calls the Bishop *Grey-beard Goff*,
     And makes his Power as meer a Scoff,
     As *Dagon*, when his Hands were off.

Heark! how he opens with full *Cry*!
Hallow my Hearts, beware of ROME.
  Cowards that are afraid to die,
Thus make domestick Broils at home.
    How quietly Great CHARLES might reign
    Would all these Hot-spurs cross the Main,
    And preach down Popery in Spain.

The starry Rule of Heaven is fixt,
There's no dissention in the Sky;
  And can there be a Mean betwixt
Confusion and Conformity?
    A Place divided never thrives;
    'Tis bad where Hornets dwell in Hives,
    But worse where Children play with Knives.

I would as soon turn back to Mass,
Or change my Phrase to *Thee* and *Thou*;
  Let the Pope ride me like an Ass,
And his Priest milk me like a Cow;
    As buckle to *Smestymnuan* Laws,[1]
    The bad effects o'th' Good Old Cause,
    That have Dove's Plumes, but Vultur's Claws.

For 'twas the *Haly Kirk* that nurs'd
The *Brownists*[2] and the *Ranters* crew;
  Foul Errors motly Vesture first
Was Oaded in a Northern blue.
    And what's the' Enthusiastick breed,
    Or men of *Knipperdoling's*[3] Creed,
    But Cov'nanters run up to feed.

Yet they all cry, they love the King,
And make boast of their Innocence:
  There cannot be so vile a thing,
But may be colour'd with Pretence.
    Yet when all's said, one thing I'll swear,
    No Subject like th' old Cavalier,
    No Traytor like *Jack Presbyter*.

[1674]

JOHN WILMOT, 2ND EARL OF ROCHESTER
(1647–80)

The son of a cavalier loyalist, who saved Charles II after the battle of Worcester, Rochester succeeded his father in 1658. He was educated at Wadham College, Oxford, and received his M.A. degree in 1661, when he was only fourteen. With the help of a grant from the king he travelled abroad with a tutor until 1664 when he came to court and at once made an impression with his good looks and wit. In 1665 he served against the Dutch as a volunteer with the fleet. He became gentleman of the bedchamber to the king and one of the chief 'wits' of the Restoration. Constantly in trouble – very often for the scurrilous libels which he perpetrated – Rochester was always eventually forgiven. During one period of banishment from court he set up as a highly successful quack-doctor. Rochester has still not received his due, though Voltaire called him 'a man of genius and a great poet'. His reputation as a writer has been overshadowed by a still greater reputation as a profligate, and all the indecent poems of the period have been fathered on him, with the result that it is difficult to establish the true canon of his work. The *Satyr* (*against Reason and Mankind*) printed below is certainly his most ambitious effort. Johnson thought it owed almost everything to the poem by Boileau on which it is modelled, but more recently Professor de Sola Pinto has described it as 'a unique expression in English poetry of the moral crisis of Western Europe at the time when the "new philosophy" had shattered the old unified world picture and man was seen as an isolated unit, miserable and insignificant in a hostile or indifferent world'.

Satyr

(against Reason and Mankind)

WERE I (who to my cost already am
    One of those strange prodigious creatures *Man*.)
A Spirit free, to choose for my own share,
What Case of Flesh, and Blood, I pleas'd to weare,
I'd be a *Dog*, a *Monkey*, or a *Bear*.
Or any thing but that vain *Animal*,
Who is so proud of being rational.

The senses are too gross, and he'll contrive
A Sixth, to contradict the other Five;
And before certain instinct, will preferr
Reason, which Fifty times for one does err.
Reason, an *Ignis fatuus*, in the *Mind*,
Which leaving light of *Nature*, sense behind;
Pathless and dang'rous wandring ways it takes,
Through errors, Fenny-*Boggs*, and Thorny *Brakes*;
Whilst the misguided follower, climbs with pain,
Mountains of Whimseys, heap'd in his own *Brain*:
Stumbling from thought to thought, falls headlong down,
Into doubts boundless Sea, where like to drown.
Books bear him up a while, and makes him try,
To swim with Bladders of *Philosophy*;
In hopes still t'oretake th'escaping light,
The *Vapour* dances in his dazling sight,
Till spent, it leaves him to eternal Night.
Then Old Age, and experience, hand in hand,
Lead him to death, and make him understand,
After a search so painful, and so long,
That all his life he has been in the wrong;
Hudled in dirt, the reas'ning *Engine* lies,
Who was so proud, so witty, and so wise.
Pride drew him in, as *Cheats*, their *Bubbles* catch,
And makes him venture, to be made a *Wretch*.
His wisdom did his happiness destroy,
Aiming to know what *World* he shou'd enjoy;
And *Wit*, was his vain frivolous pretence,
Of pleasing others, at his own expence.
For *Witts* are treated just like common *Whores*,
First they're enjoy'd, and then kickt out of *Doores*:
The pleasure past, a threatning doubt remains,
That frights th'enjoyer, with succeeding pains:
Women and *Men* of *Wit*, are dang'rous Tools,
And ever fatal to admiring Fools.
Pleasure allures, and when the *Fopps* escape,
'Tis not that they're belov'd, but fortunate,
And therefore what they fear, at least they hate.

But now methinks some formal Band, and Beard,
Takes me to task, come on Sir I'm prepar'd.
Then by your favour, any thing that's writ
Against this gibeing jingling knack call'd Wit,
Likes me abundantly, but you take care,
Upon this point, not to be too severe.
Perhaps my Muse, were fitter for this part,
For I profess, I can be very smart
On Wit, *which I abhor with all my heart:*
I long to lash it in some sharp Essay,
But your grand indiscretion bids me stay,
And turns my Tide of Ink another way.
What rage ferments in your degen'rate mind,
To make you rail at Reason, and Mankind?
Blest glorious Man! To whom alone kind Heav'n,
An everlasting Soul *has freely giv'n;*
Whom his great Maker *took such care to make,*
That from himself he did the Image *take;*
And this fair frame, in shining Reason *drest,*
To dignifie his Nature, *above Beast.*
Reason, *by whose aspiring influence,*
We take a flight beyond material sense.
Dive into Mysteries, then soaring pierce,
The flaming limits of the Universe.
Search Heav'n and Hell, find out what's acted there,
And give the World true grounds of hope and fear.

Hold mighty Man, I cry, all this we know,
From the Pathetique Pen of *Ingello*;[1]
From *P*[atrick's] *Pilgrim*,[2] *S*[ibb's][3] replys,
And 'tis this very reason I despise.
This supernatural gift, that makes a *Myte* –,
Think he is the Image of the Infinite:
Comparing his short life, void of all rest,
To the *Eternal*, and the ever blest.
This busie, puzling, stirrer up of doubt,
That frames deep *Mysteries*, then finds 'em out;
Filling with Frantick Crowds of thinking *Fools*,
Those Reverend *Beldams*, *Colledges*, and *Schools*

Borne on whose wings, each heavy *Sot* can pierce,
The limits of the boundless Universe.
So charming Oyntments, make an Old *Witch* flie,
And bear a Crippled Carcass through the Skie.
'Tis this exalted Pow'r, whose bus'ness lies,
In *Nonsense*, and impossibilities.
This made a Whimsical *Philosopher*,
Before the spacious *World*, his *Tub* prefer,
And we have modern *Cloysterd Coxcombs*, who
Retire to think, cause they have naught to do.
Where Action ceases, thoughts impertinent:
Our *Sphere* of Action, is lifes happiness,
And he who thinks Beyond, thinks like an *Ass*.
Thus, whilst 'gainst false reas'ning I inveigh,
I own right *Reason*, which I wou'd obey:
That *Reason* that distinguishes by sense,
And gives us *Rules*, of good, and ill from thence:
That bounds desires, with a reforming Will,
To keep 'em more in vigour, not to kill.
Your *Reason* hinders, mine helps t'enjoy,
Renewing Appetites, yours wou'd destroy.
My Reason is my Friend, yours is a *Cheat*,
Hunger call's out, my Reason bids me eat;
Perversly yours, your Appetite does mock,
This asks for Food, that answers what's a Clock?
This plain distinction Sir your doubt secures,
'Tis not true Reason I despise but yours.
Thus I think Reason righted, but for *Man*,
I'le nere recant defend him if you can.
For all his Pride, and his Philosophy,
'Tis evident, *Beasts* are in their degree,
As wise at least, and better far than he.
Those *Creatures*, are the wisest who attain,
By surest means, the ends at which they aim.
If therefore *Jowler*, finds, and Kills his *Hares*,
Better than M[eres],[1] supplyes Committee Chairs;
Though one's a *States-man*, th'other but a *Hound*,
Jowler, in Justice, wou'd be wiser found.

You see how far *Mans* wisedom here extends,
Look next, if humane Nature makes amends;
Whose Principles, most gen'rous are, and just,
And to whose *Moralls*, you wou'd sooner trust.
Be judge your self, I'le bring it to the test,
Which is the basest *Creature Man*, or *Beast*?
Birds, feed on *Birds*, *Beasts*, on each other prey,
But Savage *Man* alone, does *Man*, betray:
Prest by necessity, they Kill for Food,
Man, undoes *Man*, to do himself no good.
With Teeth, & Claws, by Nature arm'd they hunt,
Natures allowance, to supply their want.
But *Man*, with smiles, embraces, Friendships, praise,
Unhumanely his Fellows life betrays;
With voluntary pains, works his distress,
Not through necessity, but wantonness.
For hunger, or for Love, they fight, or tear,
Whilst wretched *Man*, is still in Arms for fear;
For fear he armes, and is of Armes afraid,
By fear, to fear, successively betray'd
Base fear, the source whence his best passion came,
His boasted Honor, and his dear bought Fame.
That lust of Pow'r, to which he's such a *Slave*,
And for the which alone he dares be brave:
To which his various Projects are design'd,
Which makes him gen'rous, affable, and kind.
For which he takes such pains to be thought wise,
And screws his actions, in a forc'd disguise:
Leading a tedious life in Misery,
Under laborious, mean *Hypocrisie*.
Look to the bottom, of his vast design,
Wherein *Mans* Wisdom, Pow'r, and Glory joyn;
The good he 'acts, the ill he does endure,
'Tis all for fear, to make himself secure.
Meerly for safety, after Fame we thirst,
For all Men wou'd be *Cowards* if they durst.
And honesty's against all common sense,
Men must be *Knaves*, 'tis in their own defence.

Mankind's dishonest, if you think it fair,
Amongst known *Cheats*, to play upon the square,
You'le be undone ⸺⸺⸺⸺
Nor can weak truth, your reputation save,
The *Knaves*, will all agree to call you *Knave*.
Wrong'd shall he live, insulted o're, opprest,
Who dares be less a *Villain*, than the rest.
Thus Sir you see what humane Nature craves,
Most Men are *Cowards*, all Men shou'd be *Knaves*:
The diff'rence lyes (as far as I can see)
Not in the thing it self, but the degree;
And all the subject matter of debate,
Is only who's a *Knave*, of the first *Rate*?

All this with indignation have I hurl'd,
At the pretending part of the proud World,
Who swolne with selfish vanity, devise,
False freedomes, holy Cheats, and formal Lyes
Over their fellow *Slaves* to tyrannize.

But if in *Court*, so just a man there be,
(In *Court*, a just man, yet unknown to me.)
Who does his needful flattery direct,
Not to oppress, and ruine, but protect;
Since flattery, which way so ever laid,
Is still a Tax on that unhappy Trade.
If so upright a *States-Man*, you can find,
Whose passions bend to his unbyass'd Mind;
Who does his Arts, and *Pollicies* apply,
To raise his *Country*, not his *Family*;
Nor while his Pride, own'd Avarice withstands,
Receives Aureal bribes, from *Friends* corrupted hands.

Is there a *Church-Man* who on *God* relyes?
Whose Life, his Faith, and Doctrine Justifies?
Not one blown up, with vain Prelatique Pride,
Who for reproof of Sins, does *Man* deride:
Whose envious heart with his obstrep'rous sawcy Eloquence,
Dares chide at *Kings*, and raile at Men of sense.
Who from his Pulpit, vents more peevish Lyes,
More bitter railings, scandals, Calumnies,

That at a Gossiping, are thrown about,
When the good *Wives*, get drunk, and then fall out.
None of that sensual *Tribe*, whose Tallents lye,
In Avarice, *Pride*, *Sloth*, and *Gluttony*.
Who hunt good Livings, but abhor good Lives,
Whose Lust exalted, to that height arrives,
They act Adultery with their own *Wives*.
And e're a score of Years compleated be,
Can from the lofty *Pulpit* proudly see,
Half a large *Parish*, their own *Progeny*.

Nor doating B[ishop] who wou'd be ador'd,
For domineering at the *Councel Board*;
A greater *Fop*, in business at Fourscore,
Fonder of serious *Toyes*, affected more,
Than the gay glitt'ring *Fool*, at Twenty proves,
With all his noise, his tawdrey Cloths, and Loves.

But a meek humble Man, of modest sense,
Who Preaching peace, does practice continence;
Whose pious life's a proof he does believe,
Misterious truths, which no *Man* can conceive.
If upon *Earth* there dwell such *God-like Men*,
I'le here recant my *Paradox* to them.
Adores those *Shrines* of *Virtue*, *Homage* pay,
And with the *Rabble World*, their *Laws* obey.
If such there are, yet grant me this at least,
Man differs more from *Man*, than *Man* from *Beast*.

[First printed as a broadside, 1675, text
from *Poems on Several Occasions*, 1680]

JOHN SHEFFIELD, 3RD EARL OF MULGRAVE, 1ST DUKE OF BUCKINGHAM AND NORMANBY

(1648–1721)

John Sheffield's long public career began in 1666, when he served as a volunteer against the Dutch in the fleet commanded by Prince Rupert and the Duke of Albemarle. By 1673 he had become a gentleman in waiting to the king, and by 1678 a Knight of the Garter. He was famous for his pride, and a notorious intriguer. In 1682 he displeased Charles II by courting the Princess (later Queen) Anne, and was banished from the court. On the accession of James he was in high favour, and did not hesitate to associate himself with the new king's most unpopular measures. He did not, however, become a Roman Catholic. On William's landing, he remained with James till the time of his flight, but later quietly submitted. In William's reign he was one of the leaders of the tories. Anne showed him marked favour on her accession, and gave him a dukedom, and on her death he was one of the lords justices appointed to carry on the administration. George I removed him from all his posts. His third wife was Catherine, the illegitimate daughter of James II, and (it is now supposed) the original of Pope's *Atossa*. The *Essay upon Satyr*, an extract from which is printed here, was the forerunner of Dryden's political satires and Dryden himself was reputed to have had a hand in it. Rochester had Dryden waylaid and beaten in revenge for the passage printed here.

From *An Essay upon Satyr*

ON ROCHESTER

Rochester I despise for his meer want of wit,
Though thought to have a Tail and Cloven Feet;
For while he mischief means to all mankind,
Himself alone the ill effects does find;
And so like Witches justly suffers shame,
Whose harmless malice is so much the same;
False are his words, affected is his wit,
So often he does aim, so seldom hit;
To every face he cringes while he speaks,

But when the Back is turn'd the head he breaks;
Mean in each Action, lewd in every Limb,
Manners themselves are mischievous in him:
A proof that chance alone makes every Creature,
A very *Killigrew*[1] without good Nature;
For what a *Bessus*[2] has he always liv'd,
And his own *Kickings* notably contriv'd:
(For there's the folly that's still mixt with fear)
Cowards more blows than any Heroe bear;
Of fighting sparks some may her pleasures say,
But 'tis a bolder thing to run away:
The World may well forgive him all his ill,
For ev'ry fault does prove his penance still:
Falsly he falls into some dangerous Noose,
And then as meanly labours to get loose;
A life so infamous is better quitting,
Spent in base injury and low submitting.

> [*The Fourth (And Last) Collection of Poems,*
> *Satyrs, Songs &c.,* 1689, written *c.* 1679]

JOHN OLDHAM

(1653–83)

The son of a nonconformist minister, Oldham entered St Edmund's
Hall in 1670. He was later an usher at Archbishop Whitgift's Free
School at Croydon, and tutor to the grandsons of a retired judge. He
is also said to have studied medicine. He died of small-pox. The
Satires upon the Jesuits, his best-known work, are an expression
of the popular panic at the time of the Popish plot. Pope, who was
probably influenced by him in his practice of making paraphrases of
classical satirists, called him 'a very indelicate writer'.

From *Satires upon the Jesuits*, I

THE JESUITS ENJOINED AGAINST PITY

SPARE not in Churches kneeling *Priests* at pray'r,
Tho interceding for you, slay ev'n there.
Spare not young *Infants* smiling at the breast,
Who from relenting Fools their mercy wrest:
Rip teeming Wombs, tear out the hated Brood,
From thence, & drown 'em in their *Mothers* blood.
Pity not *Virgins*, nor their tender cries,
Tho prostrate at your feet with melting eyes
All drown'd in tears; strike home, as 'twere in *lust*,
And force their begging hands to guide the thrust.
Ravish at th'Altar, kill when you have done,
Make them your Rapes, and Victims too in one.
Nor let gray hoary hairs protection give
To *Age*, just crawling on the verge of Life:
Snatch from its leaning hands the weak support,
And with it knock't into the grave with sport;
Brain the poor Cripple with his Crutch, then cry,
You've kindly rid him of his misery.
　　Seal up your ears to Mercy, lest their words
Should tempt a pity, ram 'em with your Swords
(Their tongues too) down their throats; let 'em not dare

To mutter for their Souls a gasping Pray'r,
But in the utt'rance choak't, and stab it there.
'Twere witty handsom Malice (could you do't)
To make 'em die, and make 'em damn'd to boot.

[1681, written 1679]

From *Satires upon the Jesuits*, III

LOYOLA'S ADVICE TO THE JESUITS

THE Credulous, and easie of Belief,
With *Miracles*, and well-fram'd Lies deceive.
Empty whole *Surius*, and the *Talmud*: drain
Saint *Francis*, and Saint *Mahomet's Alcoran*:
Sooner shall *Popes*, and *Cardinals* want Pride,
Than you a *Stock* of Lies, and Legends need.
  Tell how blest *Virgin* to come down was seen,
Like *Play-House Punk* descending in *Machine*:
How she writ *Billets Doux*, and *Love-Discourse*,
Made *Assignations*, *Visits*, and *Amours*:
How *Hosts* distrest, her *Smock* for *Banner* bore,
Which vanquish'd *Foes*, and murder'd at twelve *Score*.
Relate how *Fish* in *Conventicles met*,
And *Mackrel* were with bait of *Doctrine* caught;
How *Cattel* have *Judicious Hearers* been,
And *Stones* pathetically cry'd *Amen*:
How consecrated Hives with Bells was hung,
And Bees kept Mass, and Holy *Anthems Sung*:
How *Pigs* to th' *Ros'ry* kneel'd, and sheep were taught
To bleat *Te Deum*, and *Magnificat*:
How *Fly-Flap* of Church-Censure Houses rid
Of Insects, which at Curse of Fryer dy'd:
How travelling Saints, well mounted on a Switch,
Ride *Journeys* thro' the *Air*, like *Lapland Witch*:
And ferrying Cowls *Religious Pilgrims* bore
O're waves with the help of Sail, or Oar.
Nor let *Xavier's*[1] great *Wonders* pass conceal'd,
How *Storms* were by th' Almighty *Wafer* quell'd;

How *zealous Crab* the sacred Image bore,
And swam a *Cath'lick* to the distant *Shore*.
With Shams, like these, the giddy *Rout* mislead,
Their *Folly*, and their *Superstition* feed.

[1681, written 1679]

JOHN DRYDEN
(1631–1700)

Dryden's family had a puritan background, and he was educated at Westminster and Trinity College, Cambridge. He began his literary career with the *Heroic Stanzas* (1659) written to the memory of the Protector, but changed his tune on the Restoration with *Astraea Redux* (1660). He turned to the stage in order to make a living, and was for a time a retained writer under contract to the King's Theatre. His greatest successes were with heroic plays, and this led to his being satirized in *The Rehearsal* (1671), written by the 2nd Duke of Buckingham (for whom see the notes to *Absalom and Achitophel*). Dryden, who had been made poet laureate in 1670, is ridiculed under the name of Bayes. Dryden's own thoughts began to drift towards satire in 1678, apparently the date at which he wrote *MacFlecknoe*, which, though not published till the pirated first edition of 1682, was circulating in manuscript before that date. The success of Mulgrave's *Essay upon Satyr* (a poem Dryden is reputed to have had a hand in) perhaps helped to confirm this trend. In 1681 he took the field as a satirist on the side of the court. At that moment, Shaftesbury, having failed to carry the Exclusion Bill through the Lords, was awaiting trial for high treason. *Absalom and Achitophel* was a great success, and was followed by *The Medall*, and by the second part of *Absalom and Achitophel*, this latter mostly written by Nahum Tate, though the passages on Elkanah Settle (*Doeg*) and Shadwell (*Og*) are by Dryden. In 1685, on the accession of James II, Dryden became a Roman Catholic. He pamphleteered on the side of James, and on the fall of the king lost his office and pension as laureate, but was otherwise unmolested. A large part of his closing years were spent in labours of translation. At the end of his life he was universally recognized as the greatest of living poets, and held a small court at a coffee-house, where Congreve, Vanburgh and Addison were among his admirers. It was in these circumstances that the young Pope saw him.

From *MacFlecknoe*

FLECKNOE NAMES SHADWELL AS HIS SUCCESSOR

> ALL humane things are subject to decay,
> And when Fate Summons, Monarch's must obey;
> This *Flecknoe* found, who like *Augustus* young,
> Was call'd to Empire, and had Govern'd long;

In Prose and Verse was own'd without Dispute,
Through all the Realms of Nonsense, Absolute;
This Aged Prince now flourishing in Peace,
And blest with Issue of a large Increase,
Worn out with Business, did at length Debate,
To settle the Succession of the State,
And Pond'ring, which of all his Sons were fit
To Reign, and Wage Immortal Wars, with Wit,
Cry'd, 'tis Resolv'd (for Nature pleads, that he
Should only Rule, who most resembles me,)
Shad –¹ alone my perfect Image Bears,
Mature in Dulness from his Tender Years;
Shad – alone of all my Sons, is He
Who stands confirm'd in full Stupidity;
The rest, to some faint meaning make Pretence,
But *Shad* – never deviates into Sence;
Some Beams of Wit on other Souls may Fall,
Strike through, and make a Lucid Interval;
But *Shad* – Genuine Nights admits no Ray,
His rising Fogs prevail upon the Day;
Besides, his goodly Fabrick fills the Eye,
And seems design'd for thoughtless Majesty;
Thoughtless as Monarch-Oaks that shade the Plain,
And spread in solemn State, supinely Reign;
Heywood and *Shirly* were but Types of Thee,
Thou last great Prophet of Tautology.

[1682, written *c.* 1678]

From *Absalom and Achitophel*², Part I

PORTRAIT OF SHAFTESBURY

Of these the false *Achitophel* was first:
A Name to all succeeding Ages Curst.
For close Designs, and crooked Counsell fit;
Sagacious, Bold, and Turbulent of wit:
Restless, unfixt in Principle and Place;
In Power unpleas'd, impatient of Disgrace.

A fiery Soul, which working out its way, ⎤
Fretted the Pigmy Body to decay: ⎟
And o'r inform'd the Tenement of Clay. ⎦
A daring Pilot in extremity;
Pleas'd with the Danger, when the Waves went high
He fought the Storms; but for a Calm unfit,
Would Steer too nigh the Sands, to boast his Wit.
Great Wits are sure to Madness near ally'd;
And thin Partitions do their Bounds divide:
Else, why should he, with Wealth and Honour blest,
Refuse his Age the needful hours of Rest?
Punish a Body which he coud not please;
Bankrupt of Life, yet Prodigal of Ease?
And all to leave, what with his Toyl he won,
To that unfeather'd, two Leg'd thing, a Son:
Got, while his Soul did hudled Notions try;
And born a shapeless Lump, like Anarchy.
In Friendship False, Implacable in Hate:
Resolv'd to Ruine or to Rule the State.
To Compass this the Triple Bond he broke; ⎤
The Pillars of the publick Safety shook: ⎟
And fitted *Israel* for a Foreign Yoke. ⎦
Then, seiz'd with Fear, yet still affecting Fame,
Assum'd a Patriott's All-attoning Name.
Oh, had he been content to serve the Crown,
With vertues only proper to the Gown;
Or, had the rankness of the Soyl been freed
From Cockle, that opprest the Noble feed:
David, for him his tunefull Harp had strung,
And Heaven had wanted one Immortal song.
But wilde Ambition loves to slide, not stand;
And Fortunes Ice prefers to Vertues Land:
Achitophel, grown weary to possess
A lawfull Fame, and lazy Happiness;
Disdain'd the Golden fruit to gather free,
And lent the Croud his Arm to shake the Tree.
Now, manifest of Crimes, contriv'd long since,
He stood at bold Defiance with his Prince:

Held up the Buckler of the Peoples Cause,
Against the Crown; and sculk'd behind the Laws.
The wish'd occasion of the Plot he takes,
Some Circumstances finds, but more he makes.
By buzzing Emissaries, fills the ears
Of listning Crowds, with Jealosies and Fears
Of Arbitrary Counsels brought to light,
And proves the King himself a *Jebusite*:
Weak Arguments! which yet he knew fulwell,
Were strong with People easie to Rebell.

PORTRAIT OF THE DUKE OF BUCKINGHAM

SOME of their Chiefs were Princes of the Land:
In the first Rank of these did *Zimri*[1] stand:
A man so various, that he seem'd to be
Not one, but all Mankinds Epitome.
Stiff in Opinions, always in the wrong;
Was every thing by starts, and nothing long:
But, in the course of one revolving Moon,
Was Chymist, Fidler, States-Man, and Buffoon:
Then all for Women, Painting, Rhiming, Drinking,
Besides ten thousand freaks that dy'd in thinking.
Blest Madman, who coud every hour employ,
With something New to wish, or to enjoy!
Rayling and praising were his usual Theams;
And both (to shew his Judgment) in Extreams:
So over Violent, or over Civil,
That every man, with him, was God or Devil.
In squandring Wealth was his peculiar Art:
Nothing went unrewarded, but Desert.
Begger'd by Fools, whom still he found too late:
He had his Jest, and they had his Estate.
He laught himself from Court, then sought Releif
By forming Parties, but coud ne're be Chief:
For, spight of him, the weight of Business fell
On *Absalom* and wife *Achitophel*:

Thus, wicked but in will, of means bereft,
He left not Faction, but of that was left.

[1681]

From *Absalom and Achitophel*, Part II

PORTRAIT OF SHADWELL

NOW stop your noses Readers, all and some,
For here's a tun of Midnight-work to come,
Og[1] from a Treason Tavern rowling home.
Round as a Globe, and Liquor'd ev'ry chink,
Goodly and Great he Sayls behind his Link;
With all this Bulk there's nothing lost in *Og*
For ev'ry inch that is not Fool is Rogue:
A Monstrous mass of foul corrupted matter,
As all the Devils had spew'd to make the batter.
When wine has given him courage to Blaspheme,
He Curses God, but God before Curst him;
And if a man cou'd have reason none has more,
That made his Paunch so rich and him so poor.
With wealth he was not trusted, for Heav'n knew
What 'twas of Old to pamper up a *Jew*;
To what wou'd he on Quail and Pheasant swell,
That ev'n on Tripe and Carrion cou'd rebell?
But though Heav'n made him poor, (with rev'rence speaking,)
He never was a Poet of God's making;
The Midwife laid her hand on his Thick Skull,
With this Prophetick blessing – *Be thou Dull*;
Drink, Swear and Roar, forbear no lew'd delight
Fit for thy Bulk, doe any thing but write:
Thou art of lasting Make like thoughtless men,
A strong Nativity – but for the Pen;
Eat Opium, mingle Arsenick in thy Drink,
Still thou mayst live avoiding Pen and Ink.
I see, I see 'tis Counsell given in vain,
For Treason botcht in Rime will be thy bane;
Rhime is the Rock on which thou art to wreck,

'Tis fatal to thy Fame and to thy Neck:
Why should thy Metre good King *David* blast?
A Psalm of his will Surely be thy last.
Dar'st thou presume in verse to meet thy foes,
Thou whom the Penny Pamphlet foil'd in prose?
Doeg,[1] whom God for Mankinds mirth has made,
O'er-tops thy tallent in thy very Trade;
Doeg to thee, thy paintings are so Course,
A Poet is, though he's the Poets Horse.
A Double Noose thou on thy Neck dost pull,
For Writing Treason, and for Writing dull;
To die for Faction is a Common evil,
But to be hang'd for Non-sense is the Devil:
Hadst thou the Glories of thy King exprest,
Thy praises had been Satyr at the best;
But thou in Clumsy verse, unlickt, unpointed,
Hast Shamefully defi'd the Lord's Anointed:
I will not rake the Dunghill of thy Crimes,
For who wou'd reade thy Life that reads thy rhimes?
But of King *David's* Foes be this the Doom,
May all be like the Young-man *Absalom*;
And for my Foes may this their Blessing be,
To talk like *Doeg*, and to Write like Thee.

[1682]

SAMUEL WESLEY, THE ELDER
(1662–1735)

Samuel Wesley was the father of the founder of Methodism. He himself was the son of an independent minister, and was educated at a nonconformist academy where Defoe was among his fellow-pupils. He became a servitor at Exeter College, Oxford, in 1683, and *Maggots* was published anonymously while he was still a student. Wesley joined the established church, and struggled all his life with financial difficulties. In 1695 he became rector of Epworth in Lincolnshire, and in 1705 was imprisoned for debt in Lincoln Castle. In 1716–17 there were a series of apparently supernatural disturbances at Epworth rectory – one of the best authenticated of all poltergeist stories. Pope attacked Wesley in the first version of the *Dunciad*.

A Pindaricque[1]

On the *Grunting* of a Hog

1

FREEBORN *Pindaric* never does refuse,
    Either a lofty, or a humble Muse:
Now in proud *Sophoclæan* Buskins Sings,
    Of *Hero*'s, and of *Kings*,
    Mighty *Numbers*, mighty *Things*;
        Now out of sight she flys,
        Rowing with gaudy Wings
        A-cross the stormy Skys,
            Then down again,
            Her self she Flings,
        Without uneasiness, or Pain
    To Lice, and Dogs,
    To Cows, and Hogs,
And follows their melodious grunting o're the Plain.

2

    Harmonious *Hog* draw near!
    No bloody *Butchers* here,
        Thou need'st not fear,

130

Harmonious *Hog* draw near, and from thy *beauteous Snowt*
   Whilst we attend with Ear,
   Like thine prick't up devou't;
  To taste thy *Sugry voice*, which here, and there,
With wanton Curls, vibrates around the circling Air,
  Harmonious *Hog*! warble some *Anthem* out!
As sweet as those which quiv'ring *Monks* in days of Y'ore,
    With us did roar;
    When they alas,
  That the hard-hearted *Abbot* such a Coyl should keep,
  And cheat 'em of their first, their sweetest Sleep;
When they were ferretted up to *Midnight Mass*:
Why should not other *Piggs* on *Organs* play,
   As well as They.

3

   Dear *Hog*! thou King of Meat!
   So near thy Lord Mankind,
  The nicest Taste can scarce a difference find!
  No more may I thy glorious *Gammons* eat!
    No more,
  Partake of the *Free Farmers Christmass* store,
Black Puddings which with Fat would make your Mouths run o're:
If I, tho' should ne're so long before the Sentence stay,
And in my large Ears scale, the thing ne're so discreetly weigh,
  If I can find a difference in the Notes,
   Belcht from the applauded Throats
  Of Rotten Play house *Songsters-All-Divine*,
If any difference I can find between their Notes, and Thine:
  A Noise they keep with *Tune*, and out of *Tune*,
   And Round, and Flat,
  High, Low, and This, and That,
That *Algebra*, or Thou, or I might understand as soon.

4

  Like the confounding *Lutes* innumerable Strings,
    One of them Sings;
   Thy easier Musick's ten times more divine;

More like the one string'd, deep, Majestick *Trump-Marine*:
Prythee strike up, and cheer this drooping Heart of Mine!
    Not the sweet Harp that's claimed by *Jews*,
Nor that which to the far more Ancient *Welch* belongs,
      Nor that which the Wild *Irish* use,
Frighting even their own *Wolves* with loud *Hubbubba-boos*.
    Nor *Indian* Dance, with *Indian* Songs,
      Nor yet,
    (Which how should I so long forget?)
      The Crown of all the rest,
      The very Cream o'th' Jest:
    Amptuous Noble *Lyre* – the Tongs;
    Nor, tho' Poetick *Jordan*[1] bite his *Thumbs*,
At the bold word, my *Lord Mayors Flutes*, and *Kettle-Drums*;
    Not all this Instrumental dare,
With thy soft, ravishing, vocal Musick ever to compare.

                              [*Maggots*, 1685]

ROBERT GOULD

(fl. 1698-1709)

I have been unable to find out much about this vigorous and interesting satirist. Giles Jacob's *Poetical Register* of 1723 says that he was
'a Domestick of the late Earl of Dorset and Middlesex; who afterwards became a country school-master. He writ one play.' This play
was *The Rival Sisters*, based on Shirley's *The Maid's Revenge*, and
acted at the Theatre Royal in 1696. Gould seems to have been influenced by Swift, as one can see by comparing their respective
attacks on the female sex.

From *A Satyr Against Woman*

A FAMOUS BAWD

WHO knew not (for to whom was she unknown)
Our late Illustrious *Bewley*? (true, she's gone
To answer for the num'rous Ills sh'as done;
Who, tho' in Hell (in Hell, if any where)
Hemm'd round with all the Flames and Tortures there,
Finds 'em not fiercer, tho' she feels the worst,
Than when she liv'd, her own wild flames of Lust.)
As *Albion*'s Isle fast rooted in the Main,
Does the rough Billows raging Force disdain,
Which tho' they foam, and with loud Terrors rore,
Yet they can never reach beyond their shore.
So she with Lusts Enthusiastick Rage,
Sustain'd all the salt Stallions of the Age.
Whole Legions she encounter'd, Legions tyr'd;
Insatiate yet, still fresh Supplies desir'd.
Illustrious Bawd! whose Fame shall be display'd,
When Heroes Glories are in Silence laid,
In as profound a Silence, as the Slaves
Their conqu'ring Swords dispatch'd into their Graves.
But Bodies must decay; for 'tis too sure,
There's nothing from the Jaws of Time secure.
Yet, when she found that she could do no more,
When all her Body was one putrid Sore,
Studded with Pox, and Ulcers quite all o're;

Ev'n then, by her delusive treach'rous Wiles,
(Which show'd most specious when they most beguil'd)
Sh' enroll'd more Females in the List of Whore,
Than all the Arts of Man e're did before.
Prest with the pond'rous guilt, at length she fell;
And through the solid Centre sunk to Hell:
The murm'ring Fiends all hover'd round about,
And in hoarse howls did the great Bawd salute;
Amaz'd to see a sordid lump of Clay,
Stain'd with more various bolder Crimes than they:
Nor were her torments less; for the dire Train,
Soon sent her howling through the rowling flames,
To the sad Seat of everlasting pain.
Cresswold, and *Stratford*, the same path do tread;
In Lust's black Volumes so profoundly read,
That wheresoe're they die, we well may fear,
The very tincture of the Crimes they bear,
With strange infusion may inspire the dust,
And in the Grave commit true acts of Lust.

[1698]

From *Jack Pavy*

VISITING THE PRISONS[1]

OR shou'd you, at your Leisure, take the Pains
To visit all the *Pris'ners* in their Chains;
What Wretches doom'd to Durance wou'd you find?
For various Crimes to various *Wards* assign'd.
Our many *Bridewells*[2] we shall mention, first,
With *Hemp* and *Hunger* equally accurst;
Where of all Human Privilege debarr'd,
The *Vagrant* and the *Harlot* labour hard,
And thrice a Day are Lash'd for their Reward.
The vicious *Bench*[3] we will the next survey,
Where many Villains won't come out that may,
And needier Knaves that wou'd are forc'd to stay.[4]

But most the *Common-Side* your Eye wou'd draw,
Where fed with Basket Alms, and lodg'd on Straw,
You see the Curse of *Debt*, and Cruelty of *Law*:
Ev'n *Transportation* much a milder Doom
Than perishing, unpittied, thus at home.
Nor can you unconcern'd thro' *Ludgate* pass
Without a Conscience steel'd, or Heart of Brass;
Where, thro' the Iron Grate, a Rueful Tongue
Directs you to the *Box* below 'em hung,
To angle Farthings from the num'rous Throng;
But so successless, for one *Giver* found,
Ten thousand shove along and never hear the Sound.
But highest, *Newgate* your Concern wou'd rear,
To see 'em Batt'ning in their Dung,[1] and hear
An Everlasting Clank of Irons there:
A Nest of Villains, resolutely blind,
That neither *Present*, *Past* or *Future* mind;
But to the utmost Verge of Fate pursue
An impious Life, nor their Condition rue,
When *Tyburn* and *Damnation*'s full in view:
No least Contrition in their Eyes is seen,
But all is Brass without, and hardned Fiend within.

[*Works*, 1709]

JONATHAN SWIFT

(1667–1745)

Swift was born in Dublin, and was distantly related to Dryden. He was educated at Trinity College, Dublin, and in 1689 became secretary to Sir William Temple at Moor Park, a post he held (with one break) until his patron died in 1699. He then returned to Dublin, where he made a reputation as a wit and obtained some small church preferments – he had been ordained in 1694. In 1701 he went to England, and spent most of his time there until 1704. He was by now the friend of Pope, Steele, and Addison. In 1710 he deserted the whigs for the tories and became the editor of the *Examiner*, the chief organ of Oxford and Bolingbroke. In 1713 he was made Dean of St Patrick's, Dublin. The fall of the whigs marked the end of Swift's political hopes, and he returned to Ireland and his deanery. Coldly received at first, he turned himself into a national hero with *The Drapier's Letters* of 1724, administering in the process a humiliating defeat to the Hanoverian government. *Gulliver's Travels* was published in 1726. As he grew older Swift suffered from ever severer attacks of giddiness. He became more and more capricious and morbidly suspicious. In 1742 it was necessary to appoint guardians of his person and estate, and in September of that year came a crisis in his illness which left him a helpless wreck until his death three years later.

Verses Wrote in a Lady's Ivory Table Book

Anno. 1698

PERUSE my Leaves thro' ev'ry Part,
And think thou seest my owners Heart,
Scrawl'd o'er with Trifles thus, and quite
As hard, as senseless, and as light:
Expos'd to every Coxcomb's Eyes,
But hid with Caution from the Wise.
Here you may read (*Dear Charming Saint*)
Beneath (*A new Receit for Paint*)
Here in Beau-spelling (*tru tel deth*)
There in her own (*for an el breth*)
Here (*lovely Nymph pronounce my doom*)

There (*A safe way to use Perfume*)
Here, a Page fill'd with Billet Doux;
On t'other side (*laid out for Shoes*)
(*Madam, I dye without your Grace*)
(Item, *for half a Yard of Lace.*)
Who that had Wit would place it here,
For every peeping Fop to Jear.
To think that your Brains Issue is
Expos'd to th'Excrement of his,
In power of Spittle and a Clout
When e're he please to blot it out;
And then to heighten the Disgrace
Clap his own Nonsense in the place.
Whoe're expects to hold his part
In such a Book and such a Heart,
If he be Wealthy and a Fool
Is in all Points the fittest Tool,
Of whom it may be justly said,
He's a Gold Pencil tipt with Lead.

[*Miscellanies in Prose and Verse*, 1711]

A Satyrical Elegy

On the Death of a Late Famous General[1]

HIS GRACE! impossible! what dead!
Of old age, too, and in his bed!
And could that Mighty Warrior fall?
And so inglorious, after all!
Well, since he's gone, no matter how,
The last loud trump must wake him now:
And, trust me, as the noise grows stronger,
He'd wish to sleep a little longer.
And could he be indeed so old
As by the news-papers we're told?
Threescore, I think, is pretty high;
'Twas time in conscience he should die.

This world he cumber'd long enough;
He burnt his candle to the snuff;
And that's the reason, some folks think,
He left behind *so great a stink.*
Behold his funeral appears,
Nor widow's sighs, nor orphan's tears,
Wont at such times each heart to pierce,
Attend the progress of his herse.
But what of that, his friends may say,
He had those honours in his day.
True to his profit and his pride,
He made them weep before he dy'd.

Come hither, all ye empty things,
Ye bubbles rais'd by breath of Kings;
Who float upon the tide of state,
Come hither, and behold your fate.
Let pride be taught by this rebuke,
How very mean a thing's a Duke;
From all his ill-got honours flung,
Turn'd to that dirt from whence he sprung.

[*The Gentleman's Magazine,* 1764,
written *c.* 1722]

From *Verses on the Death of Dr Swift*

THE Time is not remote, when I
Must by the Course of Nature dye:
When I foresee my special Friends,
Will try to find their private Ends:
Tho' it is hardly understood,
Which way my Death can do them good;
Yet, thus methinks, I hear 'em speak;
See, how the Dean begins to break:
Poor Gentleman, he droops apace,
You plainly find it in his Face:
That old Vertigo in his Head,
Will never leave him, till he's dead:

Besides, his Memory decays,
He recollects not what he says;
He cannot call his Friends to Mind;
Forgets the Place where last he din'd:
Plyes you with Stories o'er and o'er,
He told them fifty Times before.
How does he fancy we can sit,
To hear his out-of-fashion'd Wit?
But he takes up with younger Fokes,
Who for his Wine will bear his Jokes:
Faith, he must make his Stories shorter,
Or change his Comrades once a Quarter:
In half the Time, he talks them round;
There must another Sett be found.

For Poetry, he's past his Prime,
He takes an Hour to find a Rhime:
His Fire is out, his Wit decay'd,
His Fancy sunk, his Muse a Jade.
I'd have him throw away his Pen;
But there's no talking to some Men.

And, then their Tenderness appears,
By adding largely to my Years:
'He's older than he would be reckon'd,
'And well remembers *Charles* the Second.

'He hardly drinks a Pint of Wine;
'And that, I doubt, is no good Sign.
'His Stomach too begins to fail:
'Last Year we thought him strong and hale;
'But now, he's quite another Thing;
'I wish he may hold out till Spring.'

Then hug themselves, and reason thus;
'It is not yet so bad with us.'

·   ·   ·   ·   ·

Here shift the Scene, to represent
How those I love, my Death lament.
Poor POPE will grieve a Month; and GAY[1]
A Week; and ARBUTHNOTT[2] a Day.

ST JOHN[3] himself will scarce forbear,
To bite his Pen, and drop a Tear.
The rest will give a Shrug, and cry,
I'm sorry; but we all must dye.
Indifference Clad in Wisdom's Guise,
All Fortitude of Mind supplies:
For how can stony Bowels melt,
In those who never Pity felt;
When *We* are lash'd, *They* kiss the Rod;
Resigning to the Will of God.

The Fools, my Juniors by a Year,
Are tortur'd with Suspence and Fear.
Who wisely thought my Age a Screen,
When death approach'd, to stand between:
The Screen remov'd, their Hearts are trembling,
They mourn for me without dissembling.

My female Friends, whose tender Hearts,
Have better learn'd to Act their Parts,
Receive the News in *doleful Dumps*,
'The Dean is Dead, (*and what is Trumps?*)
'Then Lord have Mercy on his Soul.
'(Ladies I'll venture for the *Vole*.)[4]
'Six Dean's they say must bear the Pall.
'(I wish I knew what *King* to call.)
'Madam, your Husband will attend
'The Funeral of so good a Friend.
'No Madam, 'tis a shocking Sight,
'And he's engag'd To-morrow Night!
'My Lady *Club* wou'd take it ill,
'If he shou'd fail her at *Quadrill*.

'He lov'd the Dean. (*I led a Heart.*)
'But dearest Friends, they say, must part.
'His time was come, he ran his Race;
'We hope he's in a better Place.'

[1733–9, written *c.* 1731]

DANIEL DEFOE

(c. 1659–1731)

Defoe came from a nonconformist family. His father was a butcher
and a citizen of London. After being educated at a famous nonconformist academy, Defoe seems, in 1685, to have been involved in
Monmouth's rebellion. After this, he went into business as a commission merchant, dealing especially in Spanish and Portuguese
goods. In 1692 he went bankrupt for £17,000, a sum which, in later
years, he repaid his creditors almost in full. After this venture, he
became manager and chief shareholder in a tileworks. He pamphleteered on the side of William III, his most famous effort on the
king's behalf being *The True-Born Englishman* (1701). The anonymously published *Shortest Way with the Dissenters* (1702) led to his
being imprisoned, and also put in the pillory. The mob took his
side, thanks in part to his *Hymn to the Pillory*. Harley obtained his
release, and from henceforth his career becomes a good deal more
ambiguous. In 1706–7, Defoe was a secret agent for the tory government in Scotland, working for the Union. In 1715 he was again
imprisoned, this time on a charge of libel, but again released on
condition that he worked for the government. His duties seem to
have included acting as a double-agent on a Jacobite newspaper. In
1719 the first part of *Robinson Crusoe* appeared, and other narratives
followed rapidly thereafter, including *Moll Flanders* (1721), and *The
Journal of the Plague Year* (also 1721). At this period Defoe was
prosperous, and in 1722 leased an estate from the Corporation of
Colchester, and in 1724 built himself a large house at Stoke Newing-
ton. When he died, however, he seems to have been in reduced
circumstances. We know that he had been in hiding the previous
summer, perhaps because the Jacobites had discovered what he was
up to.

From *The Reformation of Manners*

SATYR, the Arts and Mysteries forbear,
Too black for thee to write, or us to hear;
No Man, but he that is as vile as they,
Can all the Ticks and Cheats of Trade survey.
Some in Clandestine Companies combine,
Erect new Stocks to trade beyond the Line:

With Air and empty Names beguile the Town,
And raise new Credits first, then cry 'em down:
Divide the *empty nothing* into Shares,
To set the Town together by the Ears.
The Sham Projectors and the Brokers join,
And both the Cully Merchant undermine;
First he must be drawn in and then betray'd,
And they demolish the Machine they made:
So conjuring Chymists, who with a Charm and Spell,
Some wondrous Liquid wondrously exhale;
But when the gaping Mob their Money pay,
The Charm's dissolv'd, the Vapour flies away:
The wondring Bubbles stand amaz'd to see
Their Money Mountebank'd to *Mercury*.

Some fit out Ships, and double Fraights ensure,
And burn the Ships to make the Voyage secure:
Promiscuous Plunders thro' the World commit,
And *with the Money* buy their safe Retreat.

Others seek out to *Africk*'s Torrid Zone,
And search the burning Shores of *Serralone*;
There in unsufferable Heats *they fry*,
And run vast Risques to see the Gold, *and die*:
The harmless Natives basely they trepan,[1]
And barter Baubles for the *Souls of Men*:
The Wretches they to Christian Climes bring o'er,
To serve worse Heathens than they did before.
The Cruelties they suffer there are such,
Amboyna's[2] nothing, they've out-done the *Dutch*:

Cortez, Pizarro, Guzman, Penaloe,
Who drank the Blood and Gold of *Mexico*,
Who thirteen Millions of Souls destroy'd,
And left one third of God's Creation void;
By Birth for Natures Butchery design'd,
Compar'd to these are merciful and kind;

Death cou'd *their* cruellest Designs fulfil,
Blood quench't *their* Thirst, and it suffic'd to kill:
But these the tender *Coup de Grace* deny,
And make Men beg in vain for leave to die;
To more than *Spanish* Cruelty inclin'd,
Torment the Body and debauch the Mind:
The lingring Life of Slavery preserve,
And vilely teach them both to sin and serve.

[1702]

SIR RICHARD BLACKMORE

(d. 1729)

Blackmore was educated at Westminster and St Edmund's Hall,
Oxford. Later he visited France, Germany, and the Netherlands,
took a medical degree in Padua, and, on his return to England, became a member of the Royal College of Physicians. He was strongly
on the side of the Revolution, and, in 1697, was made physician-in-
ordinary to William III and knighted. He was later physician to
Anne. He was a voluminous poet in the heroic as well as the satiric
vein – Dr Johnson was unwise enough to say of his poem *Creation*
that it alone 'if he had written nothing else, would have transmitted
him to posterity as one of the first favourites of the English Muse'.
Certainly, he seems to have been far from a favourite with his contemporaries. His *Satyr against Wit* (1700) made him a swarm of
literary enemies. Swift called him 'so insipid a scoundrel', and Pope
duly immortalized him in *The Dunciad*. The extract given here is
one of many passages in English satire directed at the Irish.

From *The Kit-Cats*

In fam'd *Hibernia* on the Northern Main,
Where Wit's unknown, and Schools are built in vain.
Between two Hills, that rise with equal Pride,
And with their Tops the floating Clouds divide;
A lazy Lake, as *Lethe*, black and deep,
Secure from Storms, extended lies asleep.
Young vig'rous Winds, which heavy Tempests bear,
With fruitless Toil shove at this stagnant Air;
Their Breath all spent, they from their Labour cease,
And leave th' unweildy Fogs to rest in Peace.
The Beasts that come for Water, at the Brink,
Benumn'd stand nodding, and forget to drink;
The Birds by luckless Fortune hither brought,
Fall down and sleeping on the Waters float,
The thoughtless Boatmen, scarcely half awake,
Do never one Successful Voyage make
But yawn, and drop their Oars into the sluggish Lake.

[1708]

MATTHEW PRIOR

(1664–1721)

Prior was the son of a nonconformist joiner. He was educated at Westminster, and won a scholarship to St John's College, Oxford, where he later became a fellow. His reputation and his fortunes were made by a poem called *The City Mouse and the Country Mouse*, written in collaboration with his close friend Charles Montagu, afterwards Earl of Halifax. This, published in 1687, was a parody of Dryden's *The Hind and the Panther*. Thanks to the attention it attracted, Prior was able to embark on a career as a diplomat. In 1697 he was secretary to the plenipotentiaries who concluded the Peace of Ryswick. When Anne came to the throne he allied himself with the tories and was the principal agent in the negotiations which took place with the French court, sometimes as an openly declared ambassador, but often as a secret agent. His part in negotiating the Treaty of Utrecht led to its being nicknamed 'Matt's Peace', though he is said to have disapproved of it personally. When Anne died and the whigs came back to power, Walpole impeached Prior and he was kept in close custody for two years (1715–17).

An English Padlock

MISS *Danae*, when Fair and Young,
(As *Horace* has divinely sung)
Could not be kept from *Jove's* Embrace
By Doors of Steel, and Walls of Brass.
The Reason of the Thing is clear,
(Would *Jove* the naked Truth aver,)
Cupid was with him of the Party,
And show'd himself sincere and hearty:
For, give that Whipster but his Errand,
He takes my Lord Chief Justice' Warrant;
Dauntless as Death away he walks,
Breaks the Doors open, snaps the Locks,
Searches the Parlour, Chamber, Study,
Nor stops 'till he has *Culprit's* Body.

Since this has been Authentick Truth,
By Age deliver'd down to Youth;
Tell us, mistaken Husband, tell us,
Why so Mysterious, why so Jealous?
Does the Restraint, the Bolt, the Bar,
Make us less Curious, her less Fair?
The Spy, who does this Treasure keep,
Does she ne'er say her Pray'rs, nor Sleep?
Does she to no Excess incline?
Does she fly Musick, Mirth and Wine?
Or have not Gold and Flatt'ry Pow'r,
To purchase One unguarded Hour?

Your Care does further yet extend,
That Spy is guarded by your Friend. –
But has that Friend nor Eye, nor Heart?
May He not feel the cruel Dart
Which, soon or late, all Mortals feel?
May He not, with too tender Zeal,
Give the Fair Pris'ner Cause to see,
How much He wishes, she were free?
May He not craftily infer
The Rules of Friendship too severe,
Which chain him to a hated Trust,
Which make him Wretched, to be Just?
And may not She, this Darling She,
  Youthful and healthy, Flesh and Blood,
Easie with Him, ill us'd by Thee,
  Allow this Logic to be good?

Sir, Will your Questions never end?
I trust to neither Spy nor Friend.
In short, I keep her from the Sight
Of ev'ry Human Face. – She'll write. –
From Pen and Paper She's debarr'd. –
Has she a Bodkin and a Card?
She'll prick her Mind: – She will, you say;
But how shall She that Mind convey?

I keep her in one Room, I lock it;
The Key, look here, is in this Pocket:
The Key-hole, is that left? Most certain,
She'll thrust her Letter thro', – Sir *Martin*.

Dear angry Friend, what must be done?
Is there no Way? – There is but one.
Send her abroad, and let her see,
That all this mingled Mass, which she
Being forbidden longs to know,
Is a dull Farce, an empty Show,
Powder, and Pocket-Glass, and Beau;
A Staple of Romance and Lies,
False Tears, and real Perjuries;
Where Sighs and Looks are bought and sold,
And Love is made but to be told;
Where the fat Bawd and lavish Heir
The Spoils of ruin'd Beauty share,
And Youth seduc'd from Friends and Fame
Must give up Age to Want and Shame.
Let her behold the Frantick Scene,
The Women wretched, false the Men:
And when, these certain Ills to shun,
She would to thy Embraces run;
Receive her with extended Arms,
Seem more delighted with her Charms;
Wait on her to the Park and Play,
Put on good Humour, make her gay;
Be to her Virtues very kind,
Be to her Faults a little blind;
Let all her Ways be unconfin'd,
And clap your *Padlock* – on her Mind.

[*Poems on Several Occasions*, 1709]

EDWARD WARD

(1667–1731)

A man of humble origins and with little formal schooling, Ward visited the West Indies in his youth. Later he became a publican in Moorfields, and by 1699 had moved to a punch-shop and tavern near Gray's Inn. In 1705 he was put in the pillory for his attacks on the government in *Hudibras Redivivus* (one of the earlier imitations of Samuel Butler) and had a rough passage from the mob. He followed Butler not only in the form of his poem but also in his attacks on the whigs and the low church party. Pope duly mocks him in *The Dunciad*. Ward's voluminous works are full of information about the London of the time.

From *St Paul's Church, or The Protestant Ambulators*

A BEAU GREETS A COQUETTE

As soon as Finikin espies
The Darling of his Heart and Eyes,
Aw'd by her Charms, he walks and struts,
As she along the Pavement juts;
Heaves up her Dumplins in her Walk,
He bows, she curtsies, but no Talk;
She's proud and cunning, he's too meek,
She will not, and he cannot speak;
Thus meet, and with their Eyes reveal
The Throbs and Pit-a-pats they feel;
So parting, let their Looks betray
What vertuous Lovers fear to say.
She nimbly pacing to the Quire,
Whilst he does to some Nook retire,
To whisper forth an am'rous Pray'r
Relating to his Only Fair,
That dear Destroyer of his Rest,
That Heav'nly Charmer of his Breast,
Who fills his Head with fine Conceits
Of Honey-Moons, and nuptial Sweets,

Which skreen from e'ery Lover's Mind
The Vinegar that lurks behind.
Beauty, 'tis true, the World admires;
But still, all Roses grow on Briars;
And he that gathers without Care,
May prick his Fingers unaware.

[1716]

JOHN DURANT BREVAL

(1680?–1738)

Breval had a chequered career. The son of a prebendary of Westminster, he was a queen's scholar of Westminster School, and was
later at Trinity College, Cambridge, where he was elected a fellow
in 1702. In 1708 he was involved in a scandal over a married woman
and (perhaps unjustly) lost his fellowship. He then enlisted as a
volunteer with the army in Flanders, and soon rose to be an ensign.
At this point he attracted Marlborough's attention thanks to his
'exquisite pencil and genteel behaviour' as well as his fluency in
languages, and was sent on diplomatic missions to various German
courts, after being appointed captain. The Peace of Utrecht (1713)
put an end to his good fortune, and he began to write for the
London booksellers, chiefly under the pseudonym 'Joseph Gay'.
Later became a travelling governor to young men of position – and
during one tour was reported to have eloped with a beautiful
Milanese nun. He fell out with Pope, as a result of ridiculing the
comedy *Three Hours after Marriage*, in which Pope had had a hand,
and was duly pilloried in *The Dunciad*.

From *The Art of Dress*

   Love's Goddess now the *Furbeloe* displays,
Invents the *Flounces*, and Reforms the *Stays*;
Her Handmaid Sisters leave their old Abodes,
And make this Town *Metropolis* of Modes.
By Faction guided, Ladies patch the Face,
And to the *Watch* now add the *Twezer Case*.
White Breasts, and Shoulders bare, invade the Eye,
And Legs no more conceal'd, our Jests defy,
Those pretty Legs so Taper, and so Smart,
By which Men guess at ev'ry other *Part*.
The *Petticoat* remain'd a Point in doubt
Till WREN was forc'd to help our Beauties out;
A *Roman Cupola* he show'd in Print,
And thence of *Modern Hoops*, they took the hint;
The vast Circumference gives Air below,
At large they tread, and more Majestick show:

Thro' Lanes of ravish'd Beaus the Wonders pass,
And Names of TOASTS are Cut on conscious Glass.

To you, fair Virgin Throng, With *Myrtle* crown'd
Our Bumpers fill'd with gen'rous Wine go round;
For you, th' *Italian* Worm her Silk prepares,
And distant *India* sends her choicest Wares;
Some Toy from ev'ry Part the Sailor brings,
The Sempstress labours, and the Poet sings.

[1717]

HENRY CAREY

(d. 1743)

Is reputed to have been the illegitimate son of the famous Marquis of Halifax, who died in 1695. His mother was probably a school-mistress, and he afterwards taught music in boarding-schools for a living. He was a member of Addison's 'little senate', and the author of the famous *Sally in our Alley*. He is also credited, on rather shaky authority, with the authorship of *God Save the Queen*. Ambrose Philips (1675–1749), whom Carey burlesques so mercilessly in *Namby Pamby*, was also one of the members of the Addison circle. The immediate occasion of ridicule was a set of three poems which Philips wrote to the infant daughters of Lord Carteret, at that moment Lord Lieutenant of Ireland. One of these poems begins: 'Dimply damsel, sweetly smiling.' Pope also ridiculed Philips's lisping pastoral style.

Namby Pamby

OR

A Panegyric on the New Versification
Address'd to *A— P—* Esq

★　★　★

Nauty Pauty Jack-a-Dandy
Stole a piece of Sugar-Candy
From the Grocer's Shoppy-shop,
And away did Hoppy-Hop.

★　★　★

ALL ye Poets of the Age,
All ye Witlings of the Stage,
Learn your Jingles to reform;
Crop your Numbers, and conform:
Let your little Verses flow
Gently, sweetly, Row by Row:
Let the Verse the Subject fit;
Little Subject, Little Wit:
Namby Pamby is your Guide;
Albion's Joy, *Hibernia*'s Pride.

Namby Pamby, Pilli-pis,
Rhimy pim'd on Missy-Miss;
Tartaretta Tartaree
From the Navel to the Knee;
That her Father's Gracy-Grace
Might give him a Placy-Place.
He no longer writes of Mammy
Andromache and her Lammy
Hanging panging at the Breast
Of a Matron most distrest.
Now the Venal Poet sings
Baby Clouts, and Baby Things,
Baby Dolls, and Baby Houses,
Little Misses, Little Spouses;
Little Play-Things, Little Toys,
Little Girls, and Little Boys:
As an Actor does his Part,
So the Nurses get by Heart
Namby Pamby's Little Rhimes,
Little Jingle, Little Chimes,
To repeat to Little Miss,
Piddling Ponds of Pissy-Piss;
Cacking packing like a Lady,
Or Bye-bying in the Crady.
Namby Pamby ne'er will die
While the Nurse sings *Lullabye.*
Namby Pamby's doubly Mild,
Once a Man, and twice a Child;
To his Hanging-Sleeves restor'd;
Now he foots it like a Lord;
Now he Pumps his little Wits;
Sh—ing Writes, and Writing Sh—s,
All by little tiny Bits.
Now methinks I hear him say,
Boys and Girls, Come out to Play,
Moon do's shine as bright as Day.
Now my *Namby Pamby*'s found
Sitting on the *Friar's Ground,*

Picking Silver, picking Gold,
Namby Pamby's never Old.
Bally-Cally they begin,
Namby Pamby still keeps-in.
Namby Pamby is no Clown,
London-Bridge is broken down:
Now he *courts the gay Ladee,*
Dancing o'er the Lady-Lee:
Now he sings of *Lick-spit Liar*
Burning in the Brimstone Fire;
Lyar, Lyar, Lick-spit, lick,
Turn about the Candle-stick:
Now he sings of *Jacky Horner*
Sitting in the Chimney-corner,
Eating of a Christmas-Pie,
Putting in his Thumb, Oh, fie!
Putting in, Oh, fie! *his Thumb,*
Pulling out, Oh, strange! *a Plum.*
And again, how *Nancy Cock,*
Nasty Girl! *besh–t her Smock.*
Now he acts the *Grenadier,*
Calling for *a Pot of Beer:*
Where's his Money? He's forgot:
Get him gone, a Drunken Sot.
Now on *Cock-horse* does he ride;
And anon on Timber stride,
See-and-Saw and Sacch'ry-down,
London is a gallant Town.
Now he gathers Riches in
Thicker, faster, Pin by Pin;
Pins a-piece to see his Show;
Boys and Girls flock Row by Row;
From their Cloaths the Pins they take,
Risque a Whipping for his sake;
From their Frocks the Pins they pull,
To fill *Namby's* Cushion full.
So much Wit at such an Age,
Does a Genius great presage.

Second Childhood gone and past,
Shou'd he prove a Man at last,
What must Second Manhood be,
In a Child so Bright as he!

   Guard him, ye Poetic Powers;
Watch his Minutes, watch his Hours:
Let your Tuneful *Nine* Inspire him;
Let Poetic Fury fire him:
Let the Poets one and all
To his Genius Victims fall.

[1726]

NICHOLAS AMHURST
(1697–1742)

Educated at Merchant Taylors', and elected a scholar of St John's College, Oxford, in 1716. In 1719 was expelled from the university on charges of libertinism and misconduct, though according to himself the offence was persistent whigism and an openly expressed hatred of the toryism and high church principles which surrounded him. Much of his poetry is concerned with this affair – the piece printed here is an attack on Dr Delaune, the Master of St John's. Later Amhurst became a prominent political pamphleteer, and, under the pseudonym 'Caleb d'Anvers' edited *The Craftsman*, the most famous political journal of the age, and a thorn in the flesh of Sir Robert Walpole.

Epigram on Dr Crassus

UNFORM'D in *nature*'s shop while CRASSUS lay,
A cumbrous heap of coarse neglected clay,
Pray, Madam, says the *foreman* of the trade,
What of yon paultry *rubbish* must be made?
For it's too gross, says he, and unrefin'd,
To be the carcass of a *thinking* mind;
Then it's too lumpish and too stiff to make
A Fop, a Beau, a Witling, or a Rake;
Nor is it for a Lady's footman fit,
For Ladies footmen must have sense and wit;
A Warrior must be vigilant and bold,
And therefore claims a brisk and active mould;
A Statesman must be skill'd in various arts,
A Strumpet must have charms, a Pimp have parts.
A Lawyer, without craft, will get no fees –
This matter therefore will make none of *these*;
In short, I plainly think it good for nought;
But, Madam, I desire your better thought.

Why, TOM, says she, in a disdainful tone,
Amongst the *sweepings* let it then be thrown,
Or – make a *Parson* of the useless stuff,
'Twill serve a *preaching* blockhead well enough.

[*Poems on Several Occasions*, 1720]

EDWARD YOUNG

(1683–1765)

Young was educated at Winchester, and then successively at New
College and Corpus Christi College, Oxford. In 1708 he was
nominated as a law fellow of All Souls by Archbishop Tenison. He
graduated as B.C.L. in 1714, and D.C.L. in 1719. Around 1715 he
found a patron in the profligate Duke of Wharton, but, in 1725,
Wharton's departure for the Continent put an end to the relationship. In the same year Young began publication of the series of
satires called *The Universal Passion* – these established him with his
contemporaries as the nearest rival to Pope. In 1726 he received a
pension from Sir Robert Walpole. Soon after this he took orders,
and, in 1728, was appointed chaplain to the king. In 1730 he was presented by All Souls to the rectory of Welwyn in Hertfordshire. In
1742 he published the first of his *Night Thoughts*. His contemporaries
were much moved by the sentimental religiosity of these poems, and
they are still the work by which he is best known.

From *The Love of Fame*, Satire IV

THE SYCOPHANT

NOT gawdy butterflies are *Lico's* game;
But, in effect, his chace is much the same.
Warm in pursuit, he *levées* all the great,
Stanch to the foot of *title*, and *estate*.
Where-e'er their *Lordships* go, they never find,
Or *Lico*, or their *shadows* lagg behind;
He *sets* them sure, where-e'er their *Lordships* run,
Close at their elbows, as a *morning-dun*;
As if their grandeur, by contagion, wrought,
And *fame* was, like a *fever*, to be caught:
But after seven years dance from place to place,
The *Dane* is more familiar with his Grace.

Who'd be a *crutch* to prop a rotten peer;
Or living *pendant*, dangling at his ear,
For ever whisp'ring secrets, which were blown
For months before, by trumpets, thro' the town?

Who'd be a *glass*, with flattering grimace,
Still to reflect the temper of his face;
Or happy *pin* to stick upon his sleeve,
When my Lord's gracious, and vouchsafes *it* leave;
Or *cushion*, when his heaviness shall please
To loll, or *thump* it for his better ease;
Or a vile *butt*, for noon, or night bespoke,
When the peer *rashly* swears he'll club his joke?
Who'd shake with laughter, tho' he cou'd not find
His Lordship's jest; or, if his nose broke wind,
For blessings to the Gods profoundly bow,
That can cry *chimney-sweep*, or drive a *plough*?
With terms like these how mean the Tribe that *close*?
Scarce meaner They, who terms, like these, *impose*.

[1725–6]

From *The Love of Fame*, Satire V
On Women

THE LANGUID LADY

THE *languid* lady next appears in state,
Who was not born to carry her own weight;
She lolls, reels, staggers, 'till some foreign aid
To her own stature lifts the feeble maid.
Then, if ordain'd to so *severe* a doom,
She, by just stages, *journeys* round the room:
But knowing her own weakness, she despairs
To scale the *Alps* – that is, ascend the *stairs*.
My fan! let others say who laugh at toil;
Fan! hood! glove! scarf! is her *laconick* style.
And that is spoke with such a dying fall,
That *Betty* rather *sees*, than *hears* the call:
The motion of her lips, and meaning eye
Piece out the Idea her faint words deny.
O listen with attention most profound!
Her voice is but the shadow of a sound.
And help! O help! her spirits are so dead,

One hand scarce lifts the other to her head.
If, there, a stubborn pin it triumphs o'er,
She pants! she sinks away! and is no more.
Let the robust, and the gygantick *carve*,
Life is not worth so much, she'd rather *starve*;
But *chew* she must herself, ah cruel fate!
That *Rosalinda* can't by *proxy* eat.

THE VANITY OF THE OLD

   But adoration? give me something *more*,
Crys *Lyce*, on the borders of *threescore*;
Nought treads so silent as the foot of *Time*:
Hence we mistake our autumn for our prime;
'Tis greatly wise to know, before we're told,
The melancholy news that we *grow old*.
Autumnal *Lyce* carrys in her face
Memento mori to each publick place.
O how your beating breast a Mistress warms
Who looks thro' spectacles to see your charms!
While rival *undertakers* hover round,
And with his spade the *sexton* marks the ground,
Intent not on her own, but others doom,
She plans new conquests, and *defrauds* the tomb.
In vain the cock has summon'd *sprights* away,
She walks at noon, and blasts the bloom of day.
Gay rainbow silks her mellow charms infold,
And nought of *Lyce* but *herself* is old.
Her grizzled locks assume a *smirking* grace,
And art has *levell'd* her deep-furrow'd face.
Her strange demand no mortal can approve,
We'll ask her blessing, but can't ask her *love*.
She grants indeed a Lady *may* decline,
(All Ladies *but* herself) at *ninety-nine*.

                              [1725–6]

JAMES BRAMSTON

(1694?–1744)

One of the numerous 'scribbling parsons' of the eighteenth century,
Bramston, after being educated at Westminster and Christ Church,
Oxford, became vicar of Lurgashall, in Sussex, and later vicar of
Harling, with dispensation to hold both livings. He left behind him
a local reputation for wit. *The Man of Taste* was occasioned by Pope's
Epistle of 1731, addressed to Lord Burlington.

From *The Art of Politicks*

LIKE *South-Sea Stock*,[1] Expressions rise and fall:
King *Edward*'s Words are now no Words at all.
Did ought your Predecessors Genius cramp?
Sure ev'ry Reign may have it's proper Stamp.
All Sublunary things of Death partake;
What Alteration does a Cent'ry make?
Kings and Comedians all are mortal found,
Cæsar and *Pinkethman*[2] are under Ground.
What's not destroy'd by Time's devouring Hand?
Where's *Troy*, and where's the *May-Pole* in the *Strand*?
Pease, Cabbages, and Turnips once grew, where
Now stands new *Bond-street*, and a newer Square;
Such Piles of Buildings now rise up and down,
London itself seems going out of *Town*.
Our Fathers cross'd from *Fulham* in a Wherry,
Their Sons enjoy a Bridge at *Putney-Ferry*.
Think we that modern Words eternal are?
Toupet, and *Tompion*, *Cosins*, and *Colmar*
Hereafter will be call'd, by some plain Man,
A *Wig*, a *Watch*, a *Pair of Stays*, a *Fan*.
To Things themselves if Time such change affords,
Can there be any trusting to our Words?

[1729]

JAMES BRAMSTON

From *The Man of Taste*

T'IMPROVE in Morals *Mandevil*[1] I read,
And *Tyndal's*[2] Scruples are my settled Creed.
I travell'd early, and I soon saw through
Religion all, e'er I was twenty-two.
Shame, Pain, or Poverty shall I endure,
When ropes or opium can my ease procure?
When money's gone, and I no debts can pay,
Self-murder is an honourable way.
As *Pasaran*[3] directs I'd end my life,
And kill myself, my daughter, and my wife.
Burn but that *Bible* which the Parson quotes,
And men of spirit all shall cut their throats.
   But not to writings I confine my pen,
I have a taste for buildings, musick, men.
Young travell'd coxcombs mighty knowledge boast,
With superficial Smatterings at Most.
Not so my mind, unsatisfied with hints,
Knows more than *Budgel*[4] writes, or *Roberts* prints.
I know the town, all houses I have seen,
From *High-Park* corner down to *Bednal-Green*.
Sure wretched *Wren* was taught by bungling *Jones*,[5]
To murder mortar, and disfigure stones!
Who in *Whitehall* can symmetry discern?
I reckon *Covent-garden* Church[6] a *Barn*.
Nor hate I less thy vile Cathedral, *Paul*!
The choir's too big, the cupola's too small:
Substantial walls and heavy roofs I like,
'Tis *Vanbrug's* structures that my fancy strike:
Such noble ruins ev'ry pile wou'd make,
I wish they'd tumble for the prospect's sake.
To lofty *Chelsea* or to *Greenwich* Dome,
Soldiers and sailors all are welcom'd home.
Her poor to palaces *Britannia* brings,
St *James's* hospital may serve for kings.

Building so happily I understand,
That for one house I'd mortgage all my land.
Dorick, Ionic, shall not there be found,
But it shall cost me threescore thousand pound.
From out my honest workmen, I'll select
A *Bricklay'r*, and proclaim him architect;
First bid him build me a stupendous Dome,
Which *having finish'd*, we set out for *Rome*;
Take a weeks view of *Venice* and the *Brent*,[1]
Stare round, see nothing, and come home content.
I'll have my *Villa* too, a sweet abode,
It's situation shall be *London* road:
Pots o'er the door I'll place like Cit's[2] balconies,
Which *Bently*[3] calls the *Gardens of Adonis*.

I'll have my Gardens in the fashion too,
For what is beautiful that is not new?
Fair four-legg'd temples, theatres that vye,
With all the angles of a *Christmas*-pye.
Does it not merit the beholder's praise,
What's high to sink? and what is low to raise?
Slopes shall ascend where once a green-house stood,
And in my horse-pond I will plant a wood.
Let misers dread the hoarded gold to waste,
Expence and alteration shew a *Taste*.

In curious paintings I'm exceeding nice,
And know their several beauties by their *Price*.
Auctions and *Sales* I constantly attend,
But chuse my pictures by a *skilful friend*.
Originals and copies much the same,
The picture's value is the *painter's name*.

My taste in Sculpture from my choice is seen,
I buy no statues that are not obscene.
In spite of *Addison* and ancient *Rome*,
Sir *Cloudesly Shovel*'s[4] is my fav'rite tomb.
How oft have I with admiration stood,
To view some City-magistrate in wood?
I gaze with pleasure on a Lord May'r's head,
Cast with propriety in gilded lead.

Oh could I view through *London* as I pass,
Some broad Sir *Balaam* in *Corinthian* brass;
High on a pedestal, ye Freemen, place
His magisterial Paunch and griping Face;
Letter'd and Gilt, let him adorn *Cheapside*,
And grant the *Tradesman*, what a *King*'s deny'd.

[1733]

ALEXANDER POPE

(1688–1744)

Pope's father was a Roman Catholic linen draper, who retired from business in 1700 and went to live at Binfield in Windsor Forest. Pope had delicate health when young, and grew up a cripple. He was also brilliantly precocious and by the age of seventeen was already recognized as a prodigy, and had met many of the leading London 'wits', including the aged Wycherley. In 1709 his *Pastorals* were published, and in 1711 his reputation was put on a completely firm foundation by the *Essay on Criticism*. Pope had a great gift for friendship and for enmity – these relationships are extensively chronicled in his work. He also had a thirst for fame, a vanity and a love of intrigue which did not prevent him from being recognized as the leading poet of his day.

From *Of the Characters of Women*

PLEASURES the sex, as children Birds, pursue,
Still out of reach, yet never out of view,
Sure, if they catch, to spoil the Toy at most,
To covet flying, and regret when lost:
At last, to follies Youth could scarce defend,
It grows their Age's prudence to pretend;
Asham'd to own they gave delight before,
Reduc'd to feign it, when they give no more:
As Hags hold Sabbaths, less for joy than spight,
So these their merry, miserable Night;
Still round and round the Ghosts of Beauty glide,
And haunt the places where their Honour dy'd.
  See how the World its Veterans rewards!
A Youth of frolicks, an old Age of Cards,
Fair to no purpose, artful to no end,
Young without Lovers, old without a Friend,
A Fop their Passion, but their Prize a Sot,
Alive, ridiculous, and dead, forgot!

[1735–44]

ALEXANDER POPE

From the *Epistle to Lord Bathurst*

THE DUKE OF BUCKINGHAM

IN the worst inn's worst room,[1] with mat half-hung,
The floors of plaister, and the walls of dung,
On once a flock-bed,[2] but repair'd with straw,
With tape-ty'd curtains, never meant to draw,
The George and Garter dangling from that bed
Where tawdry yellow strove with dirty red,
Great Villiers lies – alas! how chang'd from him
That life of pleasure, and that soul of whim!
Gallant and gay, in Cliveden's[3] proud alcove,
The bow'r of wanton Shrewsbury[4] and love;
Or just as gay, at Council, in a ring
Of mimick'd Statesmen, and their merry King.
No Wit to flatter, left of all his store!
No Fool to laugh at, which he valu'd more.
There, Victor of his health, of fortune, friends,
And fame; this lord of useless thousands ends.

[1733–44]

From the *Epistle to Dr Arbuthnot*

THE CHARACTER OF ATTICUS[4]

PEACE to all such! but there were One whose fires
True Genius kindles, and fair Fame inspires,
Blest with each Talent and each Art to please,
And born to write, converse, and live with ease:
Shou'd such a man, too fond to rule alone,
Bear, like the *Turk*, no brother near the throne,
View him with scornful, yet with jealous eyes,
And hate for Arts that caus'd himself to rise;
Damn with faint praise, assent with civil leer,
And without sneering, teach the rest to sneer;
Willing to wound, and yet afraid to strike,
Just hint a fault, and hesitate dislike;

167

Alike reserv'd to blame, or to commend,
A tim'rous foe, and a suspicious friend,
Dreading ev'n fools, by Flatterers beseig'd,
And so obliging that he ne'er oblig'd;
Like *Cato*,[1] give his little Senate laws,
And sit attentive to his own applause;
While Wits and Templers ev'ry sentence raise,
And wonder with a foolish face of praise.
Who but must laugh, if such a man there be?
Who would not weep, if *Atticus* were he!

THE CHARACTER OF SPORUS[2]

LET *Sporus* tremble – 'What? that Thing of silk,
'*Sporus*, that mere white Curd of Ass's milk?[3]
'Satire or Sense alas! can *Sporus* feel?
'Who breaks a Butterfly upon a Wheel?'
Yet let me slap this Bug with gilded wings,
This painted Child[4] of Dirt that stinks and stings;
Whose Buzz the Witty and the Fair annoys,
Yet Wit ne'er tastes, and Beauty ne'er enjoys,
So well-bred Spaniels civilly delight
In mumbling of the Game they dare not bite.
Eternal Smiles his Emptiness betray,
As shallow streams run dimpling all the way.
Whether in florid Impotence he speaks,
And, as the Prompter breathes, the Puppet squeaks;
Or at the ear of *Eve*,[5] familiar Toad,
Half Froth, half Venom, spits himself abroad,
In Puns, or Politicks, or Tales, or Lyes,
Or Spite, or Smut, or Rymes, or Blasphemies.
His Wit all see-saw between *that* and *this*,
Now high, now low, now Master up, now Miss,
And he himself one vile Antithesis.
Amphibious Thing! that acting either Part,
The trifling Head, or the corrupted Heart!
Fop at the Toilet, Flatt'rer at the Board,
Now trips a Lady, and now struts a Lord.

Eve's Tempter thus the Rabbins have exprest,
A Cherub's face, a Reptile all the rest;
Beauty that shocks you, Parts that none will trust,
With that can creep, and Pride that licks the dust.

[1735, the 'Character of Atticus' written
c. 1715, and first published in 1722]

From *The Dunciad*, Book IV

THE APOTHEOSIS OF DULLNESS

NEXT bidding all draw near on bended knees,
The Queen confers her *Titles* and *Degrees.*
Her children first of more distinguish'd sort,
Who study Shakespeare at the Inns of Court,
Impale a Glow-worm, or Vertù profess,
Shine in the dignity of F.R.S.
Some, deep Free-Masons, join the silent race
Worthy to fill Pythagoras's place:
Some Botanists, or Florists at the least,
Or issue Members of an Annual feast.
Nor past the meanest unregarded, one
Rose a Gregorian, one a Gormogon.
The last, nor least in honour or applause,
Isis and Cam made Doctors of her Laws.
  Then blessing all, 'Go Children of my care!
To Practice now from Theory repair.
All my commands are easy, short, and full:
My Sons! be proud, be selfish, and be dull.
Guard my Prerogative, assert my Throne:
This Nod confirms each Privilege your own.
The Cap and Switch be sacred to his Grace;
With Staff and Pumps the Marquis lead the Race;
From Stage to Stage the licens'd Earl may run,
Pair'd with his Fellow-Charioteer the Sun;
The learned Baron Butterflies design,
Or draw to silk Arachne's subtile line;
The Judge to dance his brother Sergeant call;

The Senator at Cricket urge the Ball;
The Bishop stow (Pontific Luxury!)
An hundred Souls of Turkeys in a pye;
The sturdy Squire to Gallic masters stoop,
And drown his Lands and Manors in a Soupe.
Others import yet nobler arts from France,
Teach Kings to fiddle, and make Senates dance.
Perhaps more high some daring son may soar,
Proud to my list to add one Monarch more;
And nobly conscious, Princes are but things
Born for First Ministers, as Slaves for Kings,
Tyrant supreme! shall three Estates command,
And MAKE ONE MIGHTY DUNCIAD OF THE LAND.'
  More had she spoke, but yawn'd – All Nature nods:
What Mortal can resist the Yawn of Gods?
Churches and Chapels instantly it reached;
(St James's first, for leaden Gilbert preach'd)
Then catch'd the Schools; the Hall scarce kept awake;
The Convocation gap'd, but could not speak:
Lost was the Nation's Sense, nor could be found,
While the long solemn Unison went round:
Wide, and more wide, it spread o'er all the realm;
Ev'n Palinurus nodded at the Helm:
The Vapour mild o'er each Committee crept;
Unfinish'd Treaties in each Office slept;
And Chiefless Armies doz'd out the Campaign;
And Navies yawn'd for Orders on the Main.
  O Muse! relate (for you can tell alone,
Wits have short memories, and Dunces none)
Relate who first, who last resign'd to rest;
Whose Heads she partly, whose completely blest;
What Charms could Faction, what Ambitions lull,
The Venal quiet, and intrance the Dull;
'Till drown'd was Sense, and Shame, and Right, and Wrong –
O sing, and hush the Nations with thy Song!
  In vain, in vain, – the all-composing Hour
Resistless falls: The Muse obeys the Pow'r.
She comes! she comes! the sable Throne behold

Of Night *Primaeval*, and of *Chaos* old!
Before her, *Fancy's* gilded clouds decay,
And all its varying Rain-bows die away.
Wit shoots in vain its momentary fires,
The meteor drops, and in a flash expires.
As one by one, at dread Medea's strain,
The sick'ning stars fade off th'ethereal plain;
As Argus' eyes by Hermes' wand opprest,
Clos'd one by one to everlasting rest;
Thus at her felt approach, and secret might,
Art after *Art* goes out, and all is Night.
See skulking *Truth* to her old Cavern fled,
Mountains of Casuistry heap'd o'er her head!
Philosophy, that lean'd on Heav'n before,
Shrinks to her second cause, and is no more.
Physic of *Metaphysic* begs defence,
And *Metaphysic* calls for aid on *Sense*!
See *Mystery* to *Mathematics* fly!
In vain! they gaze, turn giddy, rave, and die.
Religion blushing veils her sacred fires,
And unawares *Morality* expires.
Nor *public* Flame, nor *private*, dares to shine;
Nor *human* Spark is left, nor Glimpse *divine*!
Lo! thy dread Empire, CHAOS! is restor'd;
Light dies before thy uncreating word:
Thy hand, great Anarch! lets the curtain fall;
And Universal Darkness buries All.

[1742–3]

RICHARD SAVAGE

(d. 1743)

The mystery of his birth was the dominating influence in Savage's unhappy life. In 1718 he made his appearance on the scene when he claimed to be the illegitimate son of the Countess of Macclesfield (later Mrs Brett), by her lover, Richard Savage, the 4th Earl Rivers. His putative mother always denied the relationship, though records show that she had a son whose birth was kept secret in January 1697. Savage blackmailed those whom he claimed as his relations, and was given a pension by Mrs Brett's nephew, Lord Tyrconnel. He set up as a dramatist and poet and had some success, but in 1727 was arrested for killing a man in a drunken quarrel, and was extricated from this scrape with some difficulty. In 1732 Queen Caroline gave him a small pension, but, at the Queen's death, having broken with Tyrconnel, he was reduced to utter poverty. Pope and others raised money to have him sent out of reach of his creditors. Savage went to Swansea, then to Bristol, where he was arrested for debt and died in a debtors' prison. Johnson's *Life* of him, published anonymously in 1744, helped to create a posthumous legend and reputation.

Fulvia, A Poem

LET Fulvia's wisdom be a slave to will,
Her darling passions, scandal and quadrille;
On friends and foes her tongue a satire known,
Her deeds a satire on herself alone.
On her poor kindred deigns she word or look?
'Tis cold respect, or 'tis unjust rebuke;
Worse when goodnatur'd than when most severe;
The jest impure then pains the modest ear.
How just the sceptic? the divine how odd?
What turns of wit play smartly on her God?

The fates, my nearest kindred, foes decree:
Fulvia, when piqu'd at them, strait pities me.
She, like benevolence, a smile bestows,
Favours to me indulge her spleen to those.
The banquet serv'd, with peeresses I sit:
She tells my story, and repeats my wit.

With mouth distorted, thro' a sounding nose
It comes, now homeliness more homely grows.
With see-saw sounds and nonsense not my own,
She skrews her features, and she cracks her tone.
How fine your Bastard? why so soft a strain?
What such a Mother? satirize again!
　　Oft I object – but fix'd is Fulvia's will –
Ah! tho' unkind, she is my mother still!
　　The verse now flows, the manuscript she claims.
'Tis fam'd – The fame, each curious fair enflames:
The wild-fire runs; from copy, copy grows:
The Brets alarm'd, a sep'rate peace propose.
'Tis ratified – How alter'd Fulvia's look?
My wit's degraded, and my cause forsook.
Thus she: What's poetry but to amuse?
Might I advise – there are more solid views.
With a cool air she adds: This tale is old:
Were it my case, it should no more be told.
Complaints – had I been worthy to advise –
You know – But when are wits, like women, wise?
True it may take, but think whate'er you list,
All love the satire, none the satirist.
　　I start, I stare, stand fix'd, then pause awhile;
Then hesitate, then ponder well, then smile.
Madam – a pension lost – and where's amends?
Sir (she replies) indeed you'll lose your friends.
Why did I start? 'twas but a change of wind –
Or the same thing – the lady chang'd her mind.
I bow, depart, despise, discern her all:
Nanny revisits, and disgrac'd I fall.
　　Let Fulvia's friendship whirl with ev'ry whim!
A reed, a weather-cock, a shade, a dream:
No more the friendship shall be now display'd
By weather-cock, or reed, or dream, or shade;
To Nanny fix'd unvarying shall it tend,
For souls, so form'd alike, were form'd to blend.

[*Works*, 1775]

SOAME JENYNS
(1704–87)

Jenyns was the son of Sir Roger Jenyns, Kt, of Bottisham Hall, near Cambridge. He entered St John's College, Cambridge, as a fellow commoner in 1722, but left without taking a degree. In 1742 he was elected M.P. for the county of Cambridge, and continued to represent either the town or the county for most of the rest of his life. In 1755 he was one of the commissioners for the Board of Trade and Plantations. In 1776 he published his most famous work, not a poem or a collection of poems but *A View of the Internal Evidence of the Christian Religion*. A long controversy raged about the book, and it had reached its tenth edition by 1798. Johnson said of it: 'a pretty book, not very theological indeed; and there seems to be an affectation of ease and carelessness, as if it were not suitable to his character to be serious about the matter.' This was by no means the least charitable thing which Johnson was to say about Jenyns.

From *An Epistle from S. J. Esq. in the Country to Lord Lovelace in Town*

THE COUNTRY VISIT

OR if with ceremony cloy'd,
You wou'd next time such plagues avoid,
And visit without previous notice,
JOHN, JOHN, a coach! – I can't think who 'tis,
My lady cries, who spies your coach,
Ere you the avenue approach;
Lord how unlucky! – washing day!
And all the men are in the hay!
Entrance to gain is something hard,
The dogs all bark, the gates are barr'd;
The yard's with lines of linen cross'd,
The hall-door's lock'd, the key is lost;
These difficulties all o'ercome,
We reach at length the drawing room,
Then there's such trampling over-head,
Madam you'd swear was brought to bed;

Miss in a hurry bursts her lock,
To get clean sleeves to hide her smock;
The servants run, the pewter clatters,
My lady dresses, calls, and chatters;
The cook-maid raves for want of butter,
Pigs squeak, fowls scream, and green geese flutter.
Now after three hours tedious waiting,
On all our neighbours faults debating,
And having nine times view'd the garden,
In which there's nothing worth a farthing,
In comes my lady, and the pudden:
You will excuse sir, – on a sudden –
Then, that we may have four and four,
The bacon, fowls, and collyflow'r
Their ancient unity divide,
The top one graces, one each side;[1]
And by and by, the second course
Comes lagging like a distanc'd horse;
A salver then to church and king,
The butler sweats, the glasses ring;
The cloth remov'd, the toasts go round,
Bawdy and politics abound;
And as the knight more tipsy waxes,
We damn all ministers and taxes.

At last the ruddy sun quite sunk,
The coachman tolerably drunk,
Whirling o'er hillocks, ruts, and stones,
Enough to dislocate one's bones,
We home return, a wond'rous token
Of heaven's kind care, with limbs unbroken.
Afflict us not, ye Gods, tho' sinners,
With many days like this, or dinners!

     [*A Collection of Poems*, 1748, written 1735]

From *The Modern Fine Lady*

BEHOLD her now in ruin's frightful jaws!
Bonds, judgments, executions ope their paws;
Seize jewels, furniture, and plate, nor spare
The gilded chariot or the tossel'd chair;
For lonely seat she's forc'd to quit the town,
And TUBBS[1] conveys the wretched exile down.

Now rumbling o'er the stones of *Tyburn-Road*,
Ne'er prest with a more griev'd or guilty load,
She bids adieu to all the well-known streets,
And envy's ev'ry cinder-wench she meets:
And now the dreaded country first appears,
With sighs unfeign'd the dying noise she hears
Of distant coaches fainter by degrees,
Then starts, and trembles at the sight of trees.
Silent and sullen, like some captive queen,
She's drawn along unwilling to be seen,
Until at length appears the ruin'd *Hall*
Within the grass-green moat and ivy'd wall,
The doleful prison where for ever she,
But not, alas! her griefs, must bury'd be.

Her coach the curate and the tradesmen meet, ⎤
Great-coated tenants her arrival greet, ⎬
And boys with stubble bonfires light the street, ⎦
While bells her ears with tongues discordant grate,
Types of the nuptial tyes they celebrate:
But no rejoycings can unbend her brow,
Nor deigns she to return one aukward bow,
But bounces in disdaining once to speak,
And wipes the trickling tear from off her cheek.

Now see her in the sad decline of life,
A peevish mistress, and a sulky wife;
Her nerves unbrac'd, her faded cheek grown pale
With many a real, and many a fancy'd ail;

Of cards, admirers, equipage bereft,
Her insolence, and title only left;
Severely humbled to her one-horse chair,
And the low pastimes of a country fair:
Too wretched to endure one lonely day,
Too proud one friendly visit to repay,
Too indolent to read, too criminal to pray.
At length half dead, half mad, and quite confin'd,
Shunning, and shun'd by all of human kind,
Ev'n rob'd of the last comfort of her life,
Insulting the poor curate's callous wife,
Pride, disappointed pride, now stops her breath,
And with true scorpion rage she stings herself to death.

[1750]

SAMUEL JOHNSON

(1709–84)

Johnson was the son of a Lichfield bookseller. He went to Oxford, and spent just over two years at Pembroke College, but in 1731 was forced by lack of money to leave the university without a degree. A miserable period in the provinces followed till, eventually, at twenty-eight, Johnson decided to try his luck in London. After a year, he got a regular appointment on the staff of *The Gentleman's Magazine*. In 1738 he at last began to make a reputation with the publication of his satire, *London*. This won the admiration of Pope, whose *Messiah* Johnson had translated into Latin verse when still an undergraduate. In 1747 Johnson set to work on the famous *Dictionary*, which was not to be finished until 1755. The *Dictionary* was received with immense enthusiasm, and in 1762, with the accession of George III, Johnson was given a pension. It was at this time that the real influence, not of his writings but of his conversation began, and Johnson became the Johnson of legend. His intimates included Goldsmith, Reynolds, Garrick, Burke, and Gibbon, as well as Boswell.

From *London*

THE cheated nation's happy fav'rites see!
Mark whom the great caress, who frown on me!
LONDON! the needy villain's gen'ral home,
The common shore[1] of Paris and of Rome;
With eager thirst, by folly or by fate,
Sucks in the dregs of each corrupted state.
Forgive my transports on a theme like this,
I cannot bear a French metropolis.
   Illustrious EDWARD![2] from the realms of day,
The land of heroes and of saints survey;
Nor hope the British lineaments to trace,
The rustick grandeur, or the surly grace,
But lost in thoughtless ease, and empty show,
Behold the warrior dwindled to a beau;
Sense, freedom, piety refin'd away,
Of France the mimick, and of Spain the prey.

All that at home no more can beg or steal,
Or like a gibbet better than a wheel;[1]
Hiss'd from the stage, or hooted from the court,
Their air, their dress, their politicks import;
Obsequious, artful, voluble and gay,
On Britain's fond credulity they prey.
No gainful trade their industry can 'scape,
They sing, they dance, clean shoes, or cure a clap;
All sciences a fasting Mounsieur knows,
And bid him go to hell, to hell he goes.

Ah! what avails it, that from slav'ry far,
I drew the breath of life in English air;
Was early taught a Briton's right to prize,
And lisp the tale of HENRY's[2] victories;
If the gull'd conqueror receives the chain,
And flattery subdues when arms are vain?

Studious to please, and ready to submit,
The supple Gaul was born a parasite:
Still to his int'rest true, where'er he goes,
Wit, brav'ry, worth, his lavish tongue bestows;
In ev'ry face a thousand graces shine,
From ev'ry tongue flows harmony divine.
These arts in vain our rugged natives try,
Strain out with fault'ring diffidence a lye,
And get a kick for awkward flattery.

Besides, with justice, this discerning age
Admires their wond'rous talents for the stage:
Well may they venture on the mimick's art,
Who play from morn to night a borrow'd part;
Practis'd their master's notions to embrace,
Repeat his maxims, and reflect his face;
With ev'ry wild absurdity comply,
And view each object with another's eye;
To shake with laughter ere the jest they hear,
To pour at will the counterfeited tear,
And as their patron hints the cold or heat,
To shake in dog-days, in December sweat.

How, when competitors like these contend,

Can surly virtue hope to fix a friend?
Slaves that with serious impudence beguile,
And lye without a blush, without a smile;
Exalt each trifle, ev'ry vice adore,
Your taste in snuff, your judgement in a whore;
Can balbo's eloquence applaud, and swear
He gropes[1] his breeches with a monarch's air.

For arts like these preferr'd, admir'd, caress'd,
They first invade your table, then your breast;
Explore your secrets with insidious art,
Watch the weak hour, and ransack all the heart;
Then soon your ill-plac'd confidence repay,
Commence your lords, and govern or betray.

By numbers here from shame or censure free,
All crimes are safe, but hated poverty.
This, only this, the rigid law pursues,
This, only this, provokes the snarling muse.
The sober trader at a tatter'd cloak,
Wakes from his dream, and labours for a joke;
With brisker air the silken courtiers gaze,
And turn the varied taunt a thousand ways.
Of all the griefs that harrass the distress'd,
Sure the most bitter is a scornful jest;
Fate never wounds more deep the gen'rous heart,
Than when a blockhead's insult points the dart.

Has heaven reserv'd, in pity to the poor,
No pathless waste, or undiscover'd shore;
No secret island in the boundless main?
No peaceful desart yet unclaim'd by SPAIN?[2]
Quick let us rise, the happy seats explore,
And bear oppression's insolence no more.
This mournful truth is ev'ry where confess'd,
SLOW RISES WORTH, BY POVERTY DEPRESS'D:
But here more slow, where all are slaves to gold,
Where looks are merchandise, and smiles are sold;
Where won by bribes, by flatteries implor'd,
The groom retails the favours of his lord.

[1738]

From *The Vanity of Human Wishes*

LET observation with extensive view,
Survey mankind,[1] from China to Peru;
Remark each anxious toil, each eager strife,
And watch the busy scenes of crouded life;
Then say how hope and fear, desire and hate,
O'erspread with snares the clouded maze of fate,
Where wav'ring man, betray'd by vent'rous pride,
To tread the dreary paths without a guide,
As treach'rous phantoms in the mist delude,
Shuns fancied ills, or chases airy good;
How rarely reason guides the stubborn choice,
Rules the bold hand, or prompts the suppliant voice;
How nations sink, by darling schemes oppress'd,
When vengeance listens to the fool's request.
Fate wings with ev'ry wish th'afflictive dart,
Each gift of nature, and each grace of art,
With fatal heat impetuous courage glows,
With fatal sweetness elocution flows,
Impeachment stops the speaker's pow'rful breath,
And restless fire precipitates on death.

. . . . .

Unnumber'd suppliants croud Preferment's gate,
Athirst for wealth, and burning to be great;
Delusive Fortune hears th' incessant call,
They mount, they shine, evaporate, and fall.
On ev'ry stage the foes of peace attend,
Hate dogs their flight, and insult mocks their end.
Love ends with hope, the sinking statesman's door
Pours in the morning worshiper no more;
For growing names the weekly scribbler[2] lies,
To growing wealth the dedicator flies,
From every room descends the painted face,
That hung the bright Palladium[3] of the place,
And smoak'd in kitchens, or in auctions sold,
To better features yields the frame of gold;

For now no more we trace in ev'ry line
Heroic worth, benevolence divine:
The form distorted justifies the fall,
And detestation rids th'indignant wall.

.   .   .   .   .

    When first the college rolls[1] receive his name,
The young enthusiast quits his ease for fame;
Through all his veins the fever of renown
Burns from the strong contagion of the gown;
O'er Bodley's dome[2] his future labours spread,
And Bacon's mansion[3] trembles o'er his head.
Are these thy views? proceed, illustrious youth,
And virtue guard thee to the throne of Truth!
Yet should thy soul indulge the gen'rous heat,
Till captive Science yields her last retreat;
Should reason guide thee with her brightest ray,
And pour on misty Doubt resistless day;
Should no false kindness lure to loose delight,
Nor Praise relax, nor Difficulty fright;
Should tempting Novelty thy cell refrain,
And Sloth effuse her opiate fumes in vain;
Should Beauty blunt on fops her fatal dart,
Nor claim the triumph of a letter'd heart;
Should no disease thy torpid veins invade,
Nor Melancholy's phantoms haunt thy shade;
Yet hope not life from grief or danger free,
Nor think the doom of man revers'd for thee:
Deign on the passing world to turn thine eyes,
And pause awhile from letters, to be wise;
There mark what ills the scholar's life assail,
Toil, envy, want, the patron,[4] and the jail.
See nations slowly wise, and meanly just,
To buried merit raise the tardy bust.[5]
If dreams yet flatter, once again attend,
Hear Lydiat's[6] life, and Galileo's end.[7]
    Nor deem, when learning her last prize bestows,
The glitt'ring eminence exempt from foes;

See when the vulgar 'scape, despis'd or aw'd,
Rebellion's vengeful talons seize on Laud.[1]
From meaner minds, tho' smaller fines content,
The plunder'd palace or sequester'd rent;
Mark'd out by dangerous parts he meets the shock,
And fatal Learning leads him to the block:
Around his tomb let Art and Genius weep,
But hear his death, ye blockheads, hear and sleep.

The festal blazes, the triumphal show,
The ravish'd standard, and the captive foe,
The senate's thanks, the gazette's pompous tale,
With force resistless o'er the brave prevail.
Such bribes the rapid Greek o'er Asia whirl'd,
For such the steady Romans shook the world;
For such in distant lands the Britons shine,
And stain with blood the Danube or the Rhine;
This pow'r has praise, that virtue scarce can warm,
Till fame supplies the universal charm.
Yet Reason frowns on War's unequal game,
Where wasted nations raise a single name,
And mortgag'd stages their grandsires wreaths regret,
From age to age in everlasting debt;
Wreaths which at last the dear-bought right convey
To rust on medals, or on stones decay.

On what foundation stands the warrior's pride,
How just his hopes let Swedish Charles[2] decide;
A frame of adamant, a soul of fire,
No dangers fright him, and no labours tire;
O'er love, o'er fear, extends his wide domain,
Unconquer'd lord of pleasure and of pain;
No joys to him pacific scepters yield,
War sounds the trump, he rushes to the field;
Behold surrounding kings their pow'r combine,
And one capitulate,[3] and one resign;[4]
Peace courts his hand, but spreads her charms in vain;
'Think nothing gain'd,' he cries, 'till nought remain,
'On Moscow's walls till Gothic standards fly,
'And all be mine beneath the polar sky.'

The march begins in military state,
And nations on his eye suspended wait;
Stern Famine guards the solitary coast,
And Winter barricades the realms of Frost;
He comes, not want and cold his course delay; –
Hide, blushing Glory, hide Pultowa's[1] day:
The vanquish'd hero leaves his broken bands,
And shews his miseries in distant lands;[2]
Condemn'd a needy supplicant to wait,
While ladies interpose, and slaves debate.
But did not Chance at length her error mend?
Did no subverted empire mark his end?
Did rival monarchs give the fatal wound?
Or hostile millions press him to the ground?
His fall was destin'd to a barren strand,
A petty fortress,[3] and a dubious hand;[4]
He left the name, at which the world grew pale,
To point a moral, or adorn a tale.

[1749]

JAMES DANCE (alias LOVE)
(1722–74)

A son of the architect George Dance the Elder, he was educated at Merchant Taylors' and at St John's College, Oxford, but left the university without taking a degree. After being disappointed in early hopes of patronage from Sir Robert Walpole, he took to the stage and to writing light comedies. He acted in Dublin and Edinburgh, and in 1762 was invited to Drury Lane. He was connected with that theatre for the rest of his life – Falstaff is reported to have been his best character. The *Dictionary of National Biography* says severely: 'It cannot be said that either as an actor or as a writer he secured or deserved much success.'

From *The Stage*

Sir *Simon*, finely cram'd with wit and knowledge,
His mother says – arrives in town from college.
In ev'ry talent, air, dress, breeding fit
To shine a *George*'s or a *Bedford* wit;[1]
When having loiter'd out the tedious day,
He dresses – yawns – and sallies to the play;
Pleas'd with the glitt'ring scene, his spirits glow,
Alarm'd with tinsel glare, and idle show.

While kind *Cordelia*, plung'd in feign'd distress,
Gives pleasing woe and painful happiness;
Compassion, duty, mingled hope and fear,
The falt'ring voice, the sadly trickling tear,
On the touch'd soul a deep impression dart,
That throbbing pleads the lovely mourner's part;
While grief and pity in soft concord join'd
With flutt'ring transports humanize the mind.

Untaught himself to feel, and yet too proud
To own his error to a diff'ring croud;
Sir Simon, fir'd with *Bacchanalian* feast,
Confirms his judgment, and avows his taste;

Remembers *Garrick*'s robe, how loose it sat,
And deifies the *button* in his hat;
But proudly whispers in his Neighbour's ear,
Shakespear's my fav'rite – Pray who wrote *King Lear*?

[*Poems on Several Occasions*, 1754]

CHARLES CHURCHILL
(1731–64)

Churchill was the son of a clergyman, and followed his father into the church, being ordained in 1756. He lived in poverty till *The Rosciad* was published in 1761. This telling satire on the stage made Churchill rich and famous. He paid his debts, made an allowance to his wife (from whom he had just been separated) and embarked on a career of loose living on a larger scale than he had hitherto been able to afford. After protests from his parishioners and his bishop, he was (1763) forced to resign his living. Churchill allied himself to Wilkes, and became assistant editor of *The North Briton*, assisting its campaign with his satires, which continued to be immensely popular. He died of a fever while on a visit to Wilkes in exile at Boulogne in 1764.

From *The Rosciad*

ON GARRICK[1]

LAST GARRICK came. – Behind him throng a train
Of snarling critics, ignorant as vain.
  One finds out, – 'He's of stature somewhat low, –
'Your Hero always should be tall you know. –
'True nat'ral greatness all consists in height.'
Produce your voucher, Critic – 'Sergeant KYTE.'[2]
  Another can't forgive the paltry arts,
By which he makes his way to shallow hearts;
Mere pieces of finesse, traps for applause. –
'Avaunt, unnat'ral start, affected pause.'
  For me, by Nature form'd to judge with phlegm,
I can't acquit by wholesale, nor condemn.
The best things carried to excess are wrong:
The start may be too frequent, pause too long;
But, only us'd in proper time and place,
Severest judgement must allow them Grace.
  If Bunglers, form'd on Imitation's plan,
Just in the way that monkies mimic man,
Their copied scene with mangled arts disgrace,
And pause and start with the same vacant face;

We join the critic laugh; those tricks we scorn,
Which spoil the scenes they mean them to adorn.
  But when, from Nature's pure and genuine source,
These strokes of Acting flow with gen'rous force;
When in the features all the soul's portray'd,
And passions, such as GARRICK's, are display'd;
To me they seem from quickest feelings caught:
Each start is Nature, and each pause is Thought.
  When Reason yields to Passion's wild alarms,
And the whole state of man is up in arms;
What, but a Critic, could condemn the Play'r,
For pausing here, when Cool Sense pauses there?
Whilst, working from the Heart, the fire I trace,
And mark it strongly flaming to the Face;
Whilst, in each sound, I hear the very man;
I can't catch words, and pity those who can.
  Let wits, like spiders, from the tortur'd brain
Fine-draw the critic-web with curious pain;
The gods, – a kindness I with thanks must pay, –
Have form'd me of a coarser kind of clay;
Nor stung with Envy, nor with Spleen diseas'd,
A poor dull creature, still with Nature pleas'd;
Hence to thy praises, GARRICK, I agree,
And, pleas'd with Nature, must be pleas'd with Thee.

[1761]

From *The Candidate*

ON HIMSELF

ENOUGH of *Self* – that darling, luscious theme,
O'er which Philosophers in raptures dream;
On which with seeming disregard they write,
Then prizing most, when most they seem to slight;
Vain proof of Folly tinctur'd strong with pride!
What Man can from himself himself divide?
For Me (nor dare I lie) my leading aim
(Conscience first satisfied) is love of Fame,

Some little Fame deriv'd from some brave few,
Who, prizing Honour, prize her Vot'ries too.
Let All (nor shall resentment flush my cheek)
Who know me well, what they know, freely speak,
So Those (the greatest curse I meet below)
Who know me not, may not pretend to know.
Let none of Those, whom bless'd with parts above
My feeble Genius, still I dare to love,
Doing more mischief than a thousand foes,
Posthumous nonsense to the world expose,
And call it mine, for mine tho' never known,
Or which, if mine, I living blush'd to own.
Know all the World, no greedy heir shall find,
Die when I will, one couplet left behind.
Let none of Those, whom I despise tho' great,
Pretending Friendship to give malice weight,
Publish my life; let no false, sneaking peer
(Some such there are) to win the public ear,
Hand me to shame with some vile anecdote,
No soul-gall'd Bishop damn me with a note.
Let one poor sprig of Bay around my head
Bloom while I live, and point me out when dead;
Let It (may Heav'n indulgent grant that pray'r)
Be planted on my grave, nor wither there;
And when, on travel bound, some riming guest
Roams thro' the Church-yard, whilst his Dinner's dress'd,
Let it hold up this Comment to his eyes;
Life to the last enjoy'd,[1] *here* Churchill lies;
Whilst (O, what joy that pleasing flatt'ry gives)
Reading my Works, he cries – *here* Churchill lives.

PORTRAIT OF SANDWICH

From his youth upwards to the present day,
When Vices more than years have mark'd him grey,
When riotous excess with wasteful hand
Shakes life's frail glass, and hastes each ebbing sand,

Unmindful from what stock he drew his birth,
Untainted with one deed of real worth,
LOTHARIO,[1] holding Honour at no price,
Folly to Folly added, Vice to Vice,
Wrought sin with greediness, and sought for shame
With greater zeal than good men seek for fame.
    Where (Reason left without the least defence)
Laughter was Mirth, Obscenity was Sense,
Where Impudence made Decency submit,
Where Noise was Humour, and where Whim was Wit,
Where rude, untemper'd License had the merit
Of Liberty, and Lunacy was Spirit,
Where the best things were ever held the worst,
LOTHARIO was, with justice, always first.
    To whip a Top, to knuckle down at Taw,
To swing upon a gate, to ride a straw,
To play at Push-Pin[2] with dull brother Peers,
To belch out Catches in a Porter's ears,
To reign the monarch of a midnight cell,
To be the gaping Chairman's Oracle,
Whilst, in most blessed union, rogue and whore
Clap hands, huzza, and hiccup out, Encore,
Whilst *grey* Authority, who slumbers there
In robes of Watchman's fur, gives up his chair,
With midnight howl to bay th'affrighted Moon,
To walk with torches thro' the streets at noon,
To force plain nature from her usual way,
Each night a vigil, and a blank each day,
To match for speed one Feather 'gainst another,
To make one leg run races with his brother,
'Gainst all the rest to take the northern wind,
BUTE[3] to ride first, and He to ride behind,
To coin new-fangled wagers, and to lay 'em,
Laying to lose, and losing not to pay 'em;
LOTHARIO, on that stock which Nature gives,
Without a rival stands, tho' MARCH[4] yet lives.
    When Folly (at that name, in duty bound,
Let subject Myriads kneel, and kiss the ground,

Whilst They who, in the presence, upright stand,
Are held as rebels thro' the loyal land)
Queen ev'ry where, but most a Queen in Courts,
Sent forth her heralds, and proclaim'd her sports,
Bade fool with fool on her behalf engage,
And prove her right to reign from age to age,
LOTHARIO, great above the common size,
With all engag'd, and won from all the prize;
Her Cap he wears, which from his Youth he wore,
And ev'ry day deserves it more and more.

[1764]

ROBERT LLOYD
(1733–64)

Robert Lloyd's father was an usher at Westminster School. Lloyd himself was educated there, and Charles Churchill, George Colman the Elder, and Warren Hastings were among his contemporaries. After attending Trinity College, Cambridge, Lloyd followed his father's footsteps and became an usher at Westminster. Renewing his friendship with Churchill, he soon took to dissipation, resigned his post and began to write for a living. In 1763 he was imprisoned for debt in the Fleet. Churchill failed to extricate him, and Lloyd was condemned to literary drudgery to keep alive. Though he found his confinement 'irksome enough', he declared that it was 'not so bad as being usher at Westminster'. But on 15 December 1764 he died while still in prison. Churchill's friendship was at once the bane and blessing of his life. It set him on the downward road, but Churchill stood by him when all his other friends deserted him, and even paid him a weekly allowance while he was in prison.

From *The Cit's Country Box*[1] (1757)

HIS WIFE SPEAKS

WELL to be sure, it must be own'd,
It is a charming spot of ground;
So sweet a distance for a ride,
And all about so *countrified*!
'Twould come to but a trifling price
To make it quite a paradise;
I cannot bear those nasty rails,
Those ugly broken mouldy pales:
Suppose, my dear, instead of these,
We build a railing, all Chinese.
Although one hates to be expos'd,
'Tis dismal to be thus inclos'd;
One hardly any object sees –
I wish you'd fell those odious trees.
Objects continual passing by
Were something to amuse the eye,
But to be pent within the walls –
One might as well be at St Paul's.

Our house beholders would adore,
Was there a level lawn before,
Nothing its views to incommode,
But quite laid open to the road;
While ev'ry trav'ler in amaze,
Should on our little mansion gaze,
And pointing to the choice retreat,
Cry, that's Sir Thrifty's Country Seat.

No doubt her arguments prevail,
For Madam's TASTE can never fail.

Blest age! when all men may procure,
The title of a Connoisseur;
When noble and ignoble herd,
Are govern'd by a single word;
Though, like the royal German dames,
It bears an hundred Christian names;
As Genius, Fancy, Judgment, Goût,
Whim, Caprice, Je-ne-scai-quoi, Virtù:
Which appellations all describe
TASTE, and the modern *tasteful* tribe.

Now bricklay'rs, carpenters, and joiners,
With Chinese artists, and designers,
Produce their schemes of alteration,
To work this wond'rous reformation.
The useful dome, which secret stood,
Embosom'd in the yew-tree's wood,
The trav'ler with amazement sees
A temple, Gothic, or Chinese,
With many a bell, and tawdry rag on,
And crested with a sprawling dragon;
A wooden arch is bent astride
A ditch of water, four foot wide,
With angles, curves, and zigzag lines,
From Halfpenny's exact designs.[1]

In front, a level lawn is seen,
Without a shrub upon the green,
Where Taste would want its first great law,
But for the skulking, sly *ha-ha*,
By whose miraculous assistance,
You gain a prospect two fields distance.
And now from Hyde-Park Corner come
The Gods of Athens, and of Rome.
Here squabby Cupids take their places,
With Venus, and the clumsy Graces:
Apollo there, with aim so clever,
Stretches his leaden bow for ever;
And there, without the pow'r to fly,
Stands fix'd a tip-toe Mercury.

The Villa thus completely grac'd,
All own, that Thrifty has a Taste;
And Madam's female friends, and cousins,
With common-council-men, by dozens,
Flock ev'ry Sunday to the Seat,
To stare about them, and to eat.

[*Poems*, 1762]

EVAN LLOYD

(1734–76)

Lloyd was educated at Jesus College, Cambridge, and proceeded B.A. in 1754. He took orders, and was for a short while a curate in London. About 1762 he was presented to the living of Llanvair Dyffryn Clwd in Denbighshire. *The Methodist* is a venomous attack on a neighbouring squire, which led to an action for libel and to the imprisonment of its author in the King's Bench. Lloyd made friends with his fellow-prisoner John Wilkes, and, through Wilkes, with David Garrick, so this misfortune was not wholly a loss to him. Wilkes later wrote his epitaph, paying tribute to his 'strong wit' and 'keen sense'.

From *The Methodist*

DEAD ALDERMEN

If *Phœbus*' rays too fiercely burn,
The *richest Wines* to *sourest* turn:
And they who living *highly fed*,
Will breed a *Pestilence when dead*.
Thus *Aldermen*, who at each Feast,
Cram Tons of Spices from the East,
Whose leading wish, and only plan,
Is to learn how to *pickle Man*;
Who more than vie with *Ægypt's* art,
And make themselves a *human Tart*,
A *walking Pastry-Shop*, a *Gut*,
Shambles by Wholesale to inglut;
And gorge each high-concocted Mess
The art of Cookery can dress:
Yet spite of all, when *Death* thinks fit
To take them off, lest t' other bit
Shou'd burst these *living Mummies*, able
Neither to eat, nor quit the Table;
Whether He Dropsy sends or Gout,
To fetch them by the Shoulders out;

Tho' living they were *Salt* and *Spice*,
The carcase is not over nice;
And all may find, who have a *Nose*,
Dead Aldermen are not a rose.

THE ENTHUSIASTS

The *Bricklay'r* throws his *Trowel* by,
And now *builds Mansions in the Sky*;
The *Cobbler*, touch'd with *holy Pride*,
Flings his *old Shoes*, and Last aside,
And now devoutly sets about
Cobbling of *Souls* that *ne'er wear out*;
The *Baker*, now a *Preacher* grown,
Finds Man *lives not by Bread alone*,
And now his Customers he feeds
With *Pray'rs*, with *Sermons*, *Groans* and *Creeds*;
The *Tinman*, mov'd by Warmth within,
Hammers the *Gospel*, just like *Tin*;
Weavers inspir'd their *Shuttles* leave,
Sermons, and *flimsy Hymns* to weave;
Barbers unreap'd will leave the Chin,
To trim, and shave the *Man within*;
The *Waterman* forgets his *Wherry*,
And opens a *celestial Ferry*;
The *Brewer*, bit by Phrenzy's Grub,
The *Mashing* for the *Preaching Tub*
Resigns, *those Waters* to explore,
Which if You drink, you *thirst no more*;
The *Gard'ner*, weary of his Trade,
Tir'd of the Mattock, and the Spade,
Chang'd to *Apollos* in a Trice,
Waters the *Plants of Paradise*;
The *Fishermen* no longer set
For *Fish* the Meshes of their Net,
But catch, like *Peter*, *Men of Sin*,
For *catching* is to *take them in*.

[1776]

CHRISTOPHER ANSTEY
(1724–1805)

Anstey was the son of a clergyman, and was educated at Eton and King's College, Cambridge. He was elected a fellow of King's in 1745. In 1754, on the death of his mother, he inherited the family estates, and in 1756 he married. For many years thereafter he seems to have lived the life of a country gentleman, combined with the pursuit of letters. A bilious fever took him to Bath, where later he made his home. In 1766 he published *The New Bath Guide*, which was an instantaneous success. Gray called it 'the only thing in fashion', and it was much admired by Horace Walpole. In 1770 Anstey removed permanently to Bath, and was one of the first residents of the Crescent. He has a firm place in literary history, as the originator of a tradition of jocular verse which continued with Barham and Moore. *The New Bath Guide* supplied Smollet with hints for *Humphrey Clinker*.

Liberality of the Decayed Macaroni[1]

1

I AM a decay'd Macaroni,
    My Lodging's up three Pair of Stairs;
My Cheeks are grown wondrously bony,
    And grey, very grey, are my Hairs:

2

My Landlady eyes me severely,
    And frowns when she opens the Door:
My Taylor behaves cavalierly –
    And my Coat will bear scouring no more:

3

Alas! what Misfortunes attend
    The Man of a *liberal* Mind!
How poor are his Thanks at the End,
    From base and ungrateful Mankind!

4

My Father, a stingy old *Rum*,
    His Fortune by Industry made,
And dying bequeath'd me a *Plum*,
    Which he meant I should double in Trade:

5

Oh! how could he destine to Trade
    A Man, of my Figure and Sense!
A Man who so early display'd
    Such a *liberal* Taste for Expence!

6

When I first came to *Years of Discretion*,
    I took a round Sum from the Stocks,
Just to keep up a *decent* Succession
    Of Race-horses, Women, and Cocks:

7

Good Company always my Aim,
    Comme il faut were my Cellars and Table:
And freely I ask'd to the same
    Ev'ry Jockey that came to my Stable:

8

No Stripling of Fortune I noted
    With a Passion for Carding and Dice,
But to Him I my Friendship devoted,
    And gave Him the best of Advice:

9

'To look upon Money as Trash,
    Not play like a pitiful Elf,
But turn all his Acres to Cash,
    And sport it as free as myself.'

10

And as Faro[1] was always my Joy,
    I set up a Bank of my own,
Just to enter a Hobbydehoy
    And give Him a Smack of the *Ton*:[2]

11

In the Morning I took him a hunting,
    At Dinner well-plyed with Champain,
At Tea gave a Lecture on punting;
    At Midnight, on throwing a Main:

12

His Friends too with Bumpers I cheer'd,
    And in Truth should have deem'd it a Sin
To have made, when a *Stranger* appear'd,
    Any Scruple of *taking Him in*.

13

As I always was kind, and soft-hearted,
    I took a rich Maiden to Wife;
And though in a Week we were parted,
    I gave Her a Pension for Life:

14

My free and humane Disposition
    (Thank Heaven) I ever have shewn
To all in a helpless Condition,
    Whose Fortunes I'd first made my own:

15

To * * * * * * with whom long ago,
    My Friendship in Childhood begun,
I presented a handsome *Rouleau*,
    When his ALL I had luckily won;

16

My Friends were much pleas'd with the Action,
　But *charm'd* when I open'd my Door
To his Wife, whom He lov'd to Distraction,
　But could not support any more.

17

The Love of my Country at last,
　In a Soul so exalted as mine
All other fond Passions surpast,
　I long'd in the Senate to shine:

18

With a *liberal* Zeal I was fir'd
　The Good of the State to promote,
And nothing more truly desir'd
　Than to make the *best Use* of my Vote:

19

I panted th' Abuses to quash
　That cast such a Slur on the Nation,
And resolv'd to dispose of my Cash,
　In buying a whole Corporation:

20

I soon heard of one to be sold,
　Such a Bargain, I could not forego it,
With the Freemen so cheap were enroll'd
　A Lawyer, a Priest, and a Poet.

21

I touch'd all the Aldermen round,
　And paid double Price for the Mayor;
But at length to my Sorrow I found
　They'd been sold long before I came there;

22

In vain for sarcastical Song
   Did my Poet his Talents display,
My Lawyer th' Election prolong,
   And the Parson get drunk ev'ry Day:

23

To my very last Farthing I treated,
   And set the whole Town in a Flame:
And since I've so basely been cheated,
   I'll publish the Truth to their Shame:

24

My Rival aloft in his Chair
   Like a Hero triumphantly rode,
My Lawyer and Priest at his Ear,
   My Poet presenting an Ode:

25

While unable to pay for their Prog,
   Their Wine, their Tobacco, and Ale,
I was forc'd to sneak off like a Dog
   With a Canister tyed to his Tail:

26

Yet how can I patiently yield
   Those Palms I so justly might claim,
When I view such a plentiful Field
   For fair Oratorical Fame?

27

'Tis true, I'm a little decayed,
   My Lungs rather husky of late,
Yet still could I throw in my Aid,
   To manage a party Debate:

28

My Legs (you observe it no Doubt)
    Partake of the general Shock;
Yet I trust they might fairly hold out
    Seven Hours by *Westminster Clock*.

29

But in vain have I studied the Art
    With Abuse to bespatter the Foe,
And shoot it like Mud from a Cart,
    With the true CICERONIAN Flow:

30

My Genius and Spirit I feel
    Depress'd by Adversity's Cup;
My Merit, alas! and my Zeal
    For my Country, hath eaten me up:

31

Yet spite of so fair of Pretension,
    Th' unfeeling, ill-judging Premier
Hath meanly deny'd me a Pension –
    Though I ask'd but a Thousand a Year.

32

Where then shall I fly from Oppression,
    Or where shall I seek an Abode,
Unskill'd in a Trade or Profession –
    Too feeble for taking the Road?

33

I'll hasten, O! Bath, to thy Springs,
    Thy Seats of the wealthy and gay,
Where the hungry are fed with good Things,
    And the rich are sent empty away:

34

With you, ye sweet Streams of Compassion,
    My Fortune I'll strive to repair,
Where so many People of Fashion
    Have Money enough, and to spare:

35

And trust, as they give it so freely,
    By private Subscription to raise,
Enough to maintain me genteely,
    And *sport with*, the rest of my Days.

[1788]

JOHN WOLCOT
(1738–1819)

Wolcot is far better known under his pseudonym, 'Peter Pindar'. He was born in Devonshire, and was originally apprenticed to his uncle, a surgeon at Fowey, and took his M.D. degree at Aberdeen in 1767. He was ordained in 1767, and went to Jamaica. In 1772, on the death of his patron, he returned to England, and set up as a physician in Truro. In 1781 he went to London, taking with him John Opie, the painter, whose talent he was the first to discover. Once in London, Wolcot soon made a huge reputation as a satirist, filling the place that Churchill had left vacant. George III was one of his favourite targets. The king was famous for his loquacity, and, when admonished for it by his doctor, during his first attack of madness, replied: 'I know that as well as you. It is my complaint, cure me of that and I shall be well.'

From *Instructions to a Celebrated Laureat*

GEORGE III VISITS WHITBREAD'S[1] BREWERY

Now did his Majesty so gracious say,
To Mister WHITBREAD, in his flying way,
  'WHITBREAD, d'ye nick th'Excisemen now and then?
'Hae, WHITBREAD, when d'ye think to leave off trade?
'Hae? what? Miss WHITBREAD's still a maid, a maid?
  'What, what's the matter with the men?

'D'ye hunt! – hae, hunt? No, no, you are too *old* –
  'You'll be Lord May'r – Lord May'r one day –
'Yes, yes, I've heard so – yes, yes, so I'm told:
  'Don't, don't the fine for Sheriff pay;
'I'll prick you ev'ry year, man, I declare:
'Yes, WHITBREAD – yes, yes – you shall be Lord May'r.

'WHITBREAD, d'ye keep a coach, or job one, pray?
  'Job, job, that's cheapest; yes that's best, that's best.
'You put your liv'ries on the draymen – hae?
  'Hae WHITBREAD? you have feather'd well your nest.
'What, what's the price now, hae, of all your stock?
'But, WHITBREAD, what's o'clock, pray, what's o'clock?'

Now WHITBREAD inward said, 'May I be curst
  'If I know what to answer first?;'
    Then searched his brains with ruminating eye:
But e'er the Man of Malt an answer found,
Quick on his heel, lo, MAJESTY turn'd round,
    Skipp'd off, and baulked the honour of reply.

Kings in inquisitiveness should be strong –
  From curiosity doth wisdom flow:
For 'tis a maxim I've adopted long,
    The more a man inquires, the more he'll know.

Reader, didst ever see a water-spout?
  'Tis possible that thou wilt answer, 'No.'
Well then! he makes a most infernal rout;
  Sucks, like an elephant, the waves below,
With huge proboscis reaching from the sky,
As if he meant to drink the ocean dry:
At length so full he can't hold one drop more –
He bursts – down rush the waters with a roar
On some poor boat, or sloop, or brig, or ship,
And almost sinks the wand'rer of the deep:
Thus have I seen a Monarch at reviews
Suck from the tribe of officers the news,
Then bear in triumph off each *wondrous* matter,
And souse it on the Queen with such a clatter!

[1787]

WILLIAM BLAKE
(1757–1827)

Blake's father was a hosier, and Blake was sent at the age of ten to Par's drawing school in the Strand. In 1771 he was apprenticed to Basire, the engraver, and in 1778 began to earn his living by engraving. Blake was always a radical, and had ridiculed fashionable society in the crude satire *An Island in the Moon* in 1787. The poem printed here can be grouped with those written in his first great creative period in the 1790s – *The Marriage of Heaven and Hell* and *Visions of the Daughters of Albion* were published in 1793; *Europe*, *Urizen* and *Songs of Experience* in 1794; *The Book of Los* in 1795. It is also perhaps worth mentioning the fact that Blake was tried (but acquitted) on a charge of treason at Chichester Assizes in January 1804; the charge was a trumped-up one, brought against him by a soldier whom he had turned out of the garden of his cottage.

Let the Brothels of Paris be Opened

'LET the Brothels of Paris be opened
'With many an alluring dance
'To awake the Pestilence thro' the city,'
Said the beautiful Queen of France.

The King awoke on his couch of gold,
As soon as he heard these tidings told:
'Arise & come, both fife & drum,
'And the Famine shall eat both crust & crumb.'

Then he swore a great & solemn Oath:
'To kill the people I am loth,
'But If they rebel, they must go to hell:
'They shall have a Priest & a passing bell.'

Then old Nobodaddy aloft
Farted & belch'd & cough'd,
And said, 'I love hanging & drawing & quartering
'Every bit as well as war & slaughtering.

'Damn praying & singing,
'Unless they will bring in
'The blood of ten thousand by fighting or swinging.

The Queen of France just touched this Globe,
And the Pestilence darted from her robe;
But our good Queen quite grows to the ground,
And a great many suckers grow all around.

Fayette[1] beside King Lewis stood;
He saw him sign his hand;
And soon he saw the famine rage
About the fruitful land.

Fayette beheld the Queen to smile
And wink her lovely eye;
And soon he saw the pestilence
From street to street to fly.

Fayette beheld the King & Queen
In tears & iron bound;
But mute Fayette wept tear for tear,
And guarded them around.

Fayette, Fayette, thou'rt bought & sold,
And sold is thy happy morrow;
Thou gavest the tears of Pity away
In exchange for the tears of sorrow.

Who will exchange his own fire side
For the steps of another's door?
Who will exchange his wheaten loaf
For the links of a dungeon floor?

O, who would smile on the wintry seas,
& Pity the stormy roar?
Or who will exchange his new born child
For the dog at the wintry door?

[c. 1793]

GEORGE CANNING
(1770–1827)

The son of a lawyer and of a not very successful actress, Canning owed his start in life to his uncle, who was a banker. He was educated at Eton, Christ Church, and Lincoln's Inn. His benefactor was a whig, but by 1792 Canning was already a supporter of Pitt. In 1794 he became member for Newport; in 1796 he was made undersecretary for foreign affairs. From 1799 to 1801 he brought out the immensely successful *Anti-Jacobin*, which completely outgunned its radical opponents. The contributors included Ellis, Frere, Lord Wellesley, Lord Carlisle, and even Pitt himself. In 1807 Canning became foreign secretary under the Duke of Portland, his brother-in-law. In 1822 he was again made foreign secretary on the death of Castlereagh (with whom he had once fought a duel). In 1827 he became prime minister, but died after a few months in office. Canning was a brilliant orator, and retained his interest in literature throughout his political career. He was a friend of Sir Walter Scott, and (in 1808) one of the principal projectors of the famous *Quarterly Review*.

Sapphics[1]
The Friend of Humanity and the Knife-grinder

Friend of Humanity:

'Needy Knife-grinder! whither are you going?
Rough is the road, your wheel is out of order –
Bleak blows the blast; your hat has got a hole in't,
                              So have your breeches!

'Weary Knife-grinder! little think the proud ones,
Who as their coaches roll along the turnpike-
road, what hard work 'tis crying all day "Knives and
                              Scissars to grind O!"

'Tell me, Knife-grinder, how came you to grind knives?
Did some rich man tyrannically use you?
Was it the squire? or parson of the parish?
                              Or the attorney?

208

'Was it the squire, for killing of his game? or
Covetous parson, for his tithes distraining?
Or roguish lawyer, made you lose your little
                              All in a lawsuit?

'(Have you not read the Rights of Man, by Tom Paine?)
Drops of compassion tremble on my eyelids,
Ready to fall, as soon as you have told your
                              Pitiful story.'

Knife-grinder:

'Story! God bless you! I have none to tell, sir,
Only last night a-drinking at the Chequers,
This poor old hat and breeches, as you see, were
                              Torn in a scuffle.

'Constables came up for to take me into
Custody; they took me before the justice;
Justice Oldmixon put me in the parish-
                              Stocks for a vagrant.

'I should be glad to drink your Honour's health in
A pot of beer, if you will give me sixpence;
But for my part, I never love to meddle
                              With politics, sir.'

Friend of Humanity:

'*I* give thee sixpence! I will see thee damned first –
Wretch! whom no sense of wrongs can rouse to vengeance –
Sordid, unfeeling, reprobate, degraded,
                              Spiritless outcast!'

(Kicks the Knife-grinder, overturns his wheel, and exit in a tran-
sport of Republican enthusiasm and universal philanthropy.)

                              [*The Anti-Jacobin*, 27 November, 1797]

From *New Morality*[1]

SUCH is the liberal JUSTICE which presides
In these our days, and modern patriots guides; –
JUSTICE, whose blood-stain'd book one sole decree,
One statute, fills – 'the People shall be Free!'
Free! By what means? – by folly, madness, guilt,
By boundless rapines, blood in oceans spilt;
By confiscation, in whose sweeping toils
The poor man's pittance with the rich man's spoils,
Mix'd in one common mass, are swept away,
To glut the short-lived tyrant of the day; –
By laws, religion, morals, all o'erthrown: –
Rouse, then, ye sovereign people, claim your own:
The license that enthrals, the truth that blinds,
The wealth that starves you, and the power that grinds!
So JUSTICE bids. – 'Twas her enlighten'd doom,
LOUIS, thy holy head devoted to the tomb!
'Twas JUSTICE claim'd, in that accursèd hour,
The fatal forfeit of too lenient power.
Mourn for the Man we may; – but for the King, –
Freedom, oh! Freedom's such a charming thing!

[*The Anti-Jacobin*, 9 July 1798]

MARY ALCOCK

(1742–98)

Information about Mary Alcock is scanty. The preface to her posthumous volume of poems informs us that she was the daughter of Dr Denison Cumberland, Bishop of Kilmore, in Ireland, and that her mother was the daughter of the great scholar Richard Bentley. Apparently she was an invalid, and for some time lived in Bath. She died and was buried at Haselbeach in Northamptonshire. The poem here printed is a satire on 'gothic' novels, of the type written by Ann Radcliffe (1764–1832). Mrs Radcliffe's most famous novel, *The Mysteries of Udolpho*, appeared in 1794.

A Receipt for Writing a Novel

WOULD you a fav'rite novel make,
Try hard your reader's heart to break
For who is pleas'd, if not tormented?
(Novels for that were first invented).
'Gainst nature, reason, sense, combine
To carry on your bold design,
And those ingredients I shall mention,
Compounded with your own invention,
I'm sure will answer my intention.
Of love take first a due proportion –
It serves to keep the heart in motion:
Of jealousy a powerful zest,
Of all tormenting passions best;
Of horror mix a copious share,
And duels you must never spare;
Hysteric fits at least a score,
Or, if you find occasion, more;
But fainting fits you need not measure,
The fair ones have them at their pleasure;
Of sighs and groans take no account,
But throw them in to vast amount;
A frantic fever you may add,
Most authors make their lovers mad;

Rack well your hero's nerves and heart,
And let your heroine take her part;
Her fine blue eyes were made to weep,
Nor should she ever taste of sleep;
Ply her with terrors day or night,
And keep her always in a fright,
But in a carriage when you get her,
Be sure you fairly overset her;
If she will break her bones – why let her:
Again, if e'er she walks abroad,
Of course you bring some wicked lord,
Who with three ruffians snaps his prey,
And to a castle speeds away;
There close confin'd in haunted tower,
You leave your captive in his power,
Till dead with horror and dismay,
She scales the walls and flies away.

    Now you contrive the lovers meeting,
To set your reader's heart a beating.
But ere they've had a moment's leisure,
Be sure to interrupt their pleasure;
Provide yourself with fresh alarms
To tear 'em from each other's arms;
No matter by what fate they're parted,
So that you keep them broken-hearted.

    A cruel father some prepare
To drag her by her flaxen hair;
Some raise a storm, and some a ghost,
Take either, which may please you most.
But this you must with care observe,
That when you've wound up every nerve
With expectation, hope and fear,
Hero and heroine must disappear.
Some fill one book, some two without 'em,
And ne'er concern their heads about 'em,
This greatly rests the writer's brain,

For any story, that gives pain,
You now throw in – no matter what,
However foreign to the plot,
So it but serves to swell the book,
You foist it in with desperate hook –
A masquerade, a murder'd peer,
His throat just cut from ear to ear –
A rake turn'd hermit – a fond maid
Run mad, by some false loon betray'd –
These stores supply the female pen,
Which writes them o'er and o'er again,
And readers likewise may be found
To circulate them round and round.

Now at your fable's close devise
Some grand event to give surprize –
Suppose your hero knows no mother –
Suppose he proves the heroine's brother –
This at one stroke dissolves each tie,
Far as from east to west they fly:
At length when every woe's expended,
And your last volume's nearly ended,
Clear the mistake, and introduce
Some tatt'ling nurse to cut the noose,
The spell is broke – again they meet
Expiring at each other's feet;
Their friends lie breathless on the floor –
You drop your pen; you can no more –
And ere your reader can recover,
They're married – and your history's over.

[*Poems*, 1799]

GEORGE GORDON BYRON, 6TH BARON BYRON

(1788–1824)

To some extent, Byron carried the tradition of the eighteenth
century over into the Romantic era. He admired and defended Pope,
and attacked the Lake poets. His work contains a great deal of satire,
without being primarily satiric, and a study of it will perhaps serve
to show why satire ceased to hold its former pre-eminent position
during the course of the nineteenth century.

From *English Bards and Scotch Reviewers*

ON WORDSWORTH[1]

NEXT comes the dull disciple of thy school,[2]
That mild apostate from poetic rule,
The simple WORDSWORTH, framer of a lay
As soft as evening in his favourite May,
Who warns his friend 'to shake off toil and trouble,[3]
And quit his books, for fear of growing double;'
Who, both by precept and example, shows
That prose is verse, and verse is merely prose;
Convincing all, by demonstration plain,
Poetic souls delight in prose insane;
And Christmas stories tortured into rhyme
Contain the essence of the true sublime.
Thus, when he tells the tale of Betty Foy,
The idiot mother of 'an idiot boy;'
A moon-struck, silly lad, who lost his way,
And, like his bard, confounded night with day;
So close on each pathetic part he dwells,
And each adventure so sublimely tells,
That all who view the 'idiot in his glory'
Conceive the Bard the hero of the story.

[1809]

From *The Vision of Judgment*

ON SOUTHEY[1]

THE varlet was not an ill-favour'd knave;
  A good deal like a vulture in the face,
With a hook nose and a hawk's eye, which gave
  A smart and sharper looking sort of grace
To his whole aspect, which, though rather grave,
  Was by no means so ugly as his case;
But that, indeed, was hopeless as can be,
Quite a poetic felony '*de se.*'

Then Michael blew his trump, and still'd the noise
  With one still greater, as is yet the mode
On earth besides; except some grumbling voice,
  Which now and then will make a slight inroad
Upon decorous silence, few will twice
  Lift up their lungs when fairly overcrow'd;
And now the bard could plead his own bad cause,
With all the attitudes of self-applause.

He said – (I only give the heads) – he said,
  He meant no harm in scribbling; 'twas his way
Upon all topics; 'twas, besides, his bread,
  Of which he butter'd both sides; 'twould delay
Too long the assembly (he was pleased to dread),
  And take up rather more time than a day,
To name his works – he would but cite a few –
'Wat Tyler' – 'Rhymes on Blenheim' – 'Waterloo'.

He had written praises of a regicide;
  He had written praises of all kings what-ever;
He had written for republics far and wide,
  And then against them bitterer than ever;
For pantisocracy he once had cried
  Aloud, a scheme less moral than 'twas clever;
Then grew a hearty anti-jacobin –
Had turn'd his coat – and would have turn'd his skin.

He had sung against all battles, and again
   In their high praise and glory; he had call'd
Reviewing 'the ungentle craft,' and then
   Became as base a critic as e'er crawl'd –
Fed, paid, and pamper'd by the very men
   By whom his muse and morals had been maul'd:
He had written much blank verse, and blanker prose,
And more of both than anybody knows.

He had written Wesley's life: – here turning round
   To Satan, 'Sir, I'm ready to write yours,
In two octavo volumes, nicely bound,
   With notes and preface, all that most allures
The pious purchaser; and there's no ground
   For fear, for I can choose my own reviewers:
So let me have the proper documents,
That I may add you to my other saints.'

Satan bow'd, and was silent. 'Well, if you
   With amiable modesty, decline
My offer, what says Michael? There are few
   Whose memoirs could be render'd more divine.
Mine is a pen of all work; not so new
   As it was once, but I would make you shine
Like your own trumpet. By the way, my own
Has more of brass in it, and is as well blown.

'But talking about trumpets, here's my Vision!
   Now you shall judge, all people! yes, you shall
Judge with my judgment, and by my decision
   Be guided who shall enter heaven or fall.
I settle all these things by intuition,
   Times present, past, to come, heaven, hell, and all,
Like King Alfonso.[1] When I thus see double,
I save the Deity some worlds of trouble.'

He ceased, and drew forth an MS.; and no
　Persuasion on the part of devils, saints,
Or angels, now could stop the torrent; so
　He read the first three lines of the contents;
But at the fourth, the whole spiritual show
　Had vanish'd, with variety of scents,
Ambrosial and sulphureous, as they sprang,
Like lightning, off from his 'melodious twang.'[1]

[1821

From *Don Juan*, Canto XII

WHY call the miser miserable? as
　I said before: the frugal life is his,
Which in a saint or cynic ever was
　The theme of praise: a hermit would not miss
Canonization for the self-same cause,
　And wherefore blame gaunt wealth's austerities?
Because, you'll say, nought calls for such a trial; –
Then there's more merit in his self-denial.

He is your only poet; – passion, pure
　And sparkling on from heap to heap, displays,
Possess'd, the ore, of which *mere hopes* allure
　Nations athwart the deep: the golden rays
Flash up in ingots from the mine obscure;
　On him the diamond pours its brilliant blaze,
While the mild emerald's beam shades down the dies
Of other stones, to soothe the miser's eyes.

The lands on either side are his; the ship
　From Ceylon, Inde, or far Cathay, unloads
For him the fragrant produce of each trip;
　Beneath his cars of Ceres groan the roads,
And the vine blushes like Aurora's lip;
　His very cellars might be kings' abodes;
While he, despising every sensual call,
Commands – the intellectual lord of all.

Perhaps he hath great projects in his mind,
  To build a college, or to found a race,
A hospital, a church, – and leave behind
  Some dome surmounted by his meagre face:
Perhaps he fain would liberate mankind
  Even with the very ore that makes them base;
Perhaps he would be wealthiest of his nation,
Or revel in the joys of calculation.

But whether all, or each, or none of these
  May be the hoarder's principle of action,
The fool will call such mania a disease: –
  What is his *own*? Go – look at each transaction,
Wars, revels, loves – do these bring men more ease
  Than the mere plodding through each 'vulgar fraction?'
Or do they benefit mankind? Lean miser!
Let spendthrifts' heirs inquire of yours – who's wiser?

How beauteous are rouleaus! how charming chests
  Containing ingots, bags of dollars, coins
(Not of old victors, all whose heads and crests
  Weigh not the thin ore where their visage shines,
But) of fine unclipt gold, where dully rests
  Some likeness, which the glittering cirque confines,
Of modern, reigning, sterling, stupid stamp:
Yes! ready money *is* Aladdin's lamp.

[1824]

THOMAS MOORE

1779–1852)

Moore was Irish, and the son of a grocer. He was educated at Trinity College, Dublin, and graduated in 1798. He then went to London to study at the Middle Temple and was an immediate social success. In 1803 he was appointed registrar of the admiralty prize-court in Bermuda, but found the life stultifying there. He appointed a deputy, and returned to London and society. In 1807 the first of the *Irish Melodies* came out – the series was to continue till 1834, and Moore sang them in all the drawing-rooms of London. In 1812 he took to writing political squibs, under the pseudonym Tom Brown. His first butt was the Prince Regent, once his friend. In 1817 he published the hugely successful *Lalla Rookh*. In 1819 his deputy in Bermuda embezzled the sum of six thousand pounds, for all of which Moore found himself liable. He was forced to retire to the Continent until 1822.

Journal of Sir Valentine Sleek

A Colonel in the —— and Finished Dandy

AWOKE at two, and call'd for tea, –
  Mem. – PIERRE forgot my strict commands
To fly *express* to JEAN DUPREE,
  For lily-water for my hands:
But delicate, and soft, their touch,
  Although *un*-wash'd; – which clearly proves
To EXQUISITES, how *very* much
  They owe to wearing chicken gloves.

Arose, and us'd my secret washes,
  (The Ladies' *envy* whilst they praise; –)
Assorted whiskers, and mustachios,
  For lounging – field – and gala days.
Mem. – PIERRE drew on my patent boots
  With six inch heels; – look'd very tall, –
Survey'd my regimental suits,
  Not meaning to attend the ball.

My pigeon breasts, and padded sleeves,
    Made my whole front *en militaire*;
Mem. – By *their* aid a youth receives
    The approbation of the Fair.
Look's *very noble* PIERRE confest,
    – *His* compliments 'all very neat,' –
And, whilst he prais'd, methought my breast
    With glowing martial ardour beat.

Five. – Visited by LANGUISH, – now
    Prime-minister, – who (ever warm
To serve me –) has convinc'd me how
    To chuse a reg'ment's uniform.
– His LORDSHIP's *hair divinely* neat! –
    Mem. – Told me, at his house a few
Staunch PATRIOTS that day would meet
    To plan distilling *Naples' Dew.*

Begg'd me to go – but I declin'd,
    Since, wearied by his LORDSHIP's call,
I felt depress'd, – so chang'd my mind,
    And thought I'd venture to the ball.
Six. – Rang for PIERRE to change my dress,
    Resolv'd to see a favour'd Beauty –
Mem. – PIERRE was arch, – and seem'd to guess
    My meaning by the toilette's duty.

But, as the *lily* grac'd my cheek,
    I grac'd the lily with the *rose*;
And, though my nerves were very weak,
    PIERRE huddled on my ball-room clothes:
Cork pumps, false calves, high collar, – stays
    That EXQUISITES with rapture view;
(Which elegance their shape displays)
    And fashionable wig – quite new.

Upon my temple saw a spot, –
   Was much alarm'd, – but found relief
From salts; – *Mem.* – PIERRE well nigh forgot
   To scent my cambric handkerchief.
A witty epigram perus'd,
   And thought of smoking a cigar, –
A vice now fashionably us'd
   By *many* GENTLEMEN OF WAR.

My brilliants *all* were well display'd, –
   My di'mond snuff-box, broche and rings;
And PIERRE'S good taste arrangements made
   For shewing fifty pretty things.
Ten. – Elegantly dress'd, – when I
   Look very delicate, but *well*;
Mem. – From my lip escap'd a sigh
   For LADY DESDÆMONA L.

Went to the ball, – oh! wondrous chance!
   Saw my ador'd ASPASIA there; –
Knew not she had return'd from France,
   And was enchanted with her air.
Mem. – Danc'd two waltzes, – saw her home, –
   In raptures! – cou'd not quit her house! –
Assur'd her I should often come
   To see her, – and grew amorous.

Mem. – Kiss'd her pretty fingers twice, –
   She told me that I *rude* had grown;
And fear'd I had *improv'd* in vice
   Since I had been *her friend in Town.*
– Got home by three, and gently wept, –
   Then rang for PIERRE, and tranquil grew;
At four, – got into bed, and slept
   Until I rose next day at two.

            [*Replies to Letters of the Fudge Family in Paris*, 1818]

PERCY BYSSHE SHELLEY

(1792–1822)

This striking but uncharacteristic poem was Shelley's response to the news of the Peterloo Massacre. On 16 August 1819 a huge but peaceful meeting took place at St Peter's Fields, Manchester, in support of parliamentary reform. The magistrates lost their heads and ordered the troops to fire on the crowd, with the result that six hundred people were killed.

From *The Masque of Anarchy*

1

As I lay asleep in Italy
There came a voice from over the Sea,
And with great power it forth led me
To walk in the visions of Poesy.

2

I met Murder on the way –
He had a mask like Castlereagh[1] –
Very smooth he looked, yet grim;
Seven blood-hounds followed him:

3

All were fat; and well they might
Be in admirable plight,
For one by one, and two by two,
He tossed them human hearts to chew
Which from his wide cloak he drew.

4

Next came Fraud, and he had on,
Like Eldon,[2] an ermined gown;
His big tears, for he wept well,
Turned to mill-stones as they fell.

5

And the little children, who
Round his feet played to and fro,
Thinking every tear a gem,
Had their brains knocked out by them.

6

Clothed with the Bible, as with light,
And the shadows of the night,
Like Sidmouth, next, Hypocrisy
On a crocodile rode by.

7

And many more Destructions played
In this ghastly masquerade,
All disguised, even to the eyes,
Like Bishops, lawyers, peers, or spies.

8

Last came Anarchy: he rode
On a white horse, splashed with blood;
He was pale even to the lips,
Like Death in the Apocalypse.

9

And he wore a kingly crown;
And in his grasp a sceptre shone;
On his brow this mark I saw –
'I AM GOD, AND KING, AND LAW!'

[1832, written *c.* 1819]

WINTHROP MACKWORTH PRAED
(1802–39)

Praed was the son of a sergeant-at-law, and was educated at Eton. Later he joined the Middle Temple, and was called to the bar in 1829. The next year he entered parliament. He was a member of the short-lived Peel administration of 1834.

Epitaph on the Late King of the Sandwich Islands:[1]

translated from the original of Crazee Rattee,[2]
His Majesty's Poet Laureate

BENEATH this marble, mud, or moss,
　Whiche'er his subjects shall determine,
Entombed in eulogies and dross,
　The Island King is food for vermin:
Preserved by scribblers, and by salt,
　From Lethe, and sepulchral vapours,
His body fills his fathers' vault,
　His character, the daily papers.

Well was he framed for royal seat;
　Kind to the meanest of his creatures,
With tender heart, and tender feet,
　And open purse, and open features;
The ladies say, who laid him out,
　And earned thereby the usual pensions,
They never wreathed a shroud about
　A corpse of more genteel dimensions.

He warred with half a score of foes,
　And shone, by proxy, in the quarrel;
Enjoyed hard fights, and soft repose,
　And deathless debt, and deathless laurel:
His enemies were scalped and flayed,
　Where'er his soldiers were victorious;
And widows wept, and paupers paid,
　To make their Sovereign Ruler glorious.

And days were set apart for thanks,
    And prayers were said by pious readers,
And laud was lavished on the ranks,
    And land was lavished on their leaders;
Events are writ by History's pen,
    And causes are too much to care for;
Fame talks about the where and when,
    And Folly asks the why and wherefore.

In peace he was immensely gay,
    And indefatigably busy;
Preparing gewgaws every day,
    And shows to make his subjects dizzy;
And hearing the reports of guns,
    And signing the reports of gaolers;
And making up recipes for buns,
    And patterns for the army tailors;

And building carriages, and boats,
    And streets, and chapels, and pavilions;
And regulating all the coats,
    And all the principles of millions;
And drinking homilies and gin,
    And chewing pork and adulation;
And looking backwards upon sin,
    And looking forwards to salvation.

The people, in his happy reign,
    Were blest beyond all other nations,
Unharmed by foreign axe or chain,
    Unhealed by civil innovations:
They served the usual logs and stones,
    With all the usual rights and terrors;
And swallowed all their fathers' bones,[1]
    And swallowed all their fathers' errors.

When a fierce mob with clubs and knives,
    Declared that nothing should content them,
But that their representatives
    Should actually represent them,
He interposed the proper checks,
    By sending troops with drums and banners,
Cut short their speeches, and their necks,
    And broke their heads, to mend their manners;

And when Dissension flung her stain
    Upon the light of Hymen's altar,
And Destiny made Cupid's chain
    As galling as the hangman's halter,
He passed a most domestic life,
    By many mistresses befriended;
And did not put away his wife,
    For fear the Priests should be offended.[1]

And thus at last he sunk to rest
    Amid the blessings of his people;
And sighs were heaved from every breast,
    And bells were tolled from every steeple;
And loud was every public throng,
    His brilliant character adorning;
And poets raised a mourning song,
    And clothiers raised the price of mourning.

His funeral was very grand,
    Followed by many robes and maces,
And all the great ones of the land,
    Struggling, as heretofore, for places.
And every loyal Minister
    Was there with signs of purse-felt sorrow,
Save POZZY,[2] his Lord Chancellor,
    Who promised to attend to-morrow.

Peace to his dust! his fostering care
  By grateful hearts shall long be cherished;
And all his subjects shall declare,
  They lost a grinder,[1] when he perished.
They who shall look upon the lead,
  In which a people's love hath shrined him,
Shall say, when all the worst is said,
  Perhaps he leaves a worse behind him!

[*The Morning Chronicle*, 3 August 1825]

Good-night to the Season
Thus runs the world away[2]
Hamlet

GOOD-NIGHT to the Season! 'tis over!
  Gay dwellings no longer are gay;
The courtier, the gambler, the lover,
  Are scatter'd like swallows away;
There's nobody left to invite one,
  Except my good uncle and spouse;
My mistress is bathing at Brighton,
  My patron is sailing at Cowes:
For want of a better employment,
  Till Ponto and Don can get out,
I'll cultivate rural enjoyment,
  And angle immensely for trout.

Good-night to the Season! – the lobbies,
  Their changes, and rumours of change,
Which startled the rustic Sir Bobbies,
  And made all the Bishops look strange:
The breaches, and battles, and blunders,
  Perform'd by the Commons and Peers;
The Marquis's eloquent thunders,
  The Baronet's eloquent ears:
Denouncings of Papists[3] and treasons,
  Of foreign dominion and oats;
Misrepresentations of reasons,
  And misunderstandings of notes.

Good-night to the Season! – the buildings
   Enough to make Inigo[1] sick;
The paintings, and plasterings, and gildings
   Of stucco, and marble, and brick;
The orders deliciously blended,
   From love of effect, into one;
The club-houses only intended,
   The palaces only begun;
The hell where the fiend, in his glory,
   Sits staring at putty and stones,
And scrambles from story to story,
   To rattle at midnight his bones.

Good-night to the Season! – the dances,
   The fillings of hot little rooms,
The glancings of rapturous glances,
   The fancyings of fancy costumes;
The pleasures which Fashion makes duties,
   The praisings of fiddles and flutes,
The luxury of looking at beauties,
   The tedium of talking to mutes;
The female diplomatists, planners
   Of matches for Laura and Jane,
The ice of her Ladyship's manners,
   The ice of his Lordship's champagne.

Good-night to the Season! – the rages
   Led off by the chiefs of the throng,
The Lady Matilda's new pages,
   The Lady Eliza's new song;
Miss Fennel's macaw, which at Boodle's[2]
   Is held to have something to say;
Mrs Splenetic's musical poodles,
   Which bark 'Batti Batti'[3] all day;
The pony Sir Araby sported,
   As hot and as black as a coal,
And the Lion his mother imported,
   In bearskins and grease, from the Pole.

Good-night to the Season! – the Toso,
  So very majestic and tall;
Miss Ayton,[1] whose singing was so-so,
  And Pasta,[2] divinest of all;
The labour in vain of the Ballet,
  So sadly deficient in stars;
The foreigners thronging the Alley,
  Exhaling the breath of cigars;
The 'loge' where some heiress, how killing,
  Environ'd with Exquisites sits,
The lovely one out of her drilling,
  The silly ones out of their wits.

Good-night to the Season! – the splendour
  That beam'd in the Spanish Bazaar;
Where I purchased – my heart was so tender –
  A card-case, – a paste-board guitar, –
A bottle of perfume, – a girdle, –
  A lithograph'd Riego[3] full-grown,
Whom Bigotry drew on a hurdle
  That artists might draw him on stone, –
A small panorama of Seville, –
  A trap for demolishing flies, –
A caricature of the Devil, –
  And a look from Miss Sheridan's[4] eyes.

Good-night to the Season! – the flowers
  Of the grand horticultural fête,
When boudoirs were quitted for bowers,
  And the fashion was not to be late;
When all who had money and leisure
  Grew rural o'er ices and wines,
All pleasantly toiling for pleasure,
  All hungrily pining for pines.
And making of beautiful speeches,
  And marring of beautiful shows,
And feeding on delicate peaches,
  And treading on delicate toes.

Good-night to the Season! – another
   Will come with its trifles and toys,
And hurry away, like its brother,
   In sunshine, and odour, and noise.
Will it come with a rose or a briar?
   Will it come with a blessing or curse?
Will its bonnets be lower or higher?
   Will its morals be better or worse?
Will it find me grown thinner or fatter,
   Or fonder of wrong or of right,
Or married, – or buried? – no matter,
   Good-night to the Season, Good-night!

           [*The New Monthly Magazine*, August 1827]

EBENEZER ELLIOTT

(1781–1849)

Ebenezer Elliott was one of a family of eleven children. His father
was in the iron trade – an extreme radical and an ultra-calvinist.
Elliott had many financial troubles to face – he lost his wife's fortune
when he invested it in his father's business, and he attributed this and
later losses to the corn laws. He was present as a delegate at the great
chartist public meeting held in Palace Yard, Westminster, in 1838,
but when O'Connor induced the chartists to repudiate the corn-law
repeal agitation, he withdrew from chartism. It was really his
passionate and over-riding hatred of the corn laws which made
Elliott seem a radical. In many ways his views were mild and conservative, and it is significant that two of his own sons became clergymen in the Church of England.

Song

WHEN working blackguards come to blows,
And give or take a bloody nose,
Shall juries try such dogs as those,
   Now Nap lies at Saint Helena?

No, let the Great Unpaid decide,
Without appeal, on tam bull's hide,
Ash-planted well, or fistified,
   Since Nap died at Saint Helena.

When Sabbath stills the dizzy mill,
Shall Cutler Tom, or Grinder Bill,
On footpaths wander where they will,
   Now Nap lies at Saint Helena?

No, let them curse, but feel *our* power;
Dogs! let them spend their idle hour
Where burns the highway's dusty shower;
   For Nap died at Saint Helena.

Huzza! the rascal Whiglings work
For better men than Hare and Burke,
And envy Algerine and Turk,
    Since Nap died at Saint Helena.

Then close each path that sweetly climbs
Suburban hills, where village chimes
Remind the rogues of other times,
    Ere Nap died at Saint Helena.

We tax their bread, restrict their trade;
To toil for us, their hands were made;
Their doom is seal'd, their prayer is pray'd;
    Nap perished at Saint Helena.

Dogs! would they toil and fatten too?
They grumble still, as dogs will do:
We conquer'd *them* at Waterloo;
    And Nap lies at Saint Helena

But shall the villains meet and prate
In crowds about affairs of state?
Ride, yeoman, ride! Act, magistrate!
    Nap perish'd at Saint Helena.

[*Corn Law Rhymes*, 1831]

EDWARD GEORGE EARLE LYTTON, 1st BARON BULWER LYTTON
(1803–73)

Lytton was educated at Trinity College and Trinity Hall, Cambridge, and showed an early inclination to dandyism. After a runaway match (which he lived to regret), he published *Pelham* (1828), a novel which gives an intimate picture of the dandy-world and which was immediately popular. This was followed by a long string of other novels, including *Eugene Aram*, *The Last Days of Pompeii*, and *The Last of the Barons*. Lytton also wrote for the stage. His plays included *The Lady of Lyons* (1838), in which Macready scored a great success at Covent Garden. Lytton pursued the career of politician as well as writer, and was eventually raised to the peerage in 1866. Tennyson bitterly resented the attack made on him in *The New Timon*, and wrote a poem in reply which is also included in this book (p. 235).

From *The New Timon*

PORTRAIT OF THE DUKE OF WELLINGTON

NEXT, with loose rein and careless canter view
Our man of men, the Prince of Waterloo;
O'er the firm brow the hat as firmly prest,
The firm shape rigid in the button'd vest;
Within – the iron which the fire has proved,
And the close Sparta of a mind unmoved!
Not his the wealth to some large natures lent,
Divinely lavish, even where misspent,
That liberal sunshine of exuberant soul,
Thought, sense, affection, warming up the whole;
The heat and affluence of a genial power,
Rank in the weed as vivid in the flower;
Hush'd at command his veriest passions halt,
Drill'd is each virtue, disciplined each fault;
Warm if his blood – he reasons while he glows,
Admits the pleasure – ne'er the folly knows;
If for our Mars his snare had Vulcan set,
He had won the Venus, but escaped the net;

His eye ne'er wrong, if circumscribed the sight,
Widen the prospect and it ne'er is right,
Seen through the telescope of habit still,
States seem a camp, and all the world – a drill!

AN ATTACK ON TENNYSON

IF to my verse denied the Poet's fame,
This merit, rare to verse that wins, I claim;
No tawdry grace shall womanize my pen!
E'vn in a love-song, man should write for men!
Not mine, not mine, (O Muse forbid!) the boon
Of borrowed notes, the mock-bird's modish tune,
The jingling medley of purloin'd conceits,
Outbaying Wordsworth, and outglittering Keats,
Where all the airs of patchwork-pastoral chime
To drowsy ears in Tennysonian rhyme!
Am I enthrall'd but by the sterile rule,
The formal pupil of a frigid school,
If to old laws my Spartan tastes adhere,
If the old vigorous music charms my ear,
Where sense with sound, and ease with weight combine,
In the pure silver of Pope's ringing line;
Or where the pulse of man beats loud and strong
In the frank flow of Dryden's lusty song?
Let School-Miss Alfred vent her chaste delight
On 'darling little rooms so warm and bright!'
Chaunt, 'I'm aweary,' in infectious strain,
And catch her 'blue fly singing i' the pane.'
Tho' praised by Critics, tho' adored by Blues,
Tho' Peel with pudding[1] plump the puling Muse,
Tho' Theban taste the Saxon's purse controuls,
And pensions Tennyson, while starves a Knowles,[2]
Rather, be thou, my poor Pierian Maid,
Decent at least, in Hayley's[3] weeds array'd,
Than patch with frippery every tinsel line,
And flaunt, admired, the Rag Fair of the Nine!

[1846]

ALFRED TENNYSON, LORD TENNYSON

(1809–1892)

This is Tennyson's furious reply to the attack made on him by Bulwer-Lytton in *The New Timon*. He afterwards grew ashamed of it, and did not include it in his collected works. Tennyson had just been established, by the two-volume edition of his *Poems*, published in 1842, as the leading poet of the age. He had also just succeeded in losing his small fortune in a 'Patent Decorative Carving Company' which went bankrupt in a few months. In September 1845 Sir Robert Peel had bestowed on Tennyson a Civil List pension of two hundred pounds a year, a fact woundingly referred to by Bulwer Lytton.

The New Timon, and the Poets

WE know him, out of SHAKESPEARE's art,
  And those fine curses which he spoke;
The old TIMON, with his noble heart,
  That, strongly loathing, greatly broke.

So died the Old: here comes the New.
  Regard him: a familiar face:
I *thought* we knew him: What, it's you,
  The padded man – that wears the stays –

Who kill'd the girls and thrill'd the boys,
  With dandy pathos when you wrote,
A Lion you, that made a noise,
  And shook a mane en papillotes.

And once you tried the Muses too;
  You fail'd, Sir: therefore now you turn,
You fall on those who are to you,
  As Captain is to Subaltern.

But men of long-enduring hopes,
  And careless what this hour may bring,
Can pardon little would-be POPES
  And BRUMMELS, when they try to sting.

An artist, Sir, should rest in Art,
    And waive a little of his claim;
To have the deep Poetic heart
    Is more than all poetic fame.

But you, Sir, you are hard to please;
    You never look but half content:
Nor like a gentleman at ease,
    With moral breadth of temperament.

And what with spites and what with fears,
    You cannot let a body be:
It's always ringing in your ears,
    'They call this man as good as *me*.'

What profits now to understand
    The merits of a spotless shirt –
A dapper boot – a little hand –
    If half the little soul is dirt?

You talk of tinsel! why we see
    The old mark of rouge upon your cheeks.
You prate of Nature! you are he
    That spilt his life about the cliques.

A TIMON you! Nay, nay, for shame:
    It looks too arrogant a jest –
The fierce old man – to take *his* name
    You bandbox. Off, and let him rest.

                  [*Punch*, 28 February 1846]

ARCHER THOMPSON GURNEY

(1820–87)

Gurney was born at Tregony, Cornwall. He began his career as a
student of law, and was called to the bar. Later he took orders,
and became curate of Holy Trinity, Exeter, in 1842. Among
his later appointments was the chaplaincy of the Court Chapel,
Paris, which he held from 1858 to 1871. Gurney was well known as
a theologian. His most successful work was *Words of Faith and Cheer*
(1874).

From *The Transcendentalists*

THE ardent patriot haply earns a smile
From his gay auditors, serene, the while
Their country's falling and the poor are dying,
Young statesmen yawn: to yawns there's no replying.
Nought so plebeian as to show rough feeling:
Conceal, until there's nothing for concealing.
Reserve, until reserve has swallowed up
The very source of life, and drain'd the cup!
O smoothly polished scions of nobility,
Must you still glory in your grand *nihility*?
Your florid insignificance of mood?
O, could I lash you into life, I would!
Let democratic battering-rams assail,
Your cheeks will blench not, you've no hearts to quail;
You'll only lisp, 'Plague take these tiresome fellows!'
Alas! that time should weaken while it mellows,
And aristocracies, when most refined,
Should revel in blank impotence of mind!

[1853]

ROBERT BARNABAS BROUGH

(1828–60)

Brough began life as a clerk in Manchester, but eventually became an extremely active London journalist. Alone, or with his brother William, he wrote a series of successful burlesques for the London stage, which were put on at such theatres as the Adelphi, the Lyceum, and the Olympic.

Vulgar Declamation

A LESSON FOR THE YOUNG

'But, Sir, I do protest against the language we have heard this evening from the Hon. Member for Aylesbury, who, while he performs what he thinks a public duty in pointing out old errors and instances of mismanagement in regard to the army, must needs tell me that this country has become the laughing-stock of Europe, and has thought proper to mingle with his observations and comments a deal of what I must call vulgar declamation against the aristocracy of this country.' (Cheers.)

Lord Palmerston's Speech

MY son, if Fate in store for you
   Should have the wond'rous bounty,
To let you live to represent
   A borough or a county –
I'd have you do your duty well,
   According to your station,
And guard, o'er all, against the use
   Of VULGAR DECLAMATION.

I hope you'll never tell the House
   That all men's rights are equal –
That woe to Nations, still must be
   Of Monarch's Wars the sequel;
Or that a pauper can be found
   In all the British nation:
For if you do, you'll be accused
   Of VULGAR DECLAMATION.

Avoid allusions to the Church,
    Except, indeed, to praise it;
Don't rail against a Bishop's pay,
    But give your vote to raise it;
Don't say that forty-pounds a-year
    Is scant remuneration
For working clergymen, because
    That's VULGAR DECLAMATION.

The Prince of Wales is just your age,
    Together you will grow up;
He'll soon want money and a wife,
    Don't – when the time comes – blow up
His marriage grant, however great,
    Or heavy on the nation –
That stinting princes is the worst
    Of VULGAR DECLAMATION.

And then when common soldiers claim
    Their share of wealth and glory,
And grudge the lions all the prize,
    Don't *you* take up the story.
And as for giving working men
    Ideas above their station,
'T is positively wrong, as well
    As VULGAR DECLAMATION.

And, lastly – if some noble name
    Should get by chance mix'd up in
Some awkward case of 'starved to death,'
    Or arsenic, a cup in,
Just hush it up, and hope, at least,
    There's some exaggeration;
But don't, for Heaven's sake, indulge
    In VULGAR DECLAMATION.

[*Songs of the Governing Classes*, 1855]

PHILIP JAMES BAILEY
(1816–1902)

Bailey is best known as the author of the gigantic poem *Festus*, which in its final form reached a length of 40,000 lines, and as the father of the so-called 'spasmodic' school of poetry. His work enjoyed a high if somewhat fluctuating reputation during his own lifetime (the Pre-Raphaelites admired it), but is now almost totally forgotten.

From *The Age*

ON POETS

To suffer in mind, body, or estate,
Or all the three at once, is no rare fate,
But these, to bards, are woes of trifling weight,
Who fainting as a fine art know, and can turn
Into their own breasts their own bull's-eye lantern.
As life-school models, philosophic misses,
Superior to their sex's prejudices,
Nude as a needle, attitudinise;
So these for our behoof will agonise;
Yea, like a zoophyte, turn inside out
Their very hearts, to illustrate a doubt.
Who studies aught with persevering skill,
His choice effects can reproduce at will.
A practised necromancer, such as you,
Can raise a ghost whene'er it suits to do.
So all these love-affairs one just regards
As so much stock in trade of bankrupt bards,
Whose books are never open to inspection
Till roguery is certain of detection.

[1858]

ARTHUR HUGH CLOUGH
(1819–61)

Clough's father was a Liverpool cotton-merchant, who emigrated to Charleston, South Carolina, in 1822. Clough was educated at Dr Arnold's Rugby, and became a favourite with Arnold, who had a great influence over him. He won a scholarship to Balliol, where he was a contemporary of Jowett, later to be Master of the College, and Matthew Arnold, son of the headmaster. In 1842 Clough became a fellow of Oriel, then one of the greatest prizes Oxford had to offer. He resigned his fellowship in 1848. He was offered the headship of University Hall, London, in 1849, but again resigned this in 1851. He sailed for America in 1852, but did not settle there, and returned to take up an examinership in the Education Office. Clough's career disappointed his contemporaries, and his two long poems, *The Bothie of Tobie na Vuig* (1849) and *Amours de Voyage* (1849) had little impact. However, he now seems a kind of type-figure of Victorian hesitation and self-doubt. James Russell Lowell shrewdly prophesied: 'We have a foreboding that Clough, imperfect as he was in many ways, and dying before he had subdued his sensitive temperament to the requirements of his art, will be thought a hundred years hence to have been the truest expression in verse of the moral and intellectual tendencies, the doubt and struggle towards settled convictions, of the period in which he lived.'

In the Great Metropolis

EACH for himself is still the rule;
We learn it when we go to school –
  The devil take the hindmost, O!

And when the schoolboys grow to men,
In life they learn it o'er again –
  The devil take the hindmost, O!

For in the church, and at the bar,
On 'Change, at court, where'er they are,
  The devil takes the hindmost, O!

Husband for husband, wife for wife,
Are careful that in married life
  The devil takes the hindmost, O!

From youth to age, whate'er the game,
The unvarying practice is the same –
  The devil takes the hindmost, O!

And after death, we do not know,
But scarce can doubt, where'er we go,
  The devil takes the hindmost, O!

Ti rol de rol, ti rol de ro,
The devil take the hindmost, O!

[*Poems*, 1862]

The Latest Decalogue

THOU shalt have one God only; who
Would be at the expense of two?
No graven images may be
Worshipped, except the currency:
Swear not at all; for, for thy curse
Thine enemy is none the worse:
At church on Sunday to attend
Will serve to keep the world thy friend:
Honour thy parents; that is, all
From whom advancement may befall;
Thou shalt not kill; but need'st not strive
Officiously to keep alive:
Do not adultery commit;
Advantage rarely comes of it:
Thou shalt not steal; an empty feat,
When it's so lucrative to cheat:

Bear not false witness; let the lie
Have time on its own wings to fly:
Thou shalt not covet, but tradition
Approves all forms of competition.

[*Poems*, 1862]

ALFRED AUSTIN

(1835-1913)

Austin's reputation has been ruined not only by his own (rather numerous) bad verses, but also by the fact that he had the ill-luck to be appointed Poet Laureate after the death of Tennyson, and this only after a humiliating interval of four years. Austin's satires are the most attractive part of his work, and *The Season* was, in fact, the poem with which he made his reputation. He edited the *National Review* for several years, and wrote leading articles for the *Standard*.

From *The Season*

THE PARADE IN HYDE PARK

STILL sweeps the long procession, whose array
Gives to the lounger's gaze, as wanes the day,
Its rich reclining and reposeful forms,
Still as bright sunsets after mists or storms,
Who sit and smile (their morning wranglings o'er,
Or dragged and dawdled through one dull day more),
As though the life of widow, wife, and girl
Were one long lapsing and voluptuous whirl.
O poor pretence! what eyes so blind but see
The sad, however elegant, ennui?
Think you that blazoned panel, prancing pair,
Befool our vision to the weight they bear?
The softest ribbon, pink-lined parasol,
Screen not the woman, though they deck the doll.
The padded corsage and the well-matched hair,
Judicious jupon spreading out the spare,
Sleeves well designed false plumpness to impart,
Leave vacant still the hollows of the heart.
Is not our Lesbia lovely? In her soul
Lesbia is troubled: Lesbia hath a mole;
And all the splendour of that matchless neck
Consoles not Lesbia for its single speck.
Kate comes from Paris, and a wardrobe brings,
To which poor Edith's are 'such common things.'
Her pet lace shawl has grown not fit to wear,
And ruined Edith dresses in despair.

AT THE OPERA

Above, around, below, are houris' eyes,
Flashing with quick, intelligent surprise,
And houris' blushes rapidly respond
To murmurous whispers deftly-dropped and fond,
Spread from the temples, eddy to the neck,
Break on the breast, and turning at the check,
In ripples weaker rally from restraint,
Creep up the cheek and on the features faint.
Their rounded, pliant, silent-straying arms
Seem sent to guard, yet manifest their charms.

AT A BALL

Louder, ye viols! shrilly, cornets! blow!
Who is this prophet that denounces woe?
Whirl fast! whirl long! ye gallants and ye girls!
Cling closer still; dance down these cursëd churls.
Be crowned, ye fair! with poppies newly-blown,
Fling loose your tresses, and relax your zone!
From floating gauze let dreamy perfumes rise,
Infuse a fiercer fervour in your eyes!
Till, head and heart and senses all on fire,
Passion presume and Modesty expire!

Bless us and save us! What tirade is this?
My choleric friend! is anything amiss?
This sparkling scene of Beauty in its bloom
Is not an Orgy, but – an auction-room.
These panting damsels, dancing for their lives,
Are only maidens waltzing into wives.
Those smiling matrons are appraisers sly,
Who regulate the dance, the squeeze, the sigh,
And each base cheapening buyer having chid,
Knock down their daughters to the noblest bid.

[1861]

From *The Golden Age*

MARRYING FOR MONEY

WHAT! wed with Virtue! Is the girl awake?
Sure, she confounds the altar with the stake.
Send for the doctor. Try a change of air.
Swear Cato drinks. In war and love all's fair.
Bring Crœsus to the front. At four he's free –
There's no one left to swindle after three.
In one brief hour behold him curled and drest,
And borne on wings of fashion to the West!
What though to regions fondly deemed refined,
He brings his City manners, City mind,
And cynics titter? – he laughs best who wins, –
A Greenwich dinner covers many sins.
What! dine with Crœsus? Surely. Is a feast
One jot the worse because the host's a beast?
He's worse than that – a snob – a cad. Agreed;
But then his goblets smack of Ganymede?
Do some strange freaks his conversation mar?
He stops your censure with a prime cigar.
A Norway stream, a shooting-lodge in Perth.
In practice look uncommonly like worth.
The Town to hear some new soprano flocks.
You long to go? Well, Crœsus has a box.
How at this hour are tickets to be got
For the Regatta? Crœsus has a yacht.
Goodwood is here. Your hopes begin to flag.
One chance awaits you: Crœsus has a drag.
You doat on Flower-shows: Crœsus has a bone.[1]
Be friends with Crœsus, and the World's your own.
Who could resist seductions such as these?
Or what could charm, if Crœsus failed to please?
Blinded and bribed, the critical are cured,
And loud extol whom late they scarce endured.

Caressed and courted, Crœsus grows the rage,
The type and glory of our Golden Age;
And Cato, Hylas, Solon, shoved aside,
Our heavenly maid is hailed as Crœsus' bride.

[1862]

WILLIAM LEECH

(*fl.* 1879)

I am unable to discover much about the author of this skilful imitation of *The Dunciad*. It was published anonymously, and the author, in his preface, claims that it was written some years prior to publication. The approximate date of composition can be deduced, first of all from the fact that it contains a violent attack on Hepworth Dixon (1821–79), in his capacity as editor of the *Athenaeum*, a post he held from 1853 to 1869, and secondly from the passage attacking Browning's *The Ring and the Book*, which is printed here. Browning's poem came out in 1868–9.

From *The Obliviad*

ON ROBERT BROWNING

But place, ye Scottish; place, ye English wits;
Here Browning, dredged from far profounder pits;
The bard that nursed, and taught betimes to rave
By Sibyl hag, in some Cimmerian cave,
Or in vast Mammoth to obscure his mind,
Where bats are biggest, and the fish are blind;
Intolerant of day, and forced to wait
Till clouds call forth to hoot articulate:
A sort of *lusus*, soon by Barnum caught,
Gazed at by crowds, and to the city brought,
There strange to jabber, in strange garment drest,
Of whom one half is cunning, fool the rest;
Some doubting much a cheat, while more debate
Or find how nonsense in the soul innate.
But vagrant next, behold him shambling go,
At once himself the showman and the show,
Street preacher of Parnassus, roll on high
His blinking orbs, and rant tautology,
While gaping multitudes around the monk
Much wonder if inspired, or simply drunk.

At length, by cast of some superior luck,
   Moping 'mid lunar light, he finds a Book,
'Tween line and hemistic which greatly grows,
And now of verse is fustian, now of prose.
Straight thumb'd by all, the students of that sort
Who read romances and Police Report,
Who deep in scandal, but whose joy, by far,
When *crim. con.* case bares each particular.
Alluring tale, much matrimonial strife,
Old, harsh, the husband, young and fair the wife;
A priest gallant, whom Caponsacchi call,
Who flings her comfits at the carnival.
Which seen, old Guido, jealous, spreads a snare,
By forged epistles to entrap the pair.
Stale trick, the lover sees what thus design'd,
Steals off the bait, and leaves the noose behind.
But, first, Pompilia, 'with that sad strange smile,'
Twists thus the metaphysic of her guile:
Since, then, my husband hates me, I shall use, –
Let have effect enough to balk his views,
And of the other's love but so much take
As stop a murd'rer, 'for his own soul's sake;'
Whence plain to all a wife without reproach,
Though midnight meet me in the hackney coach.
She comes, ah, see, in hymeneal white,
Than moon more chaste, and than the stars more bright;
How am'rous youths upon the fancy draw!
All black, ''t was her soul's whiteness which I saw.'
'Then in a tick of time,' postilions fly.
'Sprung, was beside her, she alone and I.'
What next, I pray you, to this am'rous haste?
Ungen'rous doubt, is not Pompilia chaste;
No sly approaches, heaving of the breast,
Nor e'en her hand, by jolt of coach, is press'd;
In frigid of romance they but adore,
And then to metaphysic as before.
A mystery of meaning where none is,
Set off with dash (–) and with parenthesis;

Or subtile logic such as gulls may guide,
And show but seeming is the guilty side;
With art by which unwilling wives may hope
To keep their character, and yet elope.

[1879, written *c.* 1869]

HENRY NELSON O'NEIL, A.R.A.

(1817–80)

O'Neil was born at St Petersburg, and came to England at the age of six. He entered the School of the Royal Academy, and first exhibited at the Academy in 1838. He was chiefly a historical painter, and the subjects of his pictures included 'Mozart's Last Moments', 'Esther', 'The Lay of King Canute', and 'The Landing of H.R.H. the Princess Alexandra at Gravesend'. He was elected an A.R.A. in 1860. *The Age of Stucco* is not his only effort in verse – he published some *Satirical Dialogues* in 1870. He was also an amateur musician and a good viola player.

From *The Age of Stucco*

ON ART-CRITICS

WHY marvel if a critic has not sense
To settle if 'tis power or impudence,
Which makes him, with a charity divine,
Expose the treasures of his tinsel mine?
How can he justify his self-election,
Except by ever making an objection
To rules and principles which influence
Those who are only blest with common sense?
What if his doctrines be pronounced untrue?
They have this merit, at the least they're new:
And novelty – of all means to ensure
Profit or honour – is the most secure.
And thus, Art-critics, to be thought abstruse,
Select for praise what elsewhere finds abuse;
Mere stammering they take for subtle speech,
And 'non-performance' as the highest reach
A painter can attain. Alas! for Art,
When its disciples care not to impart
Their meaning fully; but, like poor tide-waiters,
Just leave it to the whim of the spectators.

This suits the critics, for they must be bold;
From a gold-digging nuggets of pure gold
The veriest fool may reap; but to extract
Gold from a dunghill is a godlike act.

[1871]

THE COMING K— *and* THE SILIAD: ANONYMOUS

The Coming K— and *The Siliad* were each originally issued as 'Beeton's Christmas Annual' for the year in which they appeared. They were immensely popular. One reason was, quite evidently, that they helped to sum up the anti-monarchical sentiment which was prevalent in England during the 1870s, and, in particular, the disapproval felt by the public where the Prince of Wales was concerned. *The Coming K—* is a very clever parody of Tennyson's *Idylls of the King: The Holy Grail*, with three other idylls, had been published in 1869, and greeted with rather less than the usual chorus of praise. The authorship of this group of poems is something of a mystery. The British Museum catalogue attributes them to A. A. Dowty, S. R. Emerson, and Beeton himself. (S. O. Beeton was the widower of Mrs Beeton, of cookery-book fame.)

From *The Coming K—*

DELAINE CONFRONTS THE FAITHLESS LOOSEALOT AT A MARLBOROUGH HOUSE GARDEN-PARTY

ALL up the yellow gravel paths she passed,
In her right hand the umbrella, in her left
The letter – all her brown hair streaming down;
And all her polonaise was crêpe de Chine,
Drawn to the waist, and full and puffed behind,
Chaussure and skirt of blue; and for her face,
That was pure white, for she had powdered it.
With footstep measured and a face demure,
She minced her way, till came a sound of chat
And babble on the breeze; then halted she.
Now, girt with knights, round corner proximate
Came Guelpho,[1] and his courtiers following.
Sir Loosealot was there, and saw she him;
Saw he her too – all present did the same;
And not an eye but asked, 'Who is it, then?'

[1871]

From *The Siliad*

The Night Adventures of Liobed and Bersites

SUCH are the two that, lounging slowly, turn
Into a horseshoe doorway, o'er which burn
A thousand gas jets; and from out the night
They pass into a realm of lustrous light.
Peelides lingers not upon the way,
Nor stops, though doubtful houris bid him stay.
Up stairs he bounds, past mirror-hidden walls,
Past scent and glove and bon-bon covered stalls.
Till, after parley with a six-foot loon,
He and Bersites gain the great saloon.
Within is bravery of gilt, a mass,
And wealth of waving hair, and glittering glass;
A hundred rainbows cross and intertwine,
A thousand wicked eyes enchanting shine.
Lips, full of sin, yet plump and ripe withal,
Shape naughty kisses, and for liquids call.
Hands, gloved divinely, creep beneath men's arms;
Whilst shapely ankles tell of hidden charms;
Toilettes, too ravishing for mortal pen,
Flit everywhere, and prey on helpless men.
Houris in *eau de Nile*, and salmon pink,
And peacock blue, distract, and daze, and drink.
The utter stranger greet they with a smile,
So artless seeming, yet so versatile;
As some in distant corners toy and sport,
Others lap deeply lemonade and port.
While shop-boys, trying tip-top swells to be,
Have robbed the till, and call for S. and B.[1]

[1873]

ROBERT WILLIAMS BUCHANAN
(1841–1901)

Buchanan was the son of Robert Buchanan, the Owenite lecturer and journalist. He was educated at the University of Glasgow. A prolific novelist and playwright, he is now best remembered for his attack on Rossetti in the number of *The Contemporary Review* for October 1871. The article was entitled 'The Fleshly School of Poetry'.

The Ballad of Kiplingson [1]

THERE came a knock at the Heavenly Gate, where the good St
    Peter sat, –
'Hi, open the door, you fellah there, to a British rat-tat-tat!'

The Saint sat up in his chair, rubb'd eyes, and prick'd his holy ears,
'Who's there?' he muttered, 'a single man, or a regiment of
    Grenadiers?'

'A single man,' the voice replied, 'but one of prodigious size,
Who claims by Jingo, his patron Saint, the entry to Paradise!'

The good St Peter open'd the Gate, but blocking the entry scan'd
The spectacled ghost of a little man, with an infant's flag in his
    hand.

'Your name? Before I let you pass, say who and what you were!
Describe your life on the earth, and prove your claim to a place in
    there!'

'Wot! haven't you heard of Kiplingson? whose name and fame
    have spread
As far as the Flag of England waves, and the Tory prints are read?

'I was raised in the lap of Jingo, sir, till I grew to the height of man,
And a wonderful Literary Gent, I emerged upon Hindostan!

'I sounded the praise of the Empire, sir, I pitch'd out piping hot
The new old stories of British bounce (see Lever[1] and Michael
    Scott);

'And rapid as light my glory spread, till thro' Cockaigne it flew,
And I grew the joy of the Cockney cliques, and the pet of the
    Jingo Jew![2]

'For the Lord my God was a Cockney Gawd, whose voice was a
    savage yell,
A fust-rate Gawd who dropt, d'ye see, the "h" in Heaven and
    Hell!

'O I was clever beyond compare, and not like most young muffs,
Tho' I died last night, at an early age, of a plethora of puffs.

'O lollipops are toothsome things, and sweet is the log-roll'd jam,
But the last big puff of the Log-rollers has choked me, and here I
    am!

'But I was a real Phenomenon,' continued Kiplingson,
'The only genius ever born who was Tory at twenty-one!'

'Alas, and alas,' the good Saint said, a tear in his eye serene,
'A Tory at twenty-one! Good God! At fifty what *would* you have
    been?

'There's not a spirit now here in Heaven who wouldn't at twenty-
    one
Have tried to upset the very Throne, and reform both Sire and
    Son!

'The saddest sight that my eyes have seen, down yonder on earth
    or here,
Is a brat that talks like a weary man, or a youth with a cynic's leer.

'Try lower down, young man,' he cried, and began to close the
    Gate –
'Hi, here, old fellah,' said Kiplingson, 'by Jingo! just you wait –

'I've heaps of Criticisms here, to show my claims are true,
That I'm 'cute in almost everything, and have probed Creation
   through!'

'And what have you *found*?' the Saint inquired, a frown on his
   face benign –
'The Flag of England!' cried Kiplingson, 'and the thin black
   penny-a-line![I]

'Wherever the Flag of England waves, down go all other flags;
Wherever the thin black line is spread, the Bulldog bites and
   brags!

'And I warn you now, if you close that Gate, the moment it is
   done,
I'll summon an army of Cockney Gents, with a great big Gatling
   gun!

'O Gawd, beware of the Jingo's wrath! the Journals of Earth are
   mine!
Across the plains of the earth still creeps the thin black penny-a-
   line!

'For wherever the Flag of England waves' – but here, we grieve
   to state,
His voice was drown'd in a thunder-crash, for the Saint bang'd-to
   the Gate!

[*Collected Poems* (Songs of Empire), 1901]

HILAIRE BELLOC

(1870–1953)

Belloc was born in France, and was the son of a French barrister. His mother was prominent in the women's suffrage movement. He was educated at the Oratory School, Edgbaston, and, after serving in the French army, went to Balliol. In 1902 he became a British citizen. He was M.P. for Salford from 1906 to 1910, just at the period when this poem was written. He sat first as a Liberal, and then as an Independent.

Lord Lundy

Who was too Freely Moved to Tears, and thereby ruined his Political Career

I

LORD LUNDY from his earliest years
Was far too freely moved to Tears.
For instance, if his Mother said,
'Lundy! It's time to go to Bed!'
He bellowed like a Little Turk.
Or if his father, Lord Dunquerque
Said, 'Hi!' in a Commanding Tone,
'Hi, Lundy! Leave the Cat alone!'
Lord Lundy, letting go its tail,
Would raise so terrible a wail
As moved his Grandpapa the Duke
To utter the severe rebuke:
'When I, Sir! was a little Boy,
An Animal was not a Toy!'

His father's Elder Sister, who
Was married to a Parvenoo,
Confided to Her Husband, 'Drat!
The Miserable, Peevish Brat!
Why don't they drown the Little Beast!'
Suggestions which, to say the least,
Are not what we expect to hear
From Daughters of an English Peer.

His grandmamma, His Mother's Mother,
Who had some dignity or other,
The Garter, or no matter what,
I can't remember all the Lot!
Said, 'Oh! that I were Brisk and Spry
To give him that for which to cry!'
(An empty wish, alas! for she
Was Blind and nearly ninety-three).

The Dear Old Butler thought – but there!
I really neither know nor care
For what the Dear Old Butler thought!
In my opinion, Butlers ought
To know their place, and not to play
The Old Retainer night and day.
I'm getting tired and so are you,
Let's cut the Poem into two!

.   .   .   .   .

2

It happened to Lord Lundy then,
As happens to so many men:
Towards the age of twenty-six,
They shoved him into politics;
In which profession he commanded
The income that his rank demanded
In turn as Secretary for
India, the Colonies, and War.
But very soon his friends began
To doubt if he were quite the man:
Thus, if a member rose to say
(As members do from day to day),
'Arising out of that reply . . .!'
Lord Lundy would begin to cry.
A Hint at harmless little jobs
Would shake him with convulsive sobs.

While as for Revelations, these
Would simply bring him to his knees,
And leave him whimpering like a child.
It drove his Colleagues raving wild!
They let him sink from Post to Post,
From fifteen hundred at the most
To eight, and barely six – and then
To be Curator of Big Ben! . . .
And finally there came a Threat
To oust him from the Cabinet!

The Duke – his aged grand-sire – bore
The shame till he could bear no more.
He rallied his declining powers,
Summoned the youth to Brackley Towers,
And bitterly addressed him thus –
'Sir! you have disappointed us!
We had intended you to be
The next Prime Minister but three:
The stocks were sold; the Press was squared;
The Middle Class was quite prepared.
But as it is! . . . My language fails!
Go out and govern New South Wales!'

.   .   .   .   .

The Aged Patriot groaned and died:
And gracious! how Lord Lundy cried!

[*Cautionary Tales*, 1907]

SIEGFRIED SASSOON

(1886–1967)

Siegfried Sassoon was educated at Marlborough and at Cambridge, and was awarded the M.C. during the First World War. He wrote a number of superb autobiographies, including *Memoirs of a Fox-Hunting Man* and *Memoirs of an Infantry Officer*, which make it unnecessary to give any very detailed account of his life here. Of the small group of poets of the first rank produced by the war – Owen, Rosenberg, Edward Thomas and Robert Graves are the others – Sassoon is the only one who strikes me as a true satirist.

Base Details

IF I were fierce, and bald, and short of breath,
    I'd live with scarlet Majors at the Base,
And speed glum heroes up the line to death.
    You'd see me with my puffy petulant face,
Guzzling and gulping in the best hotel,
    Reading the Roll of Honour. 'Poor young chap,'
I'd say – 'I used to know his father well;
    Yes, we've lost heavily in this last scrap.'
And when the war is done and youth stone dead,
I'd toddle safely home and die – in bed.

[Counter-attack, 1918]

Memorial Tablet

(Great War)

SQUIRE nagged and bullied till I went to fight
(Under Lord Derby's scheme). I died in hell –
(They called it Passchendaele); my wound was slight,
And I was hobbling back, and then a shell
Burst slick upon the duck-boards; so I fell
Into the bottomless mud, and lost the light.

In sermon-time, while Squire is in his pew,
He gives my gilded name a thoughtful stare;
For though low down upon the list, I'm there:
'In proud and glorious memory' – that's my due.
Two bleeding years I fought in France for Squire;
I suffered anguish that he's never guessed;
Once I came home on leave; and then went west.
What greater glory can a man desire?

[*War Poems*, 1919]

EZRA POUND

(1885–   )

Mauberley is one of the most important of Pound's works. It presents an imaginary portrait of an aesthete in a world grown too philistine to harbour him. *Mr Nixon* is generally supposed to be a portrait of Arnold Bennett. H. G. Wells refers in his *Experiment in Autobiography* (1934) to Bennett's naïve pride in his yacht: 'it was a bright and lovely toy for him, and I think he felt I might just look at it, and then at him, with the wrong expression.' John J. Espey, in his *Ezra Pound's 'Mauberley'*, quotes the following from one of Pound's letters: 'Arnold Bennett knew his eggs. Whatever his interest in good writing, he never showed the public anything but his AVARICE. Consequently, they adored him.'

Mr Nixon

IN the cream gilded cabin of his steam yacht
Mr Nixon advised me kindly, to advance with fewer
Dangers of delay. 'Consider
    Carefully the reviewer.

'I was as poor as you are;
When I began I got, of course,
Advance on royalties, fifty at first,' said Mr Nixon,
'Follow me, and take a column,
Even if you have to work free.

'Butter reviewers. From fifty to three hundred
I rose in eighteen months;
The hardest nut I had to crack
Was Dr Dundas.

'I never mentioned a man but with the view
Of selling my own works.
The tip's a good one, as for literature
It gives no man a sinecure.

'And no one knows, at sight, a masterpiece.
And give up verse, my boy,
There's nothing in it.'

    .   .   .   .   .

Likewise a friend of Bloughram's once advised me:
Don't kick against the pricks,
Accept opinion. The 'Nineties' tried your game
And died, there's nothing in it.

[Mauberley, 1920]

ROY CAMPBELL

(1902–57)

Campbell was born at Durban, South Africa, and first made his reputation with *The Flying Terrapin* in 1924. A romantic and a reactionary, Campbell believed passionately in the physical life of the senses, and at different times earned his living as a seaman, fisherman, farmer, and bull-fighter. His temperament made him particularly averse to the London literary world of the twenties and thirties, and especially to the group of poets which centred on J. C. Squire and *The London Mercury*. *The Georgiad* is a last attempt to write satire in the 'traditional' manner. Campbell spent a great deal of his life in Provence, and in Spain and Portugal. His Roman Catholicism made him the champion of General Franco during the Spanish Civil War.

From *The Georgiad*

Now hawthorn blooms above the daisied slope
Where lovelorn poets after milkmaids grope,
Or troop whore-hunting down the country lanes
With flashing spectacles and empty brains,
To hang their trousers on the flowering spray
And sport with lousy Gypsies in the hay.
Here Bulbo comes his amorous hours to pass
Tickled by spiders on a tump of grass:
And sure, what blushing milkmaid would despise
Humpty's great belly and protruding eyes,
Who in his verses plainly has revealed
That when he ogles every maid must yield!
If they should fail to win the joys they sing
Or get a cuff to make their ear-drums ring,
It makes no difference, they forgive the crime
And finish off the merry feat in rhyme –
Editors are the safest go-betweens –
All maids are willing in the magazines:
More lonely hearts are linked by the Reviews
Than by the 'Link' or 'Matrimonial News',

And any one who feels a trifle flighty
Can get off in 'The London Aphrodite',
Where upon every page, always in 'hay'
These donkeys jack their mares the livelong day.

[1931]

P. WYNDHAM LEWIS

(1884–1957)

Wyndham Lewis was one of the pioneers of the Modern Movement in England, as painter, writer and (perhaps most of all) polemicist. He first made his reputation before the First World War as the leader of the Vorticists. Among his associates at this time were T. S. Eliot and Ezra Pound. *One-Way Song* is his only book of verse, and seems to belong more to the twenties than to the thirties in which it was actually published, as its radicalism is by no means conventionally left-wing. In his preface to the new edition published after the war T. S. Eliot felt obliged to defend Wyndham Lewis against the charge of fascism. He compares *One-Way Song* to the 'snarling satirists' of the Elizabethan era, and says of it: 'If we then decide that *One-Way Song* is *verse* rather than *poetry*, we shall find that it belongs to that body of high-ranking verse which is more important than most minor poetry.' This is perhaps to overvalue it, but it is certainly all of a piece with Lewis's fascinating novels, especially with *The Apes of God*, *The Wild Body*, and the *Childermass*.

If So the Man You Are

THE man I am to blow the bloody gaff
If I were given platforms? The riff-raff
May be handed all the trumpets that you will.
Not so the golden-tongued. The window-sill
Is all the pulpit they can hope to get,
Of a slum-garret, sung by Mistinguette,
Too high up to be heard, too poor to attract
Anyone to their so-called 'scurrilous' tract.
What wind an honest mind advances? Look
No wind of sickle and hammer, of bell and book,
No wind of any party, or blowing out
Of any mountain hemming us about
Of 'High Finance', or the foothills of the same.
The man I am who does *not* play the game!
Of those incalculable ones I am
Not to be trusted with free-speech to damn,
To be given enough rope – just enough to hang.
To be hobbled in a dry field. As the bird sang

Who punctured poor Cock Robin, by some sparrow
Condemned to be shot at with toy bow and arrow.
You will now see how it stands with all of those
Who strong propensities for truth disclose.
It's no use buddy – you are for it boy
If not from head to foot a pure alloy!
If so the man you are that lets the cat
Out of the bag, you're a marked fellow and that's that.

[*One-Way Song*, 1933]

EDGELL RICKWORD

(1898-   )

Edgell Rickword was educated at Colchester Grammar School and Pembroke College, Oxford. He was the editor of *The Calendar of Modern Letters* (1925–7), one of the best literary magazines of its period. (It has just been reissued complete.) He is also the author of a study of Rimbaud, and of three books of poems: *Behind the Eyes* (1921); *Invocations to Angels* (1928); *Twittingpan* (1931). A volume of *Collected Poems* appeared in 1947.

To the Wife of a Non-interventionist[1] Statesman

(March 1938)

PERMIT me, Madam, to invade,
briefly, your boudoir's pleasant shade.
Invade? No, that's entirely wrong!
I volunteered, and came along.
So please don't yell, or make a scene,
or ring for James to – intervene.
I'm here entirely for the good
of you and yours, it's understood.
No ballyhoo, what I've to say
may stand you in good stead one day.

I have to broach a matter that
less downright folk might boggle at,
but none need blush because we try
to analyse the marriage tie.

The voice that breathed o'er Eden laid
some precepts down to be obeyed:
to seek in marriage mutual trust
much more than sentiment or lust:
to base our passion on esteem
and build a home for love's young dream.
With this in mind, I'll state a case
of interest to the human race.

269

Suppose your husband yarns in bed
of plans that fill his lofty head,
think what should be a wife's reaction
if he turned out the tool of faction,
who put across the crooked schemes
of statesmen sunk in backward dreams;
whose suave compliance sealed the fate
of thousands left to Franco's hate –
(those very Basques whose fathers drowned
to keep *our* food-ships safe and sound,
sweeping for mines in furious seas).
Our Fleet stood by, but ill at ease:
restive, our sailors watched the shore
whilst hundreds drowned who'd starved before,
victims of Franco's sham blockade –
though in the way of honest trade
Potato Jones and his brave lass
had proved this husband knave or ass.

Suppose he argues: Though I swerved
from honour's course, yet peace is served?

Euzkadi's[1] mines supply the ore
to feed the Nazi dogs of war:
Guernika's[2] thermite rain transpires
in doom on Oxford's dreaming spires:
in Hitler's frantic mental haze
already Hull and Cardiff blaze,
and Paul's grey dome rocks to the blast
of air-torpedoes screaming past.
From small beginnings mighty ends,
from calling rebel generals friends,
from being taught at public schools
to think the common people fools,
Spain bleeds, and England wildly gambles
to bribe the butcher in the shambles.

Traitor and fool's a combination
to lower wifely estimation,
although there's not an Act in force
making it grounds for a divorce:
but canon law forbids at least
co-habitation with a beast.

The grim crescendo rises still
at the Black International's[1] will.
Mad with the loss of Teruel[2]
the bestial Duce looses hell;
on Barcelona slums[3] he rains
German bombs from Fiat planes.
Five hundred dead at ten a second
is the world record so far reckoned;
a hundred children in one street,
their little hands and guts and feet,
like offal round a butcher's stall,
scattered where they'd been playing ball –
because our ruling clique's pretences
rob loyal Spain of her defences,
the chaser planes and ack-ack guns
from which the prudent Fascist runs.

So time reveals what people meant
who framed a Gentlemen's Agreement,
and lest a final crime condones
fresh massacres with British loans,
should not its sponsor be outlawed
from power, position, bed and board?
Would not a thinking wife contemn
the sneaking hand that held the pen
and with a flourish signed the deed
whence all these hearts and bodies bleed?
Would not those fingers freeze the breast
where the young life should feed and rest?

Would not his breath reek of the tomb
and with cold horror seal her womb?
Could a true woman bear his brat?
The millions wouldn't.

Thanks, my hat.

[*Left Review*, March 1938]

W. H. AUDEN

(1907-)

Auden was educated at Gresham's School, Holt, and at Christ Church, Oxford. His poetry gave a characteristic tone to the literature of the thirties, and is, at this period, full of satirical comments on the condition of society. In 1938 Auden went to the United States, and later became an American citizen.

The Unknown Citizen

(To JS/07/M/378 This Marble Monument Is Erected by the State)

HE was found by the Bureau of Statistics to be
One against whom there was no official complaint,
And all the reports on his conduct agree
That, in the modern sense of an old-fashioned word, he was a saint,
For in everything he did he served the Greater Community.
Except for the War till the day he retired
He worked in a factory and never got fired,
But satisfied his employers, Fudge Motors Inc.
Yet he wasn't a scab or odd in his views,
For his Union reports that he paid his dues,
(Our report on his Union shows it was sound)
And our Social Psychology workers found
That he was popular with his mates and liked a drink.
The Press are convinced that he bought a paper every day
And that his reactions to advertisements were normal in every
way.
Policies taken out in his name prove that he was fully insured,
And his Health-card shows he was once in hospital but left it
cured.
Both Producers Research and High-Grade Living declare
He was fully sensible to the advantages of the Instalment Plan
And had everything necessary to the Modern Man,
A phonograph, a radio, a car and a frigidaire.
Our researchers into Public Opinion are content
That he held the right opinions for the time of year;
When there was peace, he was for peace; when there was war, he
went.

He was married and added five children to the population,
Which our Eugenist says was the right number for a parent of his
    generation,
And our teachers report he never interfered with their education.
Was he free? Was he happy? The question is absurd:
Had anything been wrong, we should certainly have heard.

                             [*Another Time*, 1940]

ROBERT GRAVES

(1895–)

Robert Graves served in France with the Royal Welch Fusiliers during the First World War. In the early twenties he settled in Deya, Majorca, and (except for an interruption from 1937–45) has lived there ever since. A prolific novelist and translator as well as a poet, Graves has published many books – no less than 114 titles are to be found in the 'A' list of a recent bibliography. He has, however, always regarded himself as primarily a poet.

The Persian Version

TRUTH-LOVING Persians do not dwell upon
The trivial skirmish fought near Marathon.
As for the Greek theatrical tradition
Which represents that summer's expedition
Not as a mere reconnaissance in force
By three brigades of foot and two of horse
(Their left flank covered by some obsolete
Light craft detached from the main Persian fleet)
But as a grandiose, ill-starred attempt
To conquer Greece – they treat it with contempt;
And only incidentally refute
Major Greek claims, by stressing what repute
The Persian monarch and the Persian nation
Won by this salutary demonstration:
Despite a strong defence and adverse weather
All arms combined magnificently together.

[*New Writing and Daylight*, Summer 1943]

DONALD DAVIE

(1922–)

Donald Davie was born in Yorkshire, and was educated at Barnsley Grammar School, and at St Catherine's College, Cambridge. War service with the Royal Navy took him, between 1941 and 1946, to India, Ceylon, and North Russia. He has also travelled widely since. After being a lecturer at Dublin University, and a Fellow of Gonville and Caius College, Cambridge, he is now Professor of Literature at the University of Essex. He has published four volumes of verse. His critical books include the influential *Articulate Energy*, subtitled 'An Enquiry into the Syntax of English Verse'.

The Evangelist

'MY brethren . . .' And a bland, elastic smile
Basks on the mobile features of Dissent.
No hypocrite, you understand. The style
Befits a church that's based on sentiment.

Solicitations of a swirling gown,
The sudden vox humana, and the pause,
The expert orchestration of a frown
Deserve, no doubt, a murmur of applause.

The tides of feeling round me rise and sink;
Bunyan, however, found a place for wit.
Yes, I am more persuaded than I think;
Which is, perhaps, why I disparage it.

You round upon me, generously keen:
The man, you say, is patently sincere.
Because he is so eloquent, you mean?
That test was never patented, my dear.

If, when he plays upon our sympathies,
I'm pleased to be fastidious, and you
To be inspired, the vice in it is this:
Each does us credit, and we know it too.

[*Brides of Reason*, 1955]

PETER PORTER

(1929-)

Peter Porter was born in Brisbane, Australia. He is currently an advertising copywriter in a London advertising agency. He has published two books of verse, *Once Bitten, Twice Bitten* (1961), and *Poems Ancient & Modern* (1964). He is represented in *Penguin Modern Poets 2*.

Made in Heaven

FROM Heals and Harrods came her lovely bridegrooms
(One cheque alone furnished two bedrooms),

From a pantechnicon in the dog-paraded street
Under the orange plane leaves, on workmen's feet

Crunching over Autumn, the fruits of marriage brought
Craftsman-felt wood, Swedish dressers, a court

Stool tastefully imitated and the wide bed –
(the girl who married money kept her maiden head),

As things were ticked off on the Harrods list, there grew
A middle-class maze to pick your way through –

The labour-saving kitchen to match the labour-saving thing
She'd fitted before marriage (O Love, with this ring

I thee wed) – lastly the stereophonic radiogram
And her Aunt's sly letter promising a pram.

Settled in now, the Italian honeymoon over,
As the relatives said, she was living in clover.

The discontented drinking of a few weeks stopped,
She woke up one morning to her husband's alarm-clock,

Saw the shining faces of the wedding gifts from the bed,
Foresaw the cosy routine of the massive years ahead.

As she watched her husband knot his tie for the city,
She thought: I wanted to be a dancer once – it's a pity

I've done none of the things I thought I wanted to,
Found nothing more exacting than my own looks, got through

Half a dozen lovers whose faces I can't quite remember
(I can still start the Rose Adagio, one foot on the fender)

But at least I'm safe from everything but cancer –
The apotheosis of the young wife and mediocre dancer.

[*Once Bitten, Twice Bitten*, 1961]

JOHN BETJEMAN
(1906–   )

Betjeman was educated at Marlborough and Magdalen College, Oxford. Afterwards he was a schoolmaster for a brief spell. His *Selected Poems* appeared in 1948, *A Few Late Chrysanthemums* in 1954, the *Collected Poems* in 1958, and the verse-autobiography, *Summoned by Bells* in 1960. Betjeman is also well known as an authority on architecture, especially the architecture of the Victorians.

Period Piece

ETERNAL youth is in his eyes
    Now he has freshened up his lips.
He slicks his hair and feigns surprise,
    Then glances at his fingertips.

'My dears, but yes, *of course* I know,
    Though why you think of asking *me*
I can't imagine, even though
    It rather *is* my cup of tea.

You see, my dears, I'm *old* – so old
    I'll *have* to give myself away –
So don't be flattering when you're told –
    But I was *sixty* yesterday.

And so, of course, I knew them *all*,
    And I was with them when they went
To Basil's marvellous *matelot* ball
    At Bedstead, somewhere down in Kent.

I was in decorating then,
    And Basil said the job was mine,
And though I speaks as shouldn't, when
    I'd finished, it was just *divine*.

A *hideous* house, inside and out –
  And Basil's mother – well, not *quite* –
But still, I'll say for the old trout,
  She paid my little *bill* all right.

I *stripped* the hideous painted wood,
  Stippled the corridors and halls,
And *pickled* everything I could,
  And *scrumbled* nearly all the walls.

I put Red Ensigns on the seats
  And hung Blue Peters down their backs,
And on the beds, instead of sheets,
  Enormous pairs of Union Jacks.

My dears, and *everyone* was there –
  But oh, how *old* it makes me feel
When I recall that charming pair
  In *matelot* suits of *eau de nil*.

One was Kilcock, Clonbrassil's son,
  Who died in nineteen thirty three,
(God rest his soul), the other one
  Believe it or not, was *tiny me*.

Bug Maxwell, Ropey, Rodney Park,
  Peter Beckhampton, Georges de Hem,
Maria Madeleine de Sark –
  I wonder what's become of them?

Working in some department store –
  That was the last I heard of Bug.
Ropey was always such a bore,
  And didn't Rodney go to jug?

And Georges de Hem collaborated,
  So that's the last we'll hear of *him*!
And Peter and I, though we're related,
  Are out of touch, now he's so dim.

And what's become of poor Maria?
  Patrick, I'd like another drink.'
He gazes sadly at the fire;
  His feelings make him seem to think.

Eternal age is in his eyes,
  Which watch the countless parties pass,
And, as the conversation dies,
  A seventh time we fill his glass.

[*London Magazine*, June 1964]

CHRISTOPHER LOGUE

(1926–)

Christopher Logue has always been interested in the possibilities offered by verse satire, and has been associated with the so-called 'satire movement' both through the songs he wrote for performance at the Establishment night-club and through his column in *Private Eye*. The poem printed here was written in response to a request from *Tribune*, who at the 1966 general election asked a number of people to give the reasons why they were going to vote Labour. The poem was also printed as a broadside.

I Shall Vote Labour

I SHALL vote Labour because
  God votes Labour.
I shall vote Labour in order to protect
  the sacred institution of The Family.
I shall vote Labour because
  I am a dog.
I shall vote Labour because Labour tolerates
  the traitor Ian Smith.
I shall vote Labour because
  I am on a diet.
I shall vote Labour because Ringo votes Labour.
I shall vote Labour because
  upper-class hoorays annoy me in expensive restaurants.
I shall vote Labour because if I don't
  somebody else will:

AND

I shall vote Labour because if one person does it
  everybody will be wanting to do it.
I shall vote Labour because
  my husband looks like Anthony Wedgwood Benn.
I shall vote Labour because I am obedient.
I shall vote Labour because if I do not vote Labour
  my balls will drop off.

I shall vote Labour because there are too few
  cars on the road.
I shall vote Labour because
  Mrs Wilson promised me five pounds if I did.
I shall vote Labour because I Love
  Look at Life films.
I shall vote Labour because I am
  a hopeless drug-addict.
I shall vote Labour because
  I am a Wincarnis Shareholder.
I shall vote Labour because
  I failed to be a dollar-millionaire aged three.
I shall vote Labour because Labour will build
  more maximum-security prisons.
I shall vote Labour because I want to see
  Nureyev and Fonteyn dance in Swansea Civic Centre.
I shall vote Labour because I want to shop
  in a covered precinct stretching from Yeovil to Glasgow.
I shall vote Labour because I want to rape
  an air-hostess.
I shall vote Labour because I am a hairdresser.
I shall vote Labour because
  the Queen's stamp collection is the Best in the World.
I shall vote Labour because,
  deep in my heart,
I am a Conservative.

[1966]

NOTES

Piers Plowman

p. 31, 1, *Sir Harvey:* Skelton also uses this name for a covetous man.

p. 31, 2, *eyen:* eyes.

p. 31, 3, *sydder:* lower.

p. 31, 4, *chiveled:* shivered.

p. 31, 5, *tawny tabard:* a short coat or mantle. The tawny colour was associated with Jews. In the *Essays*, Bacon says, 'usurers should have orange-tawney bonnets, because they do Judaize'.

p. 31, 6, *lopen:* leapt.

p. 31, 7, *welche:* Welsh flannel.

p. 31, 8, *a leaf other twain:* he learns to lie 'a leaf or two at a time', like one studying a book.

p. 31, 9, *Wy:* Weyhill, near Andover, where there was a famous fair.

p. 31, 10, *donet:* primer, from Aelius Donatus, the grammarian.

p. 31, 11, *lyser:* list, or edge, by which cloth was measured.

p. 31, 12, *rays:* striped or 'rayed' cloths.

p. 31, 13, *broach:* to pierce.

p. 31, 14, *plaited:* fastened.

p. 32, 1, *webbe:* weaver.

p. 32, 2, *the pound . . .:* she paid the spinners by weight, and used too heavy a weight.

p. 32, 3, *auncel:* a kind of balance. Forbidden by statute under Edward III, because there was such deceit in its use.

p. 32, 4, *Penny-ale:* the cheapest and thinnest kind of ale.

p. 32, 5, *Pudding-ale:* presumably ale thick as pudding. Covetousness tells us that there was no difference between the two when his wife brewed them.

p. 32, 6, *that lay by himself:* the ale, which was kept apart.

p. 32, 7, *bower:* an inner room.

p. 32, 8, *bummed:* tasted.

p. 32, 9, *in cupmel:* was measured out by the cup.

p. 32, 10, *Regratour:* Retailer.

p. 32, 11, *hockery:* retail trading. From the same root as 'huckster'.

p. 32, 12, *so the ik:* so may I thrive.

p. 32, 13, *Walsingham:* the famous pilgrimage centre in Norfolk.

p. 32, 14, *Rood of Bromholm:* the cross at Bromholm in Norfolk.

p. 32, 15, *restitution:* Covetousness pretends that he thinks this is French for 'robbery'.

p. 32, 16, *rifled:* a stronger word for theft then than now.

p. 32, 17, *males:* bags, cf. the French *malle*.

A Song against the Friars

p. 34, 1, *pelure:* fur.

p. 34, 2, *reverse:* dress-making term, meaning to line.

p. 34, 3, *vair:* ermine.

p. 34, 4, *gryse:* grey fur.

p. 34, 5, *bugee:* a kind of cloth.

p. 34, 6, *byse:* the so-called 'sea-silk' made from the *byssus* by which molluscs of the genus *Pinna* attach themselves to the rocks. Procopius relates that a Roman emperor offered a robe of this material to an Armenian satrap. Till recent times a material made of *byssus* woven with real silk was made in Calabria and in Sicily.

p. 34, 7, *trantes:* tricks.

p. 34, 8, *sape:* soap.

p. 34, 9, *mot:* may.

p. 35, 1, *limitour:* a friar licensed to beg within a certain district.

p. 35, 2, *blynne:* desist.

p. 35, 3, *semblaunt:* appearance.

The Prologue to The Canterbury Tales

p. 36, 1, *a fair for the maistrie:* an excellent one.

p. 36, 2, *outrider:* he rode out to oversee the estates of his monastery.

p. 36, 3, *venery:* hunting.

p. 36, 4, *There as:* where.

p. 36, 5, *cell:* daughter or subordinate monastery.

p. 36, 6, *Saint Maure:* St Maurus, a disciple of St Benedict.

p. 36, 7, *Saint Beneit:* St Benedict, who founded the Benedictine order in 529, and drew up its Rule.

p. 36, 8, *somedel:* somewhat.

p. 36, 9, *let oldè thingès pace:* let old things go their own way.

p. 36, 10, *And held . . .:* and followed the new order of things.

p. 36, 11, *He yaf not . . .:* he did not value that text at the price of a plucked hen.

p. 37, 1, *recchelees:* careless (of discipline).

p. 37, 2, *wood:* mad.

p. 37, 3, *swynken:* sweat.

p. 37, 4, *Austin:* St Augustine of Hippo.

p. 37, 5, *prikasour:* hard galloper.

p. 37, 6, *prikying:* tracking the hare.

p. 37, 7, *seigh:* saw.

p. 37, 8, *purfiled at the hand:* trimmed at the cuff.

p. 37, 9, *grys:* grey fur.

p. 37, 10, *enoynt:* anointed.

p. 37, 11, *steep:* prominent.

NOTES

p. 37, 12, *That steamed . . .* : glowed like the furnace under a cauldron.
p. 37, 13, *great estate:* good condition.
p. 37, 14, *forpyned:* tormented.

On the Death of the Duke of Suffolk

p. 38, 1, *Jack Napes:* or Jackanapes, the popular nickname of the Duke.
p. 38, 2, *on the sea:* Suffolk was arrested on his way into exile.
p. 38, 3, *Nicolas:* the name of the ship which intercepted Suffolk.
p. 38, 4, *Placebo:* 'I shall be pleasing . . .' The first word of the first antiphon at Vespers, in the Latin Office of the Dead. *Dirige* is the first word of the antiphon at Matins in the Office of the Dead. *Placebo* and *Dirige* are used by extension to mean the Office itself.
p. 39, 1, *interfectors:* slayers.
p. 39, 2, *bishop of Hertford:* Reginald Baker, promoted from the abbacy of Gloucester in 1450.
p. 39, 3, *bishop of Chester:* William Boothe, an unpopular figure in his own right. Made Bishop of Coventry and Lichfield (popularly known as the see of Chester) in 1347. Survived Suffolk's fall to become Archbishop of York in 1453.
p. 39, 4, *Salisbury:* Reginald Beauchamp, elected 1450.
p. 39, 5, *bishop of Worcester:* John Carpenter, another supporter of the church and court party.
p. 39, 6, *the cardinal:* John Kemp, Archbishop of York.
p. 39, 7, *Saint Asse:* St Asaph.
p. 39, 8, *Walter Liard:* also known as Walter Hart and Walter Lyhart, Bishop of Norwich.
p. 39, 9, *Saint Davy:* St Davids. John Delamere was consecrated bishop in 1447.
p. 39, 10, *Moleyns:* Lord Hungerford, in right of his wife Lord Molines. An ardent Lancastrian.
p. 39, 11, *Roos:* Thomas, Lord Ros, another staunch Lancastrian.
p. 40, 1, *Say:* Together with the Abbot of Gloucester and Walter Liard (of those mentioned in the poem), John Say 'esquire', of London, was one of the unpopular courtiers indicted by the triumphant Yorkists at Rochester in 1451.

The Egloges

p. 43, 1, *Muscadel, Caprike, Romney and Malvesy:* kinds of wine.
p. 43, 2, *Gene:* Genoa.
p. 44, 1, *lowne:* fool.

Speak, Parrot

p. 45, 1, *My name is Parrot:* by tradition the parrot is a wise fool.
p. 46, 1, *Quis . . . suum chaire:* 'Who taught parrot to say his hello. (*Chaire* is hello in Greek.)

p. 46, 2, *Parlez bien . . . ou parlez rien:* Speak well . . . or speak nothing.

p. 46, 3, *sable hablar Castiliano:* Parrot boasts of his knowledge of Castilian, Katharine of Aragon's native tongue.

p. 46, 4, *fidasso de cosso:* trust in yourself. A warning delivered to the Queen in her own language which helps to date the poem to the period of the divorce.

p. 46, 5, *Thrace:* at this time being over-run by the Turks, while the European powers quarrelled among themselves.

p. 46, 6, *Vis consilii expers . . . mole ruit sua:* Strength without wisdom falls by its own weight.

p. 46, 7, *Souventez foys . . . en souvenante:* many times in memory.

p. 46, 8, *Salve festa dies, toto there doth best:* When on hoilday, it's best to go the whole hog.

p. 47, 1, *Moderata juvant:* Moderation pleases us.

p. 47, 2, *Myden agan:* Nothing in excess.

p. 47, 3, *Haec res acu tangitur:* This hits the nail on the head.

p. 47, 4, *Taisez-vous . . . tenez-vous coy:* Be quiet . . . be careful.

p. 47, 5, *Que pensez-vous:* What do you think?

p. 47, 6, *Vitulus:* the (golden) calf (see Exodus 32). A hit at Wolsey, who was the son of a butcher.

p. 47, 7, *Melchizadek:* King of Salem, blessed Abraham after a victory (Genesis 14).

p. 47, 8, *cum sensu maturato; ne tropo sanno, ne tropo mato:* with a mature perception; neither too sane nor too mad.

p. 47, 9, *Aran:* probably a reference to Genesis 11, xxviii. Aran, brother of Abraham and Nachor, died in Ur of the Chaldees.

p. 47, 10, *Johab . . . Hus:* an allusion too obscure to disentangle completely. Job was from the land of Uz, and a Johab is recorded as the great-grandson of Esau (Genesis 36, xxxiii).

p. 47, 11, *The lineage of Lot:* Psalm 82, ix, laments the alliance of the Moabites and the Amorites (descendants of Lot) with the Assyrians.

p. 47, 12, *Jereboseth:* Hebrew for 'contender with the idol'.

p. 47, 13, *ebrius:* drunk.

p. 47, 14, *lyver god van hemrik, ich seg:* Hush, for God's sake, I say (in Flemish). The Flemings were proverbial for drunkenness.

p. 47, 15, *Popering:* Poperinghe was a village in Flanders, not far from Calais, which was famous for its pears. Calais itself was the scene of the mock-conference of August to November 1521, where Wolsey tried to keep Francis I of France in play, while secretly negotiating for an alliance with Charles V.

p. 47, 16, *Hob Lobin of Lowdoon:* Lot of Lothian is the King of Scots in the Arthurian cycle of romances. This and the last half of the preceding line are allusions to Scots ballads.

p. 47, 17, *The gibbet of Baldock was made for Jack Leg:* One commentator suggests that this line refers to the hanging of Jack Lincoln after the Evil May Day Riot of 1517. Another theory is that the allusion is biblical:

Baldock is the alternative name for the city of Shushan where (in the Book of Esther) Haman was hanged on the gibbet made for Mordechai.

p. 47, 18, *Ich dien:* 'I serve', the royal motto, was associated with the royal badge of a plume of ostrich feathers. Motto and badge were adopted by Edward the Black Prince from the blind King of Bohemia (Beme) who was killed at Crécy.

p. 47, 19, *byrsa:* the 'purse' over which Wolsey held power. There is also an allusion to the story of Dido, who got enough land for her new city of Carthage in Africa by asking for the earth which could be covered by a strip of leather. She then cut the leather into strips, and marked off a huge area.

p. 47, 20, *Colostrum:* the first milk after calving.

p. 47, 21, *shale:* shamble.

p. 48, 1, *moveatur terra:* let the earth move.

p. 48, 2, *Paub yn ei arver:* Each to his own liking.

p. 48, 3, *Aristippus:* a pupil of Socrates who evolved an ethical philosophy of pleasure.

p. 48, 4, *unde depromo ... Sacro vatum:* Whence I produce dilemmas taught the poet in a sacred school.

p. 48, 5, *Caesar, ave!:* 'Hail, Caesar!' According to Martial, parrots were supposed to be able to say this by nature, without being taught.

p. 48, 6, *Esebon:* Heshebon, a city of the Amorites, ruled by King Sihon, whose ally was Og of Bashan. They refused the Jews passage, and Moses defeated them (Deuteronomy 2, xxix).

p. 48, 7, *Ulala:* Alas.

p. 48, 8, *Gideon:* Gideon defeated the Amorites, killed their King, Zalmana, and executed their Princes Oreb and Zeb (Judges 7 and 8).

p. 48, 9, *Gebal, Ammon and Amaloch:* see Psalm 82, viii.

p. 49, 1, *Amorraeorum:* of the Amorites.

p. 49, 2, *coistronus Cananaeorum:* scullion of the Canaanites.

p. 49, 3, *whilom refugium miserorum:* once the refuge of the miserable.

p. 49, 4, *Non fanum, sed profanum:* not sacred, but profane.

p. 49, 5, *Japhthah:* Gideon's successor.

p. 49, 6, *Whetstone next Barnet:* Wolsey dissolved the small abbey of Bromhall, near Whetstone, on 12 September 1521.

p. 49, 7, *trim-tram:* a worthless trifle.

p. 49, 8, *chaffer far-fet:* goods fetched from afar.

p. 49, 9, *Boho:* the King.

p. 49, 10, *Hough-ho:* Wolsey.

p. 49, 11, *Scarpary:* Scarpanto or Karpathos, an island just to the east of Crete.

p. 49, 12, *Quod magnus est dominus Judas Iscariot:* How great is Lord Judas Iscariot. The general sense of the passage is that Judas (who is Wolsey) is known as far away as China to rule England with a word.

p. 49, 13, *Ptolemy:* astronomer of the second century A.D. whose explanations were only replaced by those of Copernicus.

p. 49, 14, *Haly:* Thales of Miletus, one of the Seven Sages of antiquity, famous for accurately predicting the eclipse of 585 B.C.

p. 49, 15, *volvel:* a device used to determine the setting of the sun and moon, and the state of the tides.

p. 49, 16, *tirykis:* a 'therick' or mechanical device for explaining astrological phenomenon.

p. 49, 17, *pseudo-propheta:* falsely prophesy.

p. 49, 18, *chiromancy:* the art of reading hands.

N.B. I owe the bulk of my notes on this extraordinarily complex and allusive poem to A. R. Heiserman's study, *Skelton and Satire* (University of Chicago Press, 1961). It is perhaps worthwhile to quote his summary of this particular passage, which forms the introduction to the whole poem:

A parrot . . . sits in a cage croaking bits of proverbs, Old Testament history, popular song, vague allusions to contemporary events. . . . His 'shredes of sentence' praise moderation and condemn excess; they chastise the excessive mildness of kings, and lament the resultant excessive powers of ministers; they tie together details of biblical struggles, principally those of Moses and Gideon, as does Psalm 82; they lament the inaction of Christendom before the invasion of the Turks; they allude to Poperinghe, Whetstone-next-Barnet, Dublin, Scotland, Bohemia – all 'details' of the contemporary political scene, details apparently as disjointed and insignificant as those taken from the Old Testament. The two sets of fragmentary detail, one ancient and the other contemporary, illuminate one another in such a fashion as to produce a profound aloofness.

Why Come Ye Not to Court?

p. 49, 19, *Cardinal Wolsey* (1475–1530): Wolsey was famous for his greed, love of luxury, concupiscence, and arrogance, but also for his administrative capacity and appetite for work. One diplomat accredited to the English court described him as 'the proudest prelate that ever breathed'. He abrogated to himself many of the privileges of royalty. This poem is a direct attack on Wolsey, whereas the previous poem, 'Speak, Parrot', was an indirect attack.

p. 49, 20, *Hampton Court:* On his fall, Wolsey was forced to surrender this superb palace to the king, and it has remained a royal palace.

p. 50, 1, *Yorkès Place:* Wolsey was Archbishop of York, and York Place was his official residence.

p. 50, 2, *Tancrete:* transcript.

p. 50, 3, *the Fleet . . . the Marshalsea . . . the Kingès Bench:* prisons under the jurisdiction of the king's courts at Westminster.

p. 53, 1, *Haly . . . Ptolemy:* see notes to 'Speak, Parrot'.

p. 53, 2, *Albumazar* (805–85): Arabic astronomer and astrologer at Baghdad.

p. 54, 1, *shule:* shovel.

p. 54, 2, *lechery:* Wolsey had as many illegitimate children as Henry VIII.

p. 54, 3, *starke wood:* stark mad.

Read Me and Be Not Wroth

p. 55, 1, *mules:* The mule was the characteristic mount of the high-ranking ecclesiastic. The Pope rode a white mule.

Book II, Satire VI

p. 66, 1, *truckle-bed:* a low bed which ran on castors under the main bed. It was usually given to a servant.

p. 66, 2, *bare:* with head uncovered.

CERTAIN SATIRES, III

p. 67, 1, *empery:* empire.

p. 67, 2, *the glass/Drawn full of love-knots:* drawings made with a diamond.

p. 67, 3, *pink:* an adjectival extension of the metaphor 'the pink of perfection'.

p. 67, 4, *congé:* salutation.

THE SCOURGE OF VILLAINY, V

p. 68, 1, *packstaff epithet:* a nickname expressing contempt, branding him a man as trumpery as the goods which pedlars displayed on their packstaffs.

p. 68, 2, *my wit flags . . . wits:* Hermes had the power of bringing sleep with the help of his caduceus.

p. 68, 3, *spotted kine:* Marston insolently offers to placate Hermes, the god of villains, by a sacrifice of the cattle which were spotted (by implication, spotted with sin).

p. 68, 4, *profane thee:* modern villainy, in its apishness, profanes the God of Tricks.

p. 68, 5, *gouty:* swollen, baggy.

THE SCOURGE OF VILLAINY, VIII

p. 68, 6, *souping:* sweeping.

p. 68, 7, *dye in cluttered blood:* dip his mistress's favour in blood.

p. 68, 8, *fancy's colours:* 'Fancy' has the implication of 'fickle'. 'Colours' are the ribbon-favours the lady gives to her lover.

THE SCOURGE OF VILLAINY, XI

p. 69, 1, *souls:* Marston talks both of the immortal spirit and of the spirit of reason here.

p. 69, 2, *upbrayed:* given indigestion.

p. 69, 3, *eating stews:* a pun. 'Stews' also means 'brothels'.

p. 69, 4, *music, dancing, fencing school:* Even the meanest exercises involving the use of intellect may lead to better things.

SATIRE I

p. 70, 1, *Standish:* ink-stand.

p. 70, 2, *Zopirus:* a Greek author who wrote on physiognomy (Socrates' appearance, in particular).

p. 70, 3, *Mandeville:* 'Sir John Mandeville', or 'Jehan de Mandeville', pseudonymous compiler of a book of (largely aprocryphal) travels which had an enduring popularity. His narrative was written in French, and appeared between 1357 and 1371.

p. 70, 4, *Candish:* Thomas Cavendish or Candish (1555?–92), the third circumnavigator of the globe.

p. 70, 5, *Drake:* Sir Francis Drake (1545–96), the famous English admiral.

p. 71, 1, *Anaxarchus:* Greek sceptic philosopher, a follower of Democritus. He accompanied Alexander on his Asiatic campaigns.

p. 71, 2, *Aegeus:* father of Theseus.

p. 71, 3, *Aretine:* Pietro Aretino (1492–1556), celebrated libertine author.

p. 71, 4, *varges:* verjuice, the acid juice of unripe fruit, grapes, crab-apples, etc.

SATIRE IV

p. 72, 1, *blue-coat:* the livery of both servants and beadles.

A Dwarfish Satyre

p. 76, 1, *fore-tusses:* points of hose.

Of the Moone

p. 78, 1, *Aries:* the first sign of the zodiac, corresponding to the vernal equinox.

p. 78, 2, *Aquarius:* the second to last sign.

The Distracted Puritan

A poem which picks up the convention of 'Tom O'Bedlam's Song'. The earliest version of this song seems to date from the period 1615–26.

p. 80, 1, *Festus:* Acts 26, xxv.

p. 80, 2, *Emanuel:* a centre of puritanism in Cambridge.

p. 81, 1, *Greenham:* Fellow of Pembroke College, Cambridge, and author of several Puritan religious works. His collected works were first published in 1599, and had reached a fourth edition by 1612.

p. 81, 2, *Perkins:* a Cambridge Puritan, and popular religious author. His *Golden chaine or the description of Theologie* has in it a table where the causes of damnation are shown with black zig-zag lines.

p. 81, 3, *the holy tongue of Chanaan:* the Puritan divines were often experts in Hebrew.

The Puritan and the Papist

p. 83, 1, *ship money:* This tax, levied by Charles I without the consent of Parliament, was one of the causes of the Civil War. It had its origin under the Plantagenets, who exercised the right of requiring the maritime towns and counties to furnish ships in time of war. In 1619 James I levied ship money without arousing popular opposition. In 1628 Charles I tried to repeat the levy, this time extending it inland. He met with opposition, and was forced to revoke the writ. In 1634 London and other seaports were again assessed – this time, contrary to all precedent, in time of peace. On 5 August 1635 a second writ of ship money was issued, directed at inland as well as maritime counties and towns. This excited great discontent. The suspicion that the king was determined to do away with parliamentary government was strengthened by the issue of a third writ in 1636. This led to the Hampden Case of 1638, which marked a definite stage on the road to Civil War. The illegality of ship money was declared by the Long Parliament in 1641.

p. 83, 2, *High-Commission:* The ecclesiastical Court of High Commission was used by Archbishop Laud to enforce his religious ideas. It conflicted with secular jurisdiction.

p. 83, 3, *High-Committee:* the Committee of Safety, a body consisting of members of the Lords and the Commons, chosen by vote. It was created on 4 July 1642.

p. 83, 4, *the Five:* On 4 January 1642, Charles I had tried to seize by force five members of the Commons: Pym, Hampden, Holles, Hesilrige, and Strode.

p. 83, 5, *Eighty-Eight:* 1588, the year of the Spanish Armada.

p. 83, 6, *Straffords ghost:* Thomas Wentworth, Earl of Strafford, minister of Charles I, was impeached by the Commons, and executed in 1641. Charles always regarded his consent to this execution as the greatest mistake of his life.

The Rebel Scot

p. 84, 1, *Pym's disease:* John Pym (1584–1643) was perhaps the most famous of the parliamentary leaders, architect of the constitutional revolution, and especially hated by royalists, who asserted that, like Herod, he had died 'eaten of worms'. In fact, the post-mortem makes it plain that it was cancer of the lower bowel.

p. 85, 1, *Marshal:* Stephen Marshall (1594–1655), was a Presbyterian divine and one of the greatest preachers of the age. His funeral sermon for Pym made a great impression.

p. 85, 2, *Hocus:* generic mock-latin name for a juggler.

p. 85, 3, *Montross and Crawford:* James Graham, Marquis of Montrose, (1612–50), was the most successful royalist leader in Scotland. Ludovic Lindsay, Earl of Crawford, was a much less notable figure.

p. 87, 1, *Hyperbolus:* was ostracized in 417 B.C., the last use made by the Athenians of this punishment.

p. 87, 2, *Erasmus:* Desiderius Erasmus (1466?–1536), the great humanist, tried to adopt a middle attitude towards the religious conflict of his time.

p. 87, 3, *Soland goose:* a gannet. There was a famous colony of them on the Bass Rock in the Firth of Forth.

Satyr I

p. 91, 1, *Latimer:* Hugh Latimer (1485–1554) was one of the great heroes of the Protestant cause in England. Latimer was Bishop of Worcester under Henry VIII, and a famous preacher under Edward VI. He was burnt at Oxford under Mary, together with Ridley.

p. 91, 2, *Domitian:* Roman emperor (A.D. 81–96). Domitian was morbidly suspicious and cruel, and seems in fact to have been mad towards the end of his life. The anecdote about his killing flies is related by Suetonius.

The Character of Holland

p. 92, 1, *alluvion:* legal term applied to the formation of land by the action of water.

p. 93, 1, *Mare Liberum:* title of a book by Grotius (published 1609) written against the Portuguese claim to the Eastern seas. The doctrine was revived during the Dutch Wars, when the Commonwealth laid claim to the Channel.

p. 93, 2, *Level-coyl (lever le cul):* a game in which each player was unseated in turn.

p. 93, 3, *Cabillau (kabeljauw):* Dutch for codfish.

THE LAST INSTRUCTIONS TO A PAINTER

p. 93, 4, *Castlemaine:* Barbara Villiers (1641–1709), Countess of Castlemaine and later Duchess of Cleveland, mistress to Charles II. The intrigue alluded to here is unknown, though she was at one time supposed to have been in love with Jacob Kemp, a rope-dancer.

p. 94, 1, *Porter's Den:* the Porter's lodge, where servants were whipped.

p. 94, 2, *Jermyn:* Henry Jermyn (1636–1708), nephew to the Earl of St Albans (described in 'The Last Instructions' as 'The new *Courts* pattern, stallion of the old'). Pepys records of Castlemaine, in his diary for 29 July 1667, that 'she is fallen in love with young Jermyn, who hath of late been with her oftener than the king'.

p. 94, 3, *Alexander:* Alexander the Great sent his mistress Campaspe to the painter Apelles to be painted, then, seeing that the artist had fallen in love with her, gave the girl to him (Pliny: *Historia Naturalis*, XXXV, 10).

p. 94, 4, *de Ruyter:* Michael Adrianzoon de Ruyter, celebrated Dutch Admiral.

p. 94, 5, *old:* de Ruyter was sixty.

p. 95, 1, *Sheppy Isle:* On 10 June 1667 the Dutch sailed up the Thames to a point above Canvey Island. They then returned to Sheppey, where, that evening, they bombarded Sheerness. The garrison were compelled to evacuate, and the Dutch landed and occupied the island.

p. 95, 2, *Pett:* Peter Pett (1610–70?) Commissioner of the Navy at Chatham. Sent to the Tower as a result of the disaster there.

p. 95, 3, *would not follow:* On 3 June 1665 the Duke of York failed to follow up an advantage already won.

p. 95, 4, *Bergen:* In August 1665 a convoy of Dutch ships returning from the East took refuge in the neutral harbour at Bergen. Sandwich, the English commander, negotiated instead of attacking, with the result that the Dutch escaped.

p. 95, 5, *prevented:* anticipated.

p. 95, 6, *The Fleet divided:* In 1666 the fleet was divided between the Duke of Albemarle and Prince Rupert. This nearly resulted in disaster at the Four Days' Battle in the Downs, 1–4 June.

p. 95, 7, *Languard:* the fort at Harwich, which the Dutch attacked at the same time as they sailed up the Thames.

p. 95, 8, *exposed:* Pett was blamed that the *Royal Charles* was not moored farther up the Medway.

p. 95, 9, *Phanatick:* Pett took office under the Commonwealth.

p. 96, 1, *Sea Architect:* Both Pett and his father Phineas Pett were originally shipwrights. One of his chief duties as Commissioner was to supervise shipbuilding.

p. 96, 2, *slips:* disasters.

p. 96, 3, *If no Creation:* 'Paradise Lost' was published at the end of August 1667, just as this was being written.

HUDIBRAS, Part I, Canto III

p. 98, 1, *truckle-bed:* a low bed running on truckles or castors, usually pushed under a high or 'standing' bed when not needed. Usually given to inferiors.

HUDIBRAS, Part 2, Canto III

p. 99, 1, *Opposition, Trine, and Quartile:* astrological aspects. Heavenly bodies 'in opposition' are 180 degrees distant from one another, 'in trine' 120 degrees, and 'in quartile' 80 degrees.

Tyburne Cheated

p. 105, 1, *Little-ton . . . Cooke:* Edward Littleton, Lord Littleton (1589–1645), and Sir Edward Coke (1552–1634), eminent constitutional lawyers.

p. 105, 2, *QUARLES his Dreame:* the *Regale Lectum Miseriae* by John Quarles, son of the more famous Francis, which was first printed in 1649.

John Quarles served in the King's garrison at Oxford during the Civil War; was banished to Flanders; then afterwards returned to England and died of the Plague in 1665.

The Geneva Ballad

p. 109, 1, *the tune of 48:* Charles I was executed on 27 January 1649, New Style, but 1648, Old Style.

p. 109, 2, *Laud:* William Laud, Charles I's authoritarian Archibishop of Canterbury, was attainted and executed in 1645.

p. 110, 1, *Bonner* (1500?–1569): Bishop of London under Mary and associated with the burnings of heretics in her reign.

p. 110, 2, *Kings of* Colen: Kings of Cologne, i.e. the Magi.

p. 111, 1, *Smestymnuan laws:* 'Smectymnuus' was the Latin pseudonymn, made by putting together their various initials, which was used by five Puritan divines who wrote a tract attacking Joseph Hall, Bishop of Exeter. The tract was published in March 1641. Stephen Marshall was one of the authors, and Milton had a hand in revising and enlarging the text.

p. 111, 2, *Brownists:* followers of Robert Browne (1550?–1633?), who is regarded as the founder of modern Congregationalism.

p. 111, 3, *Knipperdoling:* Bernhard Knipperdoling was leader of the Munster Anabaptists. The term came to be used generally, to denote a fanatic.

Satyr (against Reason and Mankind)

p. 114, 1, *Ingello:* Nathaniel Ingelo (1621?–83), fellow of Eton, and author of a religious romance, *Bentivolio and Urania.*

p. 114, 2, *Patrick's Pilgrim: The Parable of the Pilgrim,* by Bishop Patrick. A poor imitation of *Pilgrim's Progress.*

p. 114, 3, *Sibb's:* Richard Sibbs (1577–1635), a Puritan divine who was the author of many religious works. The one referred to is probably *Divine Meditations and Holy Contemplations* (1638).

p. 115, 1, *Meres:* Sir John Meres, M.P. for Lincoln. In 1679 he was commissioner for the Admiralty.

An Essay upon Satyr

p. 120, 1, *Killigrew:* Thomas Killigrew (1612–83), the dramatist and wit, who became Master of the Revels in 1679.

p. 120, 2, *Bessus:* the Persian satrap who assassinated the fleeing Darius after the latter had been defeated by Alexander the Great at Gaugamela.

Satires upon the Jesuits, III

p. 122, 1, *Xavier:* St Francis Xavier (1506–52), the Jesuit 'Apostle to the Indies'.

MacFlecknoe

p. 125, 1, *Shad –:* Thomas Shadwell (*c.* 1642–92), the chief satirist on the side of the whigs. Author of *The Medall of John Bayes*, a virulently personal reply to Dryden's satire *The Medall*. After the revolution of 1688 he replaced Dryden as poet laureate.

Absalom and Achitophel, Part I

p. 125, 2, *Achitophel:* Anthony Ashley Cooper, 1st Earl of Shaftesbury (1621–83). Shaftesbury was originally on the king's side in the Civil War, but went over to Parliament because he saw dangers to the Protestant religion in the king's service. By 1654 he was one of Cromwell's opponents, siding with the Presbyterians and the Republicans. He worked for the Restoration, and was one of the twelve commissioners sent to Charles at Breda, to ask him to return. He was made a baron in 1661, and became one of the chief opponents of Clarendon and the High Anglican policy. In 1672 he was rewarded with an earldom for concurring with the Declaration of Indulgence. In November 1672 he became Lord Chancellor, and was dismissed in 1673, partly for opposing grants to the king's mistresses. From 1674 onwards he became the popular leader against the court. In 1678 he had just been released from the Tower when the outbreak of the Popish Terror presented him with an unrivalled political opportunity. He put forward Monmouth, the eldest of the king's illegitimate sons (the 'Absalom' of the poem) as the Protestant candidate for the succession, and demanded that the queen be divorced and the Duke of York excluded from the succession. In June 1680 he presented the Westminster grand jury with an indictment of James as a Popish recusant. On 15 November of the same year the Exclusion Bill was defeated in the Lords. In 1681 Shaftesbury was again committed to the Tower, and in December of that year was released on bail. In 1682 he fled to Amsterdam, and died there in January 1683. He is usually considered to be the first great party leader in the modern sense.

p. 127, 1, *Zimri:* George Villiers, 2nd Duke of Buckingham (1628–87). Following the assassination of his father, the favourite of James I, he was brought up by Charles I with his own children. After being on the royalist side in the Civil War, he returned to England in 1657 and married Mary, daughter of Lord Fairfax, the commander on the side of Parliament. In 1658 he was suspected of organizing a Presbyterian plot. After the Restoration he was soon back in royal favour, and became chief minister on the fall of Clarendon. In 1675 he allied himself to the country party, but separated from the whigs on the exclusion question and was absent from the great debate in the Lords in November 1680. He was interested in alchemy, and Burnet says that for some years 'he thought he was very near finding the philosopher's stone'. As already mentioned in the introductory note on Dryden, he was the author of *The Rehearsal*, a satire on the heroic drama and on Dryden in particular. For an account of his end, see the notes to Pope, p. 300.

Absalom and Achitophel, Part 2

p. 128, 1, *Og:* Shadwell.

p. 129, 1, *Doeg:* Elkanah Settle (1648–1721), a minor satirist who began as a tory, defected to the whigs, then rejoined the tories. His career went into a decline, and he became assistant to a puppet show in Bartholomew Fair. Dryden had prophesied that he would be *master* of a puppet show!

A Pindarique

p. 130, 1, *Pindarique:* a poem written in imitation of the odes of the Greek poet Pindar.

p. 132, 1, *Jordan:* Thomas Jordan (1612?–1685), poet of the Corporation of London 1671–85. The chief duties of his post were to invent pageants for the Lord Mayor's Shows, and to compose a panegyric on the Lord Mayor elect.

Jack Pavy

p. 134, 1, *Visiting the prisons:* This passage from *Jack Pavy* gives a vivid account of prisons at the end of the seventeenth and the beginning of the eighteenth century. Prisoners, whether criminals or debtors, lived in intolerably unhealthy conditions, and had to pay their gaolers for favours at every turn.

p. 134, 2, *Bridewells:* so called from 'his house of the Bridewell' which Edward VI gave to the City of London in 1552 for use as a house of correction. The word was later used as a generic term for a house of correction, where 'sturdy beggars', prostitutes, and paupers were compulsorily employed, working for their own financial support. The Bridewells came more and more to be used for petty offenders, and the change was confirmed in 1720 by act of parliament.

p. 134, 3, *vicious* Bench: the King's Bench, one of the prisons maintained by the King's courts at Westminster, almost entirely for debtors and others confined by civil process.

p. 134, 4, *are forc'd to stay:* In some cases, men remained in prison, even when declared discharged, because they were unable to pay the discharge fees to the officials who claimed them.

p. 135, 1, *Batt'ning in their dung:* In Newgate prisoners were charged 1s. 3d. each per week for the use of shared beds and bedding.

A Satyrical Elegy

p. 137, 1, *a Late Famous General:* John Churchill, Duke of Marlborough (1650–1722).

Verses on the Death of Dr Swift

p. 140, 1, *Gay:* John Gay, the poet (1685–1732).

p. 140, 2, *Arbuthnott:* Dr John Arbuthnot (1667–1735), physician-in-ordinary to Queen Anne, and an intimate of the leading statesmen of the Harley administration. A member of the 'Scriblerus Club', with Pope, Gay, and Swift. Swift said of him that 'the doctor has more wit than we all have, and his humanity is equal to his wit'.

p. 140, 3, *St John:* Henry St John, Viscount Bolingbroke (1678–1751), Swift's particular ally in the tory ministry at the end of Anne's reign. After the accession of George I and his own dismissal, Bolingbroke fled to France and became secretary of state to the Pretender, but quarrelled with him after the failure of the Jacobite Rising of 1715. He was pardoned in 1723, but not restored to his seat in the Lords. Pope was much influenced by him, and versified some of his philosophical fragments in the *Essay on Man*.

p. 140, 4, *Vole:* To take the vole was to win all the tricks at quadrille.

The Reformation of Manners

p. 143, 1, *trepan:* to trick.

p. 143, 2, *Amboyna:* in the Moluccas. In 1623 the Dutch massacred a party of English settlers there.

The Art of Politicks

p. 162, 1, *South-Sea Stock:* The South Sea Bubble was the most famous financial scandal of the century. The crash came in 1720. Thousands of investors were ruined, and ministers of the Crown were implicated.

p. 162, 2, *Pinkethman:* an actor whose career spanned the years 1692 to 1724. He was famous for his habit of adlibbing.

The Man of Taste

p. 163, 1, *Mandevil:* Robert Mandevil (1578–1618), a puritan divine, author of *Timothie's Task*.

p. 163, 2, *Tyndal:* William Tyndale (d. 1536), translator of the Bible into English.

p. 163, 3, *Pasaran:* Alberto Radicati, Conte di Passerani, originally attached to the court of Vittorio Amadeo II of Savoy, and a violent pamphleteer against the Papacy. The attentions of the Inquisition forced him into exile in England, France, and Holland (where he died). He labelled himself a 'free thinker', and wrote in defence of suicide.

p. 163, 4, *Budgel:* Eustace Budgell (1686–1737) a Grub Street writer, somewhat disordered in his wits, who set forth his grievances in various tracts.

p. 163, 5, *Jones:* Inigo Jones (1573–1652) was the true father of English classical architecture. His most famous buildings are the Queen's House at Greenwich, and the Banqueting House in Whitehall.

p. 163, 6, *Convent-Garden Church:* The church of St Paul's, Covent Garden, was designed by Inigo Jones in a severe Tuscan style. Jones's layout for Covent Garden was one of the first examples of regulated town planning in England.

p. 164, 1, *the Brent:* the Brenta.

p. 164, 2, *Cit:* Johnson, in the *Dictionary*, defines a cit as 'a pert low townsman a pragmatical trader'.

p. 164, 3, *Bently:* 'Bently's Milton, Book 9, Ver. 439' – author's note. Richard Bentley, the famous classical scholar, made an over-ingenious edition of *Paradise Lost.*

p. 164, 4, *Sir Cloudesly Shovel:* an admiral, drowned in 1707 off the Scilly Isles. His curious tomb can still be seen in Westminster Abbey.

Epistle to Lord Bathurst

p. 167, 1, *In he worst inn's worst room:* George Villiers, 2nd Duke of Buckingham, died in 1687, in Yorkshire. Contemporaries give conflicting accounts of the circumstances. One describes him as dying 'In a little ale-house (where these eight months he hath been without meat or money, deserted of all his servants almost)'.

p. 167, 2, *flock-bed:* The aristocracy had feather beds.

p. 167, 3, *Cliveden:* a palace built by Buckingham. Evelyn remarks on 'buildings of extraordinary expense'.

p. 167, 4, *Shrewsbury:* Buckingham's mistress the Countess of Shrewsbury. He killed her husband in a duel on 16 January 1668.

Epistle to Dr Arbuthnot

p. 167, 4, *Atticus:* Joseph Addison (1672–1719), editor of the *Spectator.* The lines are an echo of an old quarrel, one cause of which was the praise given to the pastorals of Ambrose Philips by Addison's circle. For Philips see the biographical note on Henry Carey, p. 153.

p. 168, 1, *Like Cato:* In his prologue to Addison's tragedy *Cato* (1713), Pope wrote: 'While *Cato* gives his little Senate laws.'

p. 168, 2, *Sporus:* John, Baron Hervey of Ickworth (1696–1743), favourite of Queen Caroline, Walpole's agent in the court, and one of Pope's most inveterate enemies. The name is borrowed from Suetonius.

p. 168, 3, *Ass's milk:* often prescribed as a tonic.

p. 168, 4, *painted Child:* Sarah, Duchess of Marlborough, describes Hervey, in 1737, as having 'a painted face, and not a tooth in his head'.

p. 168, 5, *Eve:* Queen Caroline.

NOTES

An Epistle from S. J. Esq. in the Country

p. 175, 1, *The top one graces, one each side*: a reference to the old method of serving meals, where several dishes were put on the table at once, to be followed by a 'remove' of more dishes. Eighteenth-century cookery books give diagrams as to how the table should be arranged. The third edition (1777) of *The Lady's Assistant*, by Mrs Charlotte Mason, offers the following specimen menu: first course, pease or gravy soup and boiled chickens, flanked by bacon and greens and butter; followed by 'a ragout of pigs' feet and ears', 'fore quarter of house lamb', and orange pudding, flanked by stewed celery and 'broccoli like asparagus'. The idea of the meal being sent up a dish at a time (referred to as a *dîner à la russe*) was being mentioned as a novelty as late as 1859.

The Modern Fine Lady

p. 176, 1, *Tubbs*: 'A Person well known for supplying People of Quality with hired equipages' – author's note.

London

The poem imitates Juvenal, *Satire III*. The same satire by Juvenal influenced Elizabethan satirists of city life. Johnson's imitation has many parallels with one by John Oldham (see p. 121) published in 1682.

p. 178, 1, *shore*: sewer, cf. the definition in Johnson's *Dictionary*.

p. 178, 2, EDWARD: Edward III.

p. 179, 1, *gibbet . . . wheel*: At this period, the French method of capital punishment was breaking on the wheel.

p. 179, 2, HENRY: Henry V.

p. 180, 1, *gropes*: touches or grasps.

p. 180, 2, SPAIN: Spain still laid claim to some of the British colonies in America.

The Vanity of Human Wishes

The poem imitates Juvenal, *Satire X*.

p. 181, 1, *Let observation . . .*: Tennyson wondered why Johnson did not say: 'Let observation, with extended observation, observe extensively.

p. 181, 2, *weekly scribbler*: The political journals came out weekly.

p. 181, 3, *Palladium*: originally the image of the goddess Pallas Athene in the citadel at Troy, which ensured the safety of the city. Thence, by transference, anything which served a similarly protective function.

p. 182, 1, *When first the college rolls*: The passage is drawn from personal experience. Mrs Piozzi describes in her anecdotes, how Johnson burst into 'a passion of tears' when reading it aloud.

p. 182, 2, *Bodley's dome:* In the *Dictionary* 'dome' is defined as 'a building, a house, a fabrick'. The domed Radcliffe Camera was not opened till the year the poem was published, and did not become part of the Bodleian till 1860.

p. 182, 3, *Bacon's mansion:* the gatehouse at the northern end of Folly Bridge. Johnson notes: 'There is a tradition, that the study of friar Bacon, built on an arch over the bridge, will fall, when a man greater than Bacon shall pass under it.'

p. 182, 4, *the patron:* originally 'the garret'. Boswell relates that the change was made after Johnson's quarrel with Lord Chesterfield. The letter to Chesterfield was written in February 1755, the revised version of the poem was published in March. In the *Dictionary* (first published in April of the same year) 'patron' is defined as 'commonly a wretch who supports with insolence, and is paid with flattery'.

p. 182, 5, *tardy bust:* The bust of Milton was placed in Westminster Abbey as late as 1737.

p. 182, 6, *Lydiat:* Thomas Lydiat (1572–1646), famous mathematician and biblical scholar, who lived and died in poverty.

p. 182, 7, *Galileo's end:* In his seventieth year Galileo was forced by the Inquisition to deny the scientific creed by which he had lived.

p. 183, 1, *Laud:* Archbishop Laud (1573–1645). Here Johnson's prejudices run away with him. It was not 'fatal Learning' which led to Laud's execution.

p. 183, 2, *Swedish Charles:* Charles XII of Sweden (1686–1718). His story was well known in the England of Johnson's day through the translation of Voltaire's *Histoire de Charles XII.*

p. 183, 3, *one capitulate:* Frederick IV of Denmark.

p. 183, 4, *one resign:* Augustus II of Poland was deposed in 1704 and succeeded by Charles's nominee, Stanislas I.

p. 184, 1, *Pultowa:* Charles was defeated by Peter the Great of Russia at Pultowa, or Poltava, in 1709.

p. 184, 2, *in distant lands:* Charles fled to Bender in the Turkish Empire, and remained there till 1714.

p. 184, 3, *a petty fortress:* Charles was killed while attacking Frederikshald in Norway in 1718.

p. 184, 4, *a dubious hand:* Rumour had it that Charles was shot by his own aide-de-camp.

The Stage

p. 185, 1, *a George's or a Bedford wit:* The names are those of coffee-houses.

The Rosciad

p. 187, 1, *Garrick:* David Garrick (1717–79), the most famous actor in the history of the English stage.

p. 187, 2, *Kyte:* the recruiting sergeant in Farquhar's comedy *The Recruiting Officer.* Garrick first played the part at the age of eleven, in Lichfield.

The Candidate

p. 189, 1, *Life to the last enjoy'd:* the epitaph on Churchill's tombstone in the churchyard of St Martin's, Dover.

p. 190, 1, *Lothario:* John Montagu, 4th Earl of Sandwich (1718–92), was commonly known as 'Jemmy Twitcher' from the character of that name in *The Beggar's Opera.* He took a leading part in the prosecution of Wilkes, after having been associated with him in the corrupt fraternity of the Monks of Medmenham. He was notorious for corruption and profligacy.

p. 190, 2, *Push-Pin:* a child's game, where each player flicks a pin, with the object of crossing that of his opponent.

p. 190, 3, *Bute:* John Stuart, 3rd Earl of Bute (1713–92), favourite of the young George III, prime minister from May 1762 to April 1763, and ever after suspected of undue influence at court.

p. 190, 4, *March:* William Douglas, 3rd Earl of March and 4th Duke of Queensberry (1725–1810). Famous for his debaucheries and his fantastic wagers. Later to be nicknamed 'Old Q'.

The Cit's Country Box

p. 192, 1, *Country box:* a small country house. The phrase has the implication that the house concerned was built purely for pleasure expeditions into the country. Compare the similar 'hunting box'.

p. 193, 1, *Halfpenny's exact designs:* William Halfpenny (*fl.* 1752) was an architectural designer who published about twenty books dealing with domestic architecture, and especially with country houses in the Gothick and Chinese taste. His publications included: *New Designs for Chinese Temples* (1750–52); *Rural Architecture in the Gothic Taste* (1752); *Chinese and Gothic Architecture Properly Ornamented* (1752); and *Rural Architecture in the Chinese Taste* (1750–52).

Liberality of the Decayed Macaroni

p. 197, 1, *Macaroni:* an exquisite, especially one who affected Continental tastes and fashions.

p. 199, 1, *Faro:* a card-game, where the players laid bets on the order in which certain cards would appear when taken singly from the pack.

p. 199, 2, *Ton:* the fashionable world.

Instructions to a Celebrated Laureat

p. 204, 1, *Whitbread's:* Samuel Whitbread the Elder (*d.* 1796), the self-made brewer, who had started his career as a clerk. In politics he supported the tories.

Let the Brothels of Paris be Opened

p. 207, 1, *Fayette:* The Marquis de La Fayette (1757–1834), famous for the part he had played in the American Revolution. La Fayette also played a prominent role in the early stages of the French Revolution, and was Colonel-General of the Paris National Guard. He was, however, in favour of a limited monarchy. In 1792 the Constituent Assembly declared him a traitor, and he fled to Liège, afterwards spending five years in Prussian and Austrian prisons. Napoleon made his release one of the conditions of the Peace of Campo Formio in 1797.

Sapphics

p. 208, 1, *Sapphics:* a parody of Southey's poem in the same metre, *The Widow.* The 'Friend of Humanity' is George Tierney, M.P. for Southwark, and a prominent member of the Society of Friends of the People. Tierney was later Master of the Mint in Canning's administration of 1827.

New Morality

p. 210, 1, *New Morality:* The poem, like many others in the *Anti-Jacobin*, is a collaboration. Canning, John Hookham Frere, William Gifford, and George Ellis all had a hand in it. The publisher's copy indicates that this passage is by Canning.

English Bards and Scotch Reviewers

p. 214, 1, *Wordsworth:* Byron's notes to the fourth edition of the poem show he later considered this passage unjust.

p. 214, 2, *thy school:* Southey's.

p. 214, 3, *toil and trouble . . . growing double:* see 'The Tables Turned' in *Lyrical Ballads.*

The Vision of Judgment

p. 215, 1, *Southey:* Robert Southey (1774–1843), a particular aversion of Byron's. He had become laureate in 1813. For his own *Vision of Judgment,* also published in 1821, Southey wrote an introduction which contained a homily on the 'Satanic School'. This was obviously directed at Byron.

p. 216, 1, *Like King Alfonso:* 'Alfonso, speaking of the Ptolomean system, said that, "had he been consulted at the creation of the world, he would have spared the Maker some absurdities."' – Author's note.

p. 217, 1, *'melodious twang':* a quotation from Aubrey.

The Masque of Anarchy

p. 222, 1, *Castlereagh:* Robert Stewart, Viscount Castlereagh (1769–1821), the foreign secretary in Liverpool's government, regarded by radicals as the arch-advocate of reaction.

p. 222, 2, *Eldon:* John Scott, Earl of Eldon (1751–1838), lord chancellor 1801–6 and 1807–27, a ferocious tory die-hard, a last-ditch opponent of Catholic Emancipation and the Reform Bill. It is recorded of him that 'he wept with facility, even in public'. It was Eldon who gave judgment in the chancery suit set in motion by the father of Shelley's first wife, and ruled that Shelley was unfit to have charge of his two children.

Epitaph on the Late King of the Sandwich Islands

p. 224, 1, *Epitaph on the Late King of the Sandwich Islands:* a satirical epitaph on George IV under pretext of commemorating the death of the King of the Sandwich Islands who visited London in 1824, and died there of measles.

p. 224, 2, *Crazee Rattee:* Southey.

p. 225, 1, *father's bones:* 'In the Sandwich Islands no greater mark of respect can be paid to the parent, by the son, than the swallowing of a part of his mortal remains. More civilized nations are content with the prejudices.' – Praed's note.

p. 226, 1, *should be offended:* 'When a native of the Sandwich Islands is weary of his first spouse, he may bring home another, but may not divorce his originally chosen consort.' – Praed's note.

p. 226, 2, *Pozzy:* Lord Eldon, the famous and indestructible lord chancellor.

p. 227, 1, *a grinder:* 'When the Sovereign of the Sandwich Islands dies, each of his subjects shows his respects for the deceased Prince, by extracting a valuable tooth from his head.' – Praed's note.

Good-night to the Season

p. 227, 2, *Thus runs . . . :* misquotes *Hamlet*, Act 3, Sc. 2, 277.

p. 227, 3, *Papists:* The Catholic Emancipation Bill was passed in April 1829.

p. 228, 1, *Inigo:* Inigo Jones, architect of the Banqueting House in Whitehall.

p. 228, 2, *Boodle's:* the club.

p. 228, 3, *'Batti Batti':* Zerlina's aria in Act I of Mozart's *Don Giovanni*.

p. 229, 1, *Miss Ayton:* Fanny Ayton, who sang at the Opera in 1827.

p. 229, 2, *Pasta:* Giuditta Pasta (1798–1865), a famous singer, frequently heard in London in the years after 1824.

p. 229, 3, *Riego:* instigator of the Spanish Revolution of 1820, when Ferdinand VII was forced to grant a constitution. Executed 1823.

p. 229, 4, *Miss Sheridan:* evidently one of the three daughters of Sheridan the dramatist, known at this period as 'the three beauties'.

The New Timon

p. 234, 1, *Peel with pudding:* Peel had just given Tennyson a Civil List pension.

p. 234, 2, *Knowles:* James Sheridan Knowles (1784–1862), dramatist and actor, who was presumably a candidate for a pension at much the same time. At any rate he received one in 1848. 'Judged by literary tests alone, Knowles's plays cannot lay claim to much distinction,' says the *Dictionary of National Biography.*

p. 234, 3, *Hayley:* William Hayley (1745–1820), Blake's patron, and a poet whose work achieved some popularity. Southey wrote of him, 'Everything about that man is good except his poetry.'

The Golden Age

p. 246, 1, *a bone:* Foreigners, and perhaps even some provincials, may require to be told that a "bone" is the name given to the ivory ticket of a fellow of the Botanical Society, which represents the power of distributing admissions to its flower shows.' – Author's note.

The Coming K–

p. 253, 1, *Guelpho:* The Prince of Wales, later Edward VII.

The Siliad

p. 254, 1, *S. and B.:* brandy and soda.

The Ballad of Kiplingson

p. 255, 1, *Kiplingson:* Rudyard Kipling (1865–1936), whose imperialism is here satirized.

p. 256, 1, *Lever:* William Lever (1851–1925), the soap-magnate who was later created first Viscount Leverhulme.

p. 256, 2, *the Jingo Jew:* The word 'Jingo', used in this sense, derives from a music-hall song of 1878. Jingoes were those who supported and lauded the policy of Disraeli (by then Lord Beaconsfield) when he sent a British fleet to Turkish waters to resist the advance of Russia in that year.

p. 257, 1, *penny-a-line:* During the eighties, Kipling worked in India as a journalist.

Memorial Tablet

p. 261, 1, *Lord Derby's scheme:* In 1915, the government, alarmed by the shortage of volunteers for the trenches, appointed the Earl of Derby to devise a solution. Under the scheme which Lord Derby put forward, men were asked to attest voluntarily their willingess to serve, and then to await call-up. The scheme was in fact intended to smooth the way from the voluntary system to full conscription.

To the Wife of a Non-interventionist Statesman

p. 269, 1, *Non-interventionist:* In August 1936 twenty-seven European powers formally adhered to a non-intervention agreement concerning the Civil War in Spain. This worked greatly to the advantage of the nationalists.

p. 270, 1, *Euzkadi's:* The Basque province of Viscaya proclaimed itself the independent state of Euzkadi in the course of the Civil War.

p. 270, 2, *Guernika's:* bombed by the Germans, 26 April 1937.

p. 271, 1, *Black International's:* as opposed to the 'Red' or Communist International.

p. 271, 2, *the loss of Teruel:* Teruel, on the left bank of the Guadalaviar River, was the scene of fierce fighting. The republicans won their last major success by taking it on 9 January 1938. They lost it once more on 22 February.

p. 271, 3, *Barcelona slums:* Franco's Italian allies had established bases on Majorca, and from these Barcelona was severely bombed.

INDEX OF FIRST LINES

MORE ABOUT PENGUINS

Penguin Book News, an attractively illustrated magazine which appears every month, contains details of all the new books issued by Penguins as they are published. Every four months it is supplemented by *Penguins in Print*, which is a complete list of all books published by Penguins which are still available. (There are well over two thousand of these.)

A specimen copy of *Penguin Book News* can be sent to you free on request, and you can become a regular subscriber at 3s. for twelve issues (with the complete lists). Just write to Dept EP, Penguin Books Ltd, Harmondsworth, Middlesex, enclosing a cheque or postal order, and your name will be added to the mailing list.

Some other books published by Penguins are described on the following pages.

Note: *Penguin Book News* and *Penguins in Print* are not available in the U.S.A. or Canada

Penguin Classics

JUVENAL

THE SIXTEEN SATIRES

Translated by Peter Green

The splendour, squalor, and complexity of the Roman scene were never more vividly presented than by the satirist Juvenal (*c.* A.D. 55–130). His bitter and forcible verses were written during the reigns of Trajan and Hadrian, which Gibbon (from a safe distance) called 'the period in the history of the world during which the condition of the human race was most happy and prosperous'. To quote Peter Green's introduction, 'Juvenal does not work out a coherent ethical critique of institutions or individuals: he simply hangs a series of moral portraits on the wall and forces us to look at them.'

Some other Penguin books of Verse

*THE PENGUIN BOOK OF ANIMAL VERSE
Introduced and edited by George MacBeth

THE PENGUIN BOOK OF SICK VERSE
Introduced and edited by George MacBeth

THE PENGUIN BOOK OF WELSH VERSE
Translated with an introduction by Anthony Conran

A BOOK OF ENGLISH POETRY
Collected by G. B. Harrison

*GEORGIAN POETRY
Selected and introduced by James Reeves

*THE NEW POETRY
Selected and introduced by A. Alvarez

THE PENGUIN BOOK OF MODERN VERSE TRANSLATION
Selected and introduced by George Steiner

METAPHYSICAL POETS
Introduced and edited by Helen Gardner

*LONGER CONTEMPORARY POEMS
Introduced and edited by David Wright

*POETRY OF THE THIRTIES
Introduced and edited by Robin Skelton

* NOT FOR SALE IN THE U.S.A.

THE LOVED ONE

Evelyn Waugh

A riotous caper in the graveyards of southern California.

Set against a background of embalming-rooms and crematoria and the unforgettable Whispering Glades Memorial Park, *The Loved One* is as ludicrous as *Decline and Fall*, as incisively shocking as *Vile Bodies*, and – underneath the laughs – as moving as death itself.

THE PENGUIN
FOREIGN VERSE ANTHOLOGIES

The following foreign verse anthologies have already been published:

The Penguin Book of Spanish Verse, edited by J. M. Cohen

The Penguin Book of French Verse: (1) To the Fifteenth Century, edited by Brian Woledge

The Penguin Book of French Verse: (2) Sixteenth to Eighteenth Centuries, edited by Geoffrey Brereton

The Penguin Book of French Verse: (3) The Nineteenth Century, edited by Anthony Hartley

The Penguin Book of French Verse: (4) The Twentieth Century, edited by Anthony Hartley

The Penguin Book of German Verse, edited by L. W. Forster

The Penguin Book of Japanese Verse, edited by Geoffrey Bownas and Anthony Thwaite

The Penguin Book of Chinese Verse, edited by A. R. Davies

The Penguin Book of Russian Verse, edited by Dimitri Obolensky

The Penguin Book of Twentieth-Century German Verse, edited by Patrick Bridgewater

The Penguin Book of Italian Verse, edited by George Kay

WRITING TODAY

A new series of contemporary world literature is now being published in Penguins. It aims to bridge the cultural gaps imposed by language and distance with selections in English of the work of the best writers and poets of other lands.

Books in the series on sale or in preparation:

AFRICAN WRITING TODAY

ITALIAN WRITING TODAY

GERMAN WRITING TODAY

LATIN AMERICAN WRITING TODAY

SOUTH AFRICAN WRITING TODAY

POLISH WRITING TODAY

* THE NEW WRITING IN THE U.S.A.

AUSTRALIAN WRITING TODAY

FRENCH WRITING TODAY

WRITING IN ENGLAND TODAY

* NOT FOR SALE IN THE U.S.A.

PENGUIN MODERN POETS

* NOT FOR SALE IN THE U.S.A. OR CANADA